THE BLACK DOG MURDERS

An Inspector Abberline Mystery

By Gary Orchard

**For more information about this book or others, visit
www.emp3books.com**

Published in April 2025 by emp3books Ltd
6 Silvester Way, Church Crookham, Fleet, GU52 0TD

©Gary Orchard 2025

ISBN: 978-1-910734-60-5

Also by Gary Orchard

CHARLATAN a macabre thriller

THE THIRTEEN SHADOW SOULS OF GYRE shall darken the dawn of the new age

THE WENDIGO MURDERS the search for a missing child

LONDON'S TOWN Redemption and retribution in 1950's England

HORROR IN YOUR DREAMS supernatural evil

SOMETHING IN THE BLOOD evil never dies, it just waits

BACKGROUND

It is galling for a man who has found a profession he loves and who, all modesty aside, believes he has attained a certain proficiency in that endeavour, to be cast into the jaws of posterity for his one singular failure. My name is Frederick George Abberline, former Detective Chief Inspector with Scotland Yard and the man most notably recognised for his failure to apprehend the Whitechapel fiend known as Jack the Ripper. As I sit here in the twilight of my years, it rankles that the true facts of the Ripper case and many of my subsequent investigations have never been made public, for the simple reason that the true facts would never be believed. I am concerned that they would simply be attributed to a man who was desperate to repair his tarnished good name. Nonetheless, I am determined to set all the facts down on paper with strict instructions that they not be read until after my death. At such remove history may make of me what it will, my conscience shall be clear.'

Frederick George Abberline,
"Estcourt", 195 Holdenhurst Road,
Springbourne, Bournemouth, 1929

1

'Have you completely lost your mind, Abberline!' Police Commissioner Sir Charles Warren was a tall, raw-boned man with an overly ambitious moustache of which he was inordinately proud. It bristled now with righteous indignation.

Detective Chief Inspector Frederick Abberline, by contrast, was a man of medium height and build. His appearance had often led the casual observer to mistake him for a particularly amenable suburban bank manager. Although quietly affable in most circumstances, when it came to crime and criminality, that perception could not have been more wrong. Every good policeman has an instinct. The innate ability to assess an individual's character and motives from the minutiae of their behaviour and appearance. This instinct is commonly known as a "copper's nose". Detective Chief Inspector Abberline's "nose" was exceedingly sensitive and amazingly accurate. It was not something he could completely control. It was an intrinsic part of him like the colour of his eyes or his taste for beer. Nor was it something he could switch off. It told him now that Commissioner Warren was frustrated, angry and maybe a touch fearful. These feelings manifested themselves as a reddened complexion, bulging eyes and a general tenseness in his posture.

'Well?' Warren demanded. 'Have you gone totally mad?' Warren's voice was a roar, his cheeks suffused crimson. Abberline merely raised one quizzical eyebrow. 'Sir?' he said.

'Don't play the fool with me,' Warren snarled. 'You know damned well what I'm referring to.'

'The Cleveland Street case?' Abberline hazarded.

'The Cleveland Street debacle you mean. Whatever possessed you, man?'

Abberline cleared his throat and began to explain as if to a slightly befuddled junior officer. 'The Cleveland Street house was operating as a male brothel, something which I believe is still a criminal offence.' Warren drummed his fingers impatiently. Abberline continued. 'Upon information received I organised a raid upon that establishment. Having ascertained the claims to be correct I subsequently arrested the owner and a number of the attending clientele.'

Warren rose from his chair, leaning across his desk to roar in Abberline's face: 'You arrested a member of the Royal Family!'

'Amongst others,' Abberline agreed affably.

Warren began to pace the room, muttering under his breath. Abberline folded his arms and waited patiently. Finally, Warren ceased his pacing and resumed his seat and a modicum of his composure. 'Didn't the Ripper fiasco teach you anything, Abberline?' he asked.

'Are you suggesting that certain members of the aristocracy should be above the law?' Abberline asked.

'I'm suggesting that you use a little common sense if you value your career. There are some very important people who want your head on a platter, Abberline and I've half a mind to give it to them.' Warren took several deep breaths, clenching and unclenching his fists slowly. 'Needless to say,' he continued, 'the Cleveland case will go no further.'

Abberline opened his mouth to object but Warren raised his palm to forestall him. 'Instead you will be placed on restricted duties until this furore subsides, but be under no illusion that this is your very last chance. Keep your head down and make no more waves and you may yet have a career when this is over. Until then I will personally assign those cases that you will be allowed to take charge of. You will report to Inspector Reid for any day to day

3

procedures and that is the end of the matter.'

Abberline considered this for a few seconds. 'These cases,' he said, 'will I have any resources at my disposal?'

Warren sighed. 'One man,' he said. 'No more.'

Abberline nodded. 'I know just the man,' he said.

'I thought you might,' Warren muttered. He slid a buff folder across his desk. 'Here's something to be going on with,' he said. 'And before you do anything rash, you will report your proposals to Inspector Reid for approval. Is that clear?'

'As crystal, Commissioner.'

As Detective Chief Inspector Abberline exited the austere building where Commissioner Warren's office was housed, he was met by Police Constable William Walter John Colverson, known to his friends as Walt. Colverson was tall and wiry with dark, intelligent eyes, a smile never far from his lips. He had been Abberline's closest assistant on the Jack the Ripper case and was one of only a handful of people who knew the true facts. It had also been Colverson who had brought the Cleveland Street scandal to Abberline's attention. A telegraph boy, arrested for stealing, had admitted he also plied for trade at that establishment. After supporting witnesses had been found to corroborate his story, Abberline had organised a raid with unexpected and frustrating results. Colverson fell into step with Abberline as they strode back towards the station house.

'Do we still have a job then, sir?' Colverson asked.

A half smile twitched the corner of Abberline's mouth. 'Of sorts,' he said and took the buff file from under his arm. 'It seems we are to be hunting ghosts,' he said.

*(Note: For the full facts of the Jack the Ripper case see **Something in the Blood by Gary Orchard**)*

2

'Why me?' Jenny wanted to know.

'He asked for you special.'

Jenny made a dismissive noise. 'Can't you tell him I'm sick or summat? My arse is still sore from the last time.'

Lil Mooney, known to all and sundry as Limehouse Lil, puffed herself up to her full height of five feet two inches. 'If your arse is so special, maybe you'd like to take it back out on the street where I found you?'

'I'm only sayin' ...'

'And I'm only tellin' you. Mr Druitt is a very important man. A barrister, no less. And if he wants to take his belt to you, that's his business.'

'It's not just his belt. It's all the other stuff as well. Please Lil, don't make me.'

There were tears in Jenny's eyes as she spoke and Lil's heart melted just a fraction. She'd seen the state Montague John Druitt left the girls in that he took his pleasure with. Some couldn't work for a week. But ...

'He's a good tipper,' Lil told her. 'And a regular customer. We can't afford to upset him. Still, I'll tell you what I'll do. I'll let Sally go in with you. Tell him it's a special offer. Two for the price of one. You'll have to share the fee mind, but you'll also share the beating. How's that?'

Jenny pouted and moaned but Lil knew she'd agree in the end. So would Sally. It wasn't as if they had a choice.

3

Montague John Druitt was feeling very pleased with himself. His meeting with a notoriously difficult client had been protracted and laborious but ultimately successful. The documents in his briefcase would put him in good stead with his employer and ease his ascendancy to a higher position, of that he was sure. His success spurred him to indulge in his little eccentricity and he was most pleased with the result.

Two girls for the price of one! A rare treat. It opened up all sorts of possibilities. He'd managed to use the full range of accoutrement that he carried in a small leather bag, now safely hidden beneath papers of a more legal nature in his briefcase. The restraints, the devices that, once inserted, delivered as much pain as pleasure. But sometimes the simplest things were the best. He'd ordered the girls to strip and, once naked, had them wrestle each other. The girl Sally had enjoyed that. He could see it in her eyes. The inflicting of pain on another human being had ignited something in her. The sound of flesh on flesh as they struggled and hit out at their opponent had inflamed something in Druitt as well until he could resist it no more and joined the fray, lashing out with his broad leather belt until both girls lay panting and whimpering at his feet. And then the fun really began.

He had left a more than generous tip, thanking Lil for her consideration and making a mental note to request two playthings on his next visit. He could afford it after all.

The night air refreshed him as he walked along the embankment. Even the unpleasant odours rising from waters of the Thames did not diminish his good mood. If he'd been a whistling man he would have whistled a happy tune. Had he done so he might not have heard it. The sound of carriage wheels on the cobbles. Not an uncommon sound, but the streets were empty at this time of night and the sound amplified and echoed out of all proportion. He stopped for a second and glanced around. Far back, in the shadows of a side street, the dark bulk of a hansom had drawn up. The driver dismounted and stood, silently waiting. Unusual, but no matter. It was none of his concern and he walked on.

That was when he heard the other sound. A most unusual sound. A more sinister sound. A soft padding as of muffled footsteps and a heavy, panting voice. He stopped. The footsteps stopped. He glanced back. There, in the shadows across the street. A darker mass of night. He could not make out the form. But it was large. And then a slight movement, black on black and two red pinpoints glared directly at him. Druitt's breath caught in his throat. Another subtle movement and he knew for certain what it was.

A dog.

No, not a dog. A hound. A huge, black hound. Bigger than any hound he had ever seen. Bigger than any mortal hound had any right to be.

And then it growled.

A deep, rumbling vibration that seemed to shake the very ground beneath Druitt's feet. A cold, clammy sweat broke out on his forehead. He took two tentative steps. The hound kept pace with him. As he sped up, so did the hound. Druitt let out a whimper and began to run. He had no breath to scream although he dearly wanted to. He could hear the padding footfalls of his pursuer, feel his hot breath on his heels.

Desperate, he swung his briefcase but the beast simply snapped his jaws and tore it from his grasp. The beast could easily overtake

7

him and bring him down, but it did not. It contented itself with snapping at his heels, ripping his coat with his fangs. Teeth and claws drawing blood from back and legs. Druitt screamed his pain and terror to the night, stumbled and almost fell, but managed to keep going until fatigue leeched every last ounce of strength from his limbs. He slowed and sank back against the stone parapet bordering the river. The brute stopped also and stared at him. Huge, black pelt with devil red eyes and yellowed fangs dripping saliva.

'Please,' Druitt whispered. 'Don't hurt me.'

The hound cocked his great, shaggy head and seemed almost to be considering Druitt's plea. Then it began to growl and Druitt knew that his plea had fallen on deaf ears. He cast around frantically for a means of escape but none seemed apparent. The streets were empty. No help was coming from any quarter. It was just him and the beast. Faced with no other option, Druitt took the only course of action open to him. He turned and hoisted himself upon the parapet. The hound leaped forward and snapped at Druitt's ankles, catching and ripping his trouser cuff as Druitt launched himself into the welcoming embrace of the Thames.

4

A day spent perusing the shelves of the British Library is seldom wasted. Detective Chief Inspector Frederick Abberline found this particular day especially informative.

The folder given to him by Commissioner Warren outlined the case of Lord Alfred Haversham. The details had been brought to Commissioner Warren's attention by Lord Haversham's son, the Right Honourable Rupert Haversham. Following the death of Lord Haversham's wife, Lady Felicity, the venerable gentleman had, not surprisingly, descended into melancholy and despair. When his mood suddenly lifted and a smile once more graced his lips and a spring was noticeable in his step, his son breathed a sigh of relief. To have lost one parent was sorrow enough to bear, but to lose two in quick succession was impossible to contemplate and yet, that was precisely what Rupert Haversham feared would be the case. His joy at his father's uplift of mood was short lived however when he discovered the source of Lord Haversham's revived disposition.

Unable to contain his grief any longer, Lord Haversham had sought solace in the form of a society medium known as "Madame Olga". Her growing reputation in society circles had, it seems, persuaded many others in Lord Haversham's situation to seek out her services. Promising, as she did, to establish contact with the late Lady Felicity so that her husband may find the consolation he so badly needed by a continuing relationship of sorts with his wife from beyond the grave, Lord Haversham was prepared to pay any price for such a service. And a high price it was indeed. Compared to a policeman's salary it wasn't quite a King's ransom, but it did make Abberline's "copper's nose" twitch, especially as many other clients were also men of considerable resources who were no doubt paying similar amounts on a regular basis.

Rupert Haversham believed the whole thing to be a sham. A parlour game elevated to the level of fraud and extortion. Inclined to dismiss any religious or spiritual connotations as hogwash and unable to convince his father that he was being cheated out of considerable amounts of cash, he had used his gentleman's club contacts to bring the case to the attention of Commissioner Warren. And from Warren to Abberline. Which is why Abberline spent an instructive day researching spiritualism and the many and varied tricks of that particular trade that may simulate genuine psychic activity. A fascinating subject in itself, Abberline felt he was reasonably well prepared to detect any subterfuge that may take place at one of Madame Olga's séances. Now all he had to do was arrange an invitation to one such occasion. For that he would need the unwitting connivance of Lord Haversham himself. Posing as a bereaved husband, which indeed he had been, and using a false name, Abberline had persuaded Rupert Haversham to present his credentials to Lord Haversham himself and beg his indulgence by arranging such an invitation. The good Lord was only too pleased to intervene on Abberline's behalf and the time and place of the encounter had been fixed. Whether Lord Haversham would be as pleased after the meeting as he was now remained to be seen. Whatever the outcome, Abberline felt as prepared as he was ever going to be. All psychic phenomenon aside, Abberlne trusted his "copper's nose" to see a just and righteous outcome to the proceedings.

5

It had been a disappointing evening. The cards had played him false. Again. Now, through the persistent drizzle, Dr Thomas Neill Cream espied two hulking figures lurking in the shadows of his lodgings, attempting, and failing, to look inconspicuous. He recognised them as two of Reilly's men.

Patrick Reilly.

The smiling Irishman behind all that was illegal or immoral in the city. Cream was familiar with him in his capacity as a money lender. An affable enough agreement. Unless you were unable to pay him back. With interest.

Cream pressed himself into an alley. The two shadows hadn't moved. They had yet to see him. His one piece of good luck the entire evening. Quietly, he retraced his steps and melted back into the night.

The persistent drizzle transformed into a thin, driving, rain which only served to deepen Cream's anger. That Reilly's men would return on the morrow he knew with a nagging certainty that clawed at his soul. The seething anger at his own weakness stirred a need within him, a need to take his revenge upon a savage and uncaring fate in the only way that gave him any peace. He didn't think of them as victims. Accomplices maybe. Partners in a perverse pleasure. A pleasure that would see them transported from this life of pain and drudgery whilst he achieved a measure of satisfaction, a measure of complete control and ultimate mastery. He just needed to find a willing doxie. No, not willing. They were all willing. She just needed to be convenient.

He cursed the rain that had driven even the most hardened strumpet indoors, plying their trade in taverns, where, for him, the risk of witnesses was too great. The streets were his hunting ground. The back alleys and darkened doorways where no-one could see and no-one would care, but even they seemed strangely deserted. He was on the verge of giving up when he saw her. A bedraggled bloom wilting in a doorway. She would do. He approached her, seeking permission to share her sparse shelter. She played the coquette but he had no time for such a charade and asked her price outright. She faltered, gauging, no doubt, how much he was worth. She named a sum almost beyond his means to pay but the urge inside him did not lend itself to haggling, besides, it would only be a loan and easily retrievable once his business was concluded. He would do it here, he decided. Nothing fancy. The thrill of her death exciting enough; just up with her skirts and complete the transaction. He agreed and parted with coin. She made to lift her skirts but he stopped her.

'A little something to warm us first,' he suggested and produced a flask.

She readily agreed and took a swallow. 'Take these,' he said, producing two pills from his waistcoat pocket.

'What are they?' Suspicion crawled across her features.

'Just something to relax you. Keeps out the cold better than gin. Go on.'

She took the tablets and eyed them dubiously. 'Later,' she said. 'I'll take 'em later. Still got a long night ahead of me.'

'Take them now,' he demanded, his voice taking on a hard edge.

'You gonna do the bizness or not? If not, there's plenty others who will.'

'Take the pills and I'll service you like no-one before,' he promised.

She laughed. 'I've heard that one before. You're a time-waster, that's what you are. Sling yer hook.'

'Give me back my money and I'll gladly find another more willing.'

'No chance. You paid and I'm willing, so no returns.'

She made to move past him. He grabbed her arm. 'You filthy trollop!' he shouted.

She turned quickly, her knee coming up swiftly between his legs. Pain shot through him. He gagged and retched, doubling over against the wall as she sallied forth into the night. 'Thanks for the drink,' she laughed.

6

The rain had increased in intensity. Cream's hat and coat provided inadequate protection. Since going home was out of the question until he was sure that the hulking bruisers had themselves become so aggrieved at the downpour that they had given up at last and retreated to a welcoming hostelry, Cream needed some other form of shelter.

The glowing lights of the Alhambra Theatre beckoned him with the promise of a dry refuge from the inclement weather and the stormy vicissitudes of his own life. He had just enough coins in his pocket for the price of admission. He barely glanced at the poster outside. Prominent above the list of singers, jugglers and comedians was a representation of a severe Chinaman with dark, piercing eyes and a long, drooping moustache. The poster proclaimed him as top of the bill, by name, "Wu Feng, master of magic and mysticism". A pleasing enough diversion Cream decided. He purchased his ticket and went inside.

7

As Cream was taking his seat, in another, more salubrious part of town, Detective Chief Inspector Abberline knocked on an ornately carved door seeking entertainment of an entirely different sort.

The house was situated in Mayfair. The whole neighbourhood spoke of wealth and privilege. Abberline knew that appearances were often deceptive.

PC Colverson was safely ensconced across the road beneath the branches of a mature oak tree taking advantage of whatever protection its branches offered from the steady rain and easily within earshot of a police whistle should his services be required.

Abberline's mission was clear. Expose Madame Olga as a fraud and thus free Lord Haversham from her influence. The fact that this would dash the elderly Lord's most cherished hopes and destroy what happiness these sessions provided from his grief seemed not to be taken into consideration. Abberline had his duty to perform and he would do so to the best of his ability.

He raised his hand and knocked a trifle more aggressively than was perhaps necessary. After a few seconds the door was opened by a tall, stoop-shouldered figure dressed as a butler.

'Eric Wise,' Abberline told him. 'I have an appointment.'

'Ah, yes,' the butler replied. 'Do come in. The other guests have already arrived. Madame Olga will commence her reading momentarily.'

Abberline stepped inside as the butler closed the door behind him. His hat and coat were passed to a young housemaid of some fourteen summers Abberline guessed. As she took his garments, her fingers brushed briefly against his hand. Abberline felt a sharp tingle and a blue spark, brief as a firefly on a summer's night,

15

passed between his hand and the girl's. The girl drew back with a small 'Oh!' sound.

'This way, sir, if you would be so kind.' The butler ushered Abberline towards a set of double doors. As he followed, Abberline glanced back at the young housemaid. There was something in her glance. Puzzlement and maybe something more but Abberline had no time to explore the situation as he was led into a sumptuously furnished sitting room. Several guests mingled, sipping sherry. Abberline politely refused any refreshment. He spotted Lord Haversham immediately but the others were strangers. He scanned the room quickly. A morning spent in the British Library had left him well versed in the many and varied tricks of the false medium's trade. He noted several possible opportunities for subterfuge: the heavy drapes at the windows, the ornately lacquered screen that masked one corner of the room, the rich cloth that covered the central table down to the floor, the many framed paintings on the wall. All this and more he filed away as he began to introduce himself to his fellow attendees.

Of the famous Madame Olga there was no sign but Abberline felt sure she would make her entrance before long and then the performance would commence in earnest.

'Wise. Eric Wise.' Abberline introduced himself to Lord Haversham, who beamed and shook his hand.

'Ah, yes,' he said. 'Rupert, my son, mentioned you.'

'It was kind of you to arrange this invitation for me your lordship.'

'Think nothing of it. Any friend of Rupert and all that. I can assure you that Madame Olga will not disappoint. Now, let me introduce you to the rest of the group.'

As Haversham led him to each attendee in turn, Abberline made a mental note of each one, knowing that fake psychics used "plants" among their congregation to facilitate the authenticity of their act.

The tall, well-built young man with a heavy moustache was Arthur Conan Doyle, a doctor and aspiring author whose first story concerning a "consulting detective" had recently been published in Beetons Christmas Annual. Abberline considered the tale a little fanciful and nothing like real police work, consisting of lucky guesses and far-fetched leaps of intricate but implausible logic. It had not been terribly well received and Abberline doubted there would be another. Abberline's "nose" positively twitched with the sense of anticipation and delight of a possible new convert which came off Doyle in waves. Little chance of a co-conspirator there Abberline decided.

More difficult to read were two slim women whose names were given as Katherine Bradley, the older of the two, in her early forties Abberline surmised, and her companion, in her mid-twenties, Edith Cooper. They smiled coquettishly as though at some intimate secret. Deep in Abberline's mind a connection was made. They too were writers of some renown, working together under the name of Michael Field. It remained to be seen if they shared any other secret.

The next member of the select group was a plump faced young man who introduced himself as William Warner. As they shook hands Warner turned Abberline's hand palm up and stared at it intently. Abberline was about to protest at this familiarity when Warner confessed that his interest lay in palmistry and the prediction of the future. 'You have a very interesting palm Mr Wise,' he said. 'But you see this line here, where it bisects your lifeline? That indicates change is coming and very soon. If you would like to know more, perhaps we can arrange a private consultation?'

Abberline drew his hand back from Warner's grasp. 'Thank you, but no,' he said. 'I find the present provides all the knowledge I can handle. Foreknowledge would be entirely too burdensome.'

Warner chuckled and gave a slight bow of acknowledgement. 'As you wish, Mr Wise. As you wish.'

Although rather unsettling, Abberline could detect nothing from the man's words or demeanour to suggest any sort of criminal motive for his presence here. In fact, Warner was as close to a void as Abberline had ever encountered.

The final member of the congregation was a bulky, dark haired man who introduced himself in a distinctive American accent as: 'Pinkerton. William Pinkerton. Pleased to make your acquaintance, Mr Wise.' He engulfed Abberline's hand in a massive grip and Abberline was relieved when the handshake terminated. The man's eyes were shrewd, his smile professional. A sceptic, Abberline deduced. No, not quite a sceptic. This is a man who requires proof and is not easily convinced. Given his surname, that was hardly surprising if Abberline's notion as to the man's identity was correct. As Abberline massaged life back into his fingers, he tested his theory.

'Pinkerton?' he said. 'Would that be any relation to Allan Pinkerton of Pinkerton's Detective Agency?'

The American smiled broadly. 'My father,' he said. 'You are well informed, Mr Wise.'

Abberline shrugged. 'I merely take an interest in the news from abroad. I was saddened to hear of your father's passing. He was a great innovator in the world of deductive techniques.'

'That he was and I thank you kindly for your condolences.'

'Have you taken over the family business, as it were?'

'That I have. With my brother, Robert. In fact, I am here to establish a London branch of the Pinkerton Detective Agency. I have been studying the methods of Scotland Yard and have been heartily impressed to the extent that I feel a London branch of Pinkertons will supplement their activities most effectively.'

'Then I wish you well in your endeavours, but isn't this is an unusual setting to find a level headed detective such as yourself, Mr Pinkerton?' Abberline said, gesturing around the room and its esoteric set dressing. 'Are you hoping to contact your father, perhaps? Do you require his assistance on a particularly puzzling case maybe?'

Pinkerton gave a smile that didn't quite reflect in his eyes and wagged his finger. 'You are an astute individual Mr Wise. I like that in a man but I assure you my presence here is nothing more than idle curiosity.'

Abberline nodded. There was a mystery here. The man was obviously not quite as he seemed. An invitation to one of Madame Olga's séances was no easy thing to come by, not even for a visiting American celebrity, which, in certain circles at least, William Pinkerton certainly was. Before he could ponder further, a gong sounded. A signal that the evening's performance was about to commence.

The main doors to the salon opened and a slim, elegant figure dressed in a long silk patterned robe entered silently and gracefully. Her dark hair fell loose about her shoulders, her dark eyes gleamed with intelligence and, Abberline thought, not a little cunning. She had high cheekbones and full, red lips. In all respects she was a stunning beauty. She smiled and held out her hands. 'My friends,' she said, her voice thickly accented Russian that Abberline doubted was natural. 'Welcome,' she said. 'Welcome to you all. I am Madame Olga and I am here to make your fondest desires come true.'

Olga moved around the room greeting her supplicants individually by name. If this was indeed a confidence trick, prior knowledge of those attending the sitting was essential if the performance was to pass their scrutiny. For that reason, Abberline had contrived a last minute invitation and a false identity so as not to provide the supposed medium with any additional information.

When it became his turn to be introduced, Olga grasped his hand in a warm, strong grip and stared into his eyes. After a few seconds she said; 'I see you are troubled Mr Wise, but have no fear. The spirits will calm your fears I am sure.'

'I look forward to it, Madame'

She smiled and released his hand. 'My friends,' she announced, 'it is time for the unveiling. For the benefit of our newest guests, let me explain. Many charlatans practice sleight of hand with many devices and tricks hidden about their person and in the folds of their clothing. For that reason I conduct my séances in a state that denies me access to any such trickery.'

So saying, she stripped the gown from her shoulders and let it fall to the floor. Beneath it, she was entirely naked. Abberline raised an eyebrow. Tonight would certainly be an unusual encounter, of that he was sure.

8

The singers were tuneless, the jugglers uncoordinated and the comedian lacking in wit. But at least it was dry. The star attraction however, quelled the restless congregation. From his first entrance in an explosion of smoke and flame as the curtains parted, through a panoply of fire-breathing, levitating miscellaneous objects, vanishing assistants and knife throwing, the crowd were mystified and entertained. As the applause subsided, Wu Feng prepared for his grand finale. His two scantily clad female assistants wheeled on a full size guillotine to an appreciative "Oooooh!" from the audience. As they fixed the lethal looking device in place, Wu Feng produced a large cabbage and demonstrated the guillotines efficiency by using it to slice the unfortunate vegetable in half. As his assistants winched the wicked blade back into position he approached the footlights and spoke for the first time in the entire performance in a lilting, sing-song oriental accent.

'For the final demonstration of my powers I require a volunteer.' A nervous ripple ran through the audience. Wu Feng placed long fingers against his brow and concentrated. 'This will be no ordinary volunteer. This must be someone of courage and faith who entrusts their very life to the magnificent Wu Feng.' With a sudden movement, Wu Feng shot out one taloned forefinger and pointed. 'You, sir. The spirits tell me that you are such a fearless individual. Will you join Wu Feng in a journey into the unknown?'

Nervous faces turned to see who Wu Feng was pointing at. As his two assistants hurried into the audience to escort the "volunteer" onto the stage, Cream realised with a sinking feeling in his stomach that Wu Feng was pointing directly at him.

'No, no…' he began but the two young ladies had him in a surprisingly strong grip and led him, stumbling and protesting onto the stage. The audience applauded mightily with no little relief. Wu Feng's assistants whispered encouraging words in his ear as they led him into position.

Kneeling, with his head securely fastened in place, they stepped back. Sweat ran freely down Cream's face as the sinister Chinaman advanced towards him, lowering his lips to Cream's ear as he spoke.

'Hello, Creamy,' he whispered. And smiled.

9

Thomas Cream despised Francis Tumblety with every fibre of his being. They had first become acquainted when Cream was a lowly medical student with barely enough money to buy his instruments. Thrown into the company of rich, advantaged, confident young men in richly tailored suits who looked down on this raggedy pauper who had appeared unbidden in their midst, Cream had lacked confidence and was the frequent butt of their jokes and ridicule. It was perhaps the most miserable time of his life and he thought many times of giving up. Then, at his lowest ebb, Francis Tumblety took him under his wing. It was his patronage, nay, his friendship, that enabled Cream to rise above his humble beginnings. Had he known at the time that Tumblety was simply playing a more subtle game than the rest of his fellows and was using Cream for his own amusement, much as you would a pet parakeet that you had taught to say obscene words, he would have cursed himself for a fool and more and broken off any further contact. But he was blissfully unaware. He accepted the invitation to join Tumblety's circle and participate in their pastimes of drinking and gambling with alacrity, but showed no great skill or ability in either. When funds were short – and when were they not? – Tumblety was always there with a loan. A guinea here, a few shillings there, the promise that he would be repaid brushed aside with a fulsome: 'Think nothing of it, old chap. That's what friends are for.'

Friends. It is doubtful that Francis Tumblety ever had a true friend in his life. Acquaintances certainly. Hangers-on who wanted to bask in his reflected glory. Schemers who wanted to use his name to further their own careers. But friends? The fact that Cream himself was being treated like a performing monkey never occurred to him even as he noticed the unsavoury traits in others of Tumblety's circle. Indeed, he tried to warn Tumblety of their less that noble intentions and, in that act, proved his credentials as perhaps the only true friend Tumblety may have had. But it was to no avail. Tumblety was oblivious. In an attempt to curry favour, Cream resorted to being a "good sport", always up for a jolly jape. Stealing a rival school's mascot; plugging the Professor's stethoscope with candle wax; singing ribald songs outside the nurse's boarding house. All these and more did Cream willingly undertake to perform because it pleased his lord and master that he did so. And his reward was not long in coming. It was the nature of that reward that would forever change Cream's life.

In a moment of too candid intimacy over a snifter of brandy or two in Tumblety's club, Cream had admitted that his success with the fairer sex had been limited to holding hands and a chaste peck on the cheek from a baker's daughter when his father's drapery business had still been a going concern. With its demise, the source of funding that had seen his brother, James, through this very same medical school had evaporated, leaving Cream with no choice but to take on supplementary employment to pay his fees leaving precious little time or money for romance.

'Wot, never popped your cherry?' Tumblety exclaimed. 'Dear me, we can't have that. Just you leave it to your Uncle Francis. I'll have you sorted in two shakes of a lamb's tail.'

Cream spent the next few weeks in a state of nervous anticipation. Tumblety's family had extensive connections in both society and business and Cream entertained romantic notions of a lord's daughter or the product of a well-to-do business family being introduced to him as his prospective partner at a sophisticated soiree where a string quartet played waltzes as they danced the night away in each other's arms before retiring for a discrete tryst in some luxurious hotel where no-one is ever referred to by their real name.

Poor, deluded, ridiculous Cream. His dreams were shattered after a night of drinking and cards in a seedy hotel in the poorest part of town. Tumblety and three of his cronies, Paulson, Reedy and Smythe, insisted that he accompany them with the promise of a surprise. The individual behind the desk waved them through with a resigned scowl, obviously used to their patronage. 'Not so much noise this time,' he admonished. 'Had all sorts of complaints after last time.'

Tumblety and his friends ignored him and ushered Cream to a room on the second floor. Tumblety threw open the door with a flourish and pushed Cream inside, his fellows crowding in behind him. The room was sparsely furnished and dirty, containing just a bed, a table and a chair with a broken leg. One other item did it also contain.

A girl.

She had blonde curls and was pretty enough in a plump sort of way. She wore a dirty cotton shift, the rest of her clothes piled untidily on the broken chair.

Tumblety grasped Cream's shoulders with both hands. 'Meet Doris,' he said.

'Daisy,' the girl said. 'My name's Daisy.'

'Daisy, Doris, who cares? What do you think of her, eh, Cream? She'll do, won't she?'

'Do?' Cream stammered.

'Yes, "do". For your first. She'll do well enough won't she? She's clean, I promise. Well, she's never given me the clap anyway.'

Tumblety's cronies hooted with laughter at that but Cream felt his soul shrivel inside. This was not what he had in mind at all. He wanted to run but knew they would never let him. He was trapped. Trapped by his own stupidity. Why-oh-why had he ever been foolish enough to admit to never having had a girl before?

Tumblety slapped him on the back. 'Come on, Creamy,' he said, using the nickname that Cream had always loathed. 'Get your pecker out, the girl's not going to tupp herself you know.'

'I can if you want,' Daisy offered and they all roared with merriment. All except Cream who was paralysed by fear and embarrassment. They began to chant then.

'Creamy, Creamy, Creamy.'

'He's shy, Daisy,' Tumblety called. 'Give him a little encouragement.'

Obligingly, Daisy came and knelt at Cream's feet and undid his fly buttons. She thrust her hand inside his trousers and began searching for signs of life. After a few seconds, she frowned. 'Are you sure he's got one?' she asked. More raucous screams of mirth. Cream squeezed his eyes shut tight to stop the tears from flowing.

'She thinks you're a ruddy eunuch, Creamy!' Tumblety roared. 'Come on, don't let the side down. Stand to attention man.'

'Oh, I found something now,' Daisy informed them to more hysterical laughter. 'It's only small though. Hardly seems worth the trouble.'

Seized with uncontrollable anger, Cream grabbed the girl by the shoulders and hauled her to her feet. Grabbing her shift by the collar he tore it straight down the middle, baring her body for all to see.

'That's the spirit, Creamy!' Tumblety guffawed. 'You give her what for.'

Cream shoved the girl down onto the bed. She lay there, supine, her legs spread, her breasts lolling indolently.

26

Having gone thus far, Cream had no real idea what to do next. In desperation he flung himself on top of her, dragging his flaccid member from his trousers, pushing and heaving against her in the hopes of some miraculous act of spontaneous coupling. It was not to be. After a minute or two of sweaty ineffectiveness, he rolled off of her and onto the floor, covering his face with his hands, sobbing helplessly.

His companions seemed to find his discomfiture even more amusing.

'Wot's up wiv 'im?' Daisy asked. 'I had a wash and everything and he don't even know where to put it.'

'Stone me, maybe he is a eunuch,' Tumblety said. 'Is that it, Creamy? Not got enough meat and two veg to do the deed? Maybe you just need to see how it's done, eh?' With that, the four roaring boys dropped their trousers and took turns to heave themselves onto the un-protesting Daisy. When they had finished, they pulled up their trousers and trooped out of the room, still laughing. Daisy took a few more minutes to get her breath back, then dressed and followed them out leaving Cream alone, broken and betrayed.

Nor did Cream's torment end there. The tale, much embellished, about how he had failed to satisfy even the most compliant of cheap whores was soon disseminated amongst his fellow students who took to sniggering behind his back and passing pointed comments within his hearing. Even his professors gave knowing looks and smug smiles in his presence. As his life became a living hell, it was only some miniscule crumb of comfort that the architect of his misery soon removed himself from Cream's orbit. Having wrung whatever amusement there was from their association, Francis Tumblety cut Cream adrift and before long abandoned all pretence at study, leaving for good to take up a career of drunkenness and profligation.

If Cream's torment lessened after Tumblety's departure, replaced in the public interest by newer scandals and salacious gossip, it left him with one other debilitating vice that he could not cure.

Gambling.

A hopeless addict to cards and dice, Cream took a succession of supplementary tasks in order to pay his way. Selling his services to staff and students alike, he prepared lecture rooms, theatres, copied notes, provided research as well as acting as a pharmacy clerk and assisting the coroner in the morgue. The last, a particularly odious task that only the most desperate would consider undertaking, nonetheless provided Cream with an insight into the workings of his own soul that would shape the rest of his life. It was also the place where he next encountered Daisy.

It was a bitter winter's night when the stars were rimmed with frost that the coroner left him in charge with the instruction to prepare three corpses for his attention in the morning. A perfunctory if unpleasant task that entailed nothing more than removing the corpse's clothing, washing the bodies and making note of any obvious marks or characteristics prior to the Coroner's post mortem dissection the next day.

The three corpses lay on tables covered with dirty linen sheets. Cream set to his task with as much perfunctory diligence as was required. He completed the first two well enough; the one a dock labourer who had been crushed by a barrel, the other an old woman mown down by a hansom cab and removed the sheet from his third customer. It was then that he stopped, frozen in mid action and stared at the face looking up at him from the table. Though death had robbed her of her robust colouration there was no ignoring the mass of blonde curls and the rounded cheeks.

Daisy.

The shame and anguish he had experienced during their last encounter enfolded him like a cocoon and he stood, quivering with impotent rage. It was some minutes before he could compose himself sufficiently to begin his work. Fate, he reasoned, had meted out a far harsher punishment upon her than any he could devise and had, in addition, given him the opportunity to witness her final degradation. Taking a deep breath to calm his shaking fingers, Cream began to remove her clothing, twisting her body this way and that to assist the process. When he had finished and Daisy lay naked before him, he found himself to be sweating despite the coldness of the morgue. He cast a professional eye upon her naked form. No obvious injuries presented themselves. Cause of death was probably due to alcohol, a not uncommon occurrence particularly with women of her profession. He took his time taking in every aspect of her features, the arrangement of her limbs. He reached out and ran his fingers down the smooth, cold skin of her arms, placed his palms against her rounded belly. Making a small, strangulated, whimper, he wiped sweat from his eyes and cupped one full breast in each hand, lifting them, feeling their weight, pressing thumbs against the mottled nipples. Moving down then to trail his fingers in the forest of pubic hair that dominated the apex of her thighs. That this was more than his professional duty required he had tried to deny but now there was no way to gainsay it. The awful, inevitable truth of the matter was that here, naked and dead on a mortuary slab, Cream found her more desirable than he ever had when the warmth and vitality of life had animated her luscious flesh.

Finding himself painfully aroused, Cream stepped back and loosened his trousers lest they should strangle him. Thus freed, his passion did not ebb; if anything it increased. With slow, hesitant movements, Cream levered himself upon the table, parted Daisy's mottled thighs and insinuated himself between them. With sudden urgency he crawled forward and applied himself most vigorously to that act which he had been unable to perform in the squalid hotel upon their last meeting.

After he had finished, with a gasping cry of satisfaction, he took some minutes to compose himself and adjust his attire. A strange, un-natural calm possessed him. He knew that what he had done was wrong by any sane, rational, definition, but he did not care. He was elated. Fulfilled. Complete. He had, at last, solved one mystery that had tormented him for his entire life. Cream smiled. He whistled a gay tune to himself as he carefully, almost lovingly, washed Daisy's body. As he once more covered her with the soiled cotton shroud he placed a kiss upon her lips. And why not? After all, she was his first. She would not be the last.

Cream's duties at the morgue continued to provide him with opportunities to indulge in his new-found passion, although not with the frequency he would have liked. The aesthetic nature of his prospective dalliances also left something to be desired, but, beggars could not be choosers. It was only after he had graduated and taken up his medical practice that he devised a more reliable method to satisfy his predilection. A rare good fortune at the card table had endowed him with the means to engage the services of one of Daisy's sisters of the streets. A thin, sharp-featured girl with missing teeth, she had taken him to her room where Cream had ordered her to remove her clothes and lie on the bed under instruction not to move or make a sound. Once she had complied, Cream tried to apply himself with his accustomed vigour but found it impossible. Even if the girl had been able to stop herself from involuntary twitches or grunting, the very fact of her breathing, the cacophonous beating of her heart disturbed and upset him. He left unsatisfied.

The next time he attempted to find satisfaction he persuaded the girl to take some ether. Once she was unconscious, a fact he confirmed by pinching her flesh in many sensitive places as hard as he could, and therefore incapable of any involuntary movement, he judged things would go more smoothly. He was wrong. The warmth of her flesh repulsed him and he was unable to perform. There seemed only one inescapable conclusion. In order to satisfy his passion, his partner needed to be bereft of all life. No longer with access to the morgue, his plight seemed desperate, but desperate men adopt desperate measures and Cream began to formulate a plan that would provide him with as many satisfactory playmates as he wanted.

All these thoughts raced through Cream's mind as Wu Feng whispered the fateful words: 'Hello, Creamy' in his ear. That voice! That same, detested voice! In that instant Thomas Cream knew that Wu Feng was none other than Francis Tumblety. He twisted his head to stare up at the leering, grinning face that loomed above him. The erstwhile Chinaman grinned a devilish grin and gave the shouted instruction: 'Release the blade!'

Everything went dark.

10

'Martha sends her love.'

Until those words were spoken, the evening had progressed in much the same way as Abberline had anticipated. Except, of course, for Madame Olga's flagrant disregard for clothing. Having disrobed completely, she made a point of mingling with her patrons, explaining as she did so that the more disreputable psychic mediums even went so far as to secrete items within their own body cavities so as to bring them forth at opportune moments. Having proved that she had no clothing within which to hide such paraphernalia she invited anyone who wished to do so to subject her to whatever intimate search they felt was required to ascertain that she did not have anything hidden within or about her person. This request elicited much discrete coughing and reddening of the cheeks amongst the male attendees and much excited twittering amongst the two ladies, who seemed as though they may just take her up on her offer until Dr Doyle spoke up. He claimed that, as a medical man, he was well acquainted with human anatomy and could state quite categorically that Madame Olga's body would not be suitable for the housing of such devices.

Thanking him for his assurance, and at the obvious disappointment of the two ladies, Madame Olga bade her guests to be seated at the table. Once seated she asked that they hold hands with the person on either side of them and to remain as silent as possible unless communicating with the spirits directly. The gas lamps were dimmed so that the room was cast in deep shadow. The butler took up his station at the door, presumably to prevent any wayward spirits from escaping and the séance began.

First the dramatic and expected deep breathing exercise that Madame Olga practiced to cleanse her mind and to put her in touch with the spirit world. The fact that this caused her bare bosoms to heave and sway in a most salacious manner was simply a bonus and a likely distraction for any underhand practices that may be about to come into play.

'Is there anybody there?' she asked. When silence was her only reply, she took another deep breath and tried again. 'Spirits, if you hear me knock twice I implore you.'

After another moment's silence there came two strong knocks upon the table which caused those present to jump in alarm. Madame Olga simply smiled. 'Thank you spirits,' she said, 'but the connection is weak, the veil is not fully torn asunder and I beg you to make your presence felt more strongly.'

Another moment's silence and then the table began to tremble and then to shake and finally to rise up a good six inches into the air. Amidst gasps of surprise, the table stayed in suspension for a moment or two and then lowered itself back to the floor.

'Ah, that's better,' Madame Olga purred. 'And now we can begin in earnest.'

Manifestations aplenty followed. A trumpet and a vase that had been lying supine on the dresser rose into the air, a glowing spectral image purporting to be a spirit guide called White Feather, appeared out of the gloom and a voice, thin and echoing, gave solace to Lord Haversham who received a loving and heartfelt message from his dearly departed wife. White Feather then dispensed some insights into the past and present life and times of Doyle, Warren and Pinkerton, none of whom had any specific connection to the afterlife that they wanted to pursue. And then it was Abberline's turn.

'Martha sends her love.'

Such gentle, comforting words. If Abberline had been able to believe in their veracity they would have brought solace to a heart that still ached for her loss. His first wife, Martha, had been the love of his life but had died of tuberculosis just a few short weeks after their marriage. Abberline had been broken by that loss and had only survived by immersing himself totally in his work. Ironically, that dedication had much to do with his current reputation and position. For many months, Abberline was of the opinion that this was the form his life would take from now on. He would live out his days as a widower, pursuing his career at all costs. Emma Beament had other ideas. From their first chance meeting after her purse had been snatched in the street she had made it clear that she would not be adverse to further visits of a more social nature from the concerned policeman. The culprit was a known thief and it did not take long for him to be apprehended and Emma's property returned to her. Why Abberline had chosen to return said property himself, a task far beneath his rank, had often perplexed him. Was there some chemistry at work even then that urged him, against his avowed intention to eschew all female company, to put himself in such a position? Whatever the reason, what began as a formal acquaintance progressed to less formal chance meetings engineered, Abberline now knew, by Emma herself, until that spark of mutual attraction blossomed into more fiery emotions. Within six months Abberline and Emma married, the space in his heart forever occupied by Martha still extant and the pain of her loss never extinguished, but eased by the extent of his attachment to Emma.

Hearing Martha's name now, in a voice thin and echoing in that temple of false hope, brought no comfort. Instead, it provoked a rage that boiled over into dramatic action. With a roar, Abberline erupted from his seat, ripping the embroidered cloth from the table. People screamed. Shouts were heard.

'What the devil?'

'He's gone mad!'

'Someone call the police.'

Abberline saved them the trouble. He withdrew a police whistle from his pocket and blew three long, loud blasts. Shrugging off any attempt to restrain him he set about demolishing the room. Ripping down the draperies exposed several wires and mechanisms attached to various objects that had purported to be floating above the patron's heads during the séance. The destruction of the lacquered screen revealed a hidden door, which, when flung open further disclosed a small space containing a chair, a table and a speaking tube at which sat the young maid who had taken Abberine's coat upon his entrance. Upon being discovered, the girl pushed through a thick velvet curtain which led into the hallway. Abberline followed only to be met by the enraged butler. In the ensuing tussle, Constable Colverson barged through the front door only to collide with Madame Olga herself, still naked, running for the stairs. Colverson's eyes went wide.

'Blimey!' he said.

'Don't let her get away!' Abberline shouted breathlessly as a skilful uppercut put paid to the butler's intervention.

Olga struggled ferociously in Colverson's grip, her bare skin giving him nothing to get hold of in order to restrain her. Nonetheless, he persevered manfully in his task and eventually managed to pin the spitting, kicking, swearing, fighting would-be spiritualist to the floor, where, ever the gentleman, he covered her with his cape once the worst of her tantrums had subsided and he had been able to fasten handcuffs upon her. In the meantime, the remaining patrons were streaming into the hall, talking and shouting and demanding to know what was going on. The maid took advantage of the chaos to make her escape through the front door. Finally, largely due to the intervention of William Pinkerton, the tumult subsided and Abberline was able to provide those attending the aborted séance with an explanation.

11

Lord Haversham shook Abberline by the hand, even though the grief and shame of his belief in the callous deception made his expression a hollow mask.

'My dear fellow, I cannot thank you enough. What a fool I've been.'

'Not at all your lordship. Grief is a terrible thing that undermines us all. If your love for your wife hadn't been so great, the deception would not have been so easy to establish. The fault is entirely theirs for taking advantage of your noble emotions.'

'Thank you, thank you,' Haversham muttered and drifted away to be consoled by the two lady writers who seemed disappointed that the sham had ended so soon, their interest fuelled, Abberline had no doubt, more by Madame Olga's state of undress than any spiritual inclination they may have.

As Colverson arranged transportation for the butler and his employer to the police station, only Warner, Doyle and Pinkerton remained. Warner was the first to speak.

'Well, Inspector, you certainly know how to liven up an evening.'

'My apologies if it was a trifle "unforeseen", Mr Warner.'

Warner chuckled. 'You jest, Inspector, but I take it in good part. I hope we meet again.'

'Who knows what the fates hold, Mr Warner.'

Chuckling, Warner left the group and retrieved his hat and coat before making his way into the night.

'A most instructive lesson in the deductive mind, Inspector,' Doyle said. 'Most instructive indeed.'

'Diligent research and simple observation, I assure you,' Abberline said. 'The floating objects were obviously manipulated by that butler chap, using hidden wires behind the draperies.'

'But what about the glowing face that appeared at one point, how do you explain that?'

'Quite simply. The butler used a hidden mechanism to pull back one of the many pictures to reveal a face beneath. He simply closed it again when the illusion had done its work.'

'And the spectral glow?'

'Phosphorus oil. You may have detected a slight smell of garlic in the room? White phosphorus glows in the dark and smells like burnt matches or garlic.'

'Astounding!' Doyle chuckled. 'You are a credit to your profession, Inspector and I thank you for removing a blight from all true psychic believers.'

'I have a question,' Pinkerton said.

'Yes?'

'The floating table.'

'By jove, yes!' Doyle said. 'We all felt the table rise and lower itself several times. You cannot explain that by hidden mechanisms Inspector.'

Abberline pulled on his earlobe as he considered the question. 'No, that was not due to hidden mechanisms, but I believe I have a much more simple explanation. If you would assist me, gentlemen?'

Abberline led the way into the now wrecked parlour. Nothing remained intact save the table itself. A large round base and a circular top that the participants had been seated around.

'If you would be so kind as to take hold of the table edges, gentlemen and lift if you would.'

Following Abberline's instructions, the three men lifted the heavy table top. With some little resistance the top was pulled clear of the base and laid to one side. Abberline leaned over the table's base which was revealed to be hollow.

'Gentlemen, allow me to introduce you to one Shunty Magruider.'

Abberline reached into the hollow base and hauled a stocky individual no more than four feet tall out by his collar.

Doyles eyes went wide. 'Goodness gracious me!' he said.

Pinkerton began to laugh. 'Astounding, Inspector, simply astounding. But how did you know?'

Abberline deposited the squirming Magruider on the floor. 'It was the only possible answer, Mr Pinkerton. Beside, Shunty and I are old acquaintances, isn't that right Shunty?'

'As you say Mr Abberline, as you say,' Magruider admitted.

'Shunty here is an expert cat burglar. His small stature making him ideal to squeeze in through small windows carelessly left ajar. Go and find Constable Colverson, Shunty. He'll give you a lift to the station and, if you can convince us that you knew nothing of the more larcenous aspects of your employment, we may be neglectful in pressing charges.'

'You're a gentleman Mr A. God bless you.'

So saying, Magruider waddled off in search of the constable.

'As generous as you are astute, Inspector,' Pinkerton said.

'We have the big fish. Shunty is harmless enough and now feels obliged should we need information on any matters that may fall within his sphere of influence.'

'Most practical, Inspector,' Doyle said, extending his hand for a farewell handshake. 'I hope we meet again.'

'As do I, Mr Doyle and best of luck with your writing endeavours.'

'Thank you, I … how did you know I was a writer?'

'Research and observation, Mr Doyle. Research and observation.'

Doyle took his leave, smiling and shaking his head in amusement, leaving Pinkerton and Abberline alone.

'I take it you too, will want to be on your way, Mr Pinkerton? There is no reason to detain you. I think my testimony will be sufficient to bring charges.'

'Of course, of course, but I would like to thank you for a most instructive evening and to give you my card.' Pinkerton took a card case from his pocket and passed an embossed calling card to Abberline. 'I've written the name of my hotel on the back in case you do need to contact me. I hope we will meet again, Inspector, in fact I'm sure we will, because you have just given me the answer to a question that has been vexing me ever since I arrived on these shores. Until then, I wish you goodnight.' So saying, the tall American marched out into the night streets.

'Now, what on earth did he mean by that?' Abberline wondered.

12

'Oh, Creamy, your face as the blade came down? What a picture!' Tumblety roared with laughter. They were sequestered in Tumblety's dressing room drinking brandy. Cream drank to steady his nerves, Tumblety because it was his habit to do so. His wig, moustache, and false nails lay haphazardly on a small table along with the remnants of his stage costume. Sitting in his underwear in front of a mirror, Tumblety swiped at his face, removing the last traces of Wu Feng to reveal his own features beneath. 'The audience loved it,' he continued. 'And then you fainted dead away! Priceless! If you think you can do that every night I could make you part of the act.'

'I think not,' Cream muttered.

'No? The bright lights of the music hall not to your taste?' Tumblety turned and refilled their glasses. 'Be just like old times, eh? Oh, the fun we had back then, eh Creamy? Do you remember?'

Cream remembered only too well but chose to say nothing. It fleetingly crossed his mind that Tumblety came from a rich family and, for the sake of those old times he seemed to be so fond of, he might be able to offer Cream a way out of his present financial dilemma. Then the thought of being beholden to this repulsive individual once more drove those thoughts out of his mind. Tumblety seemed not to notice, or maybe not care about, Cream's unease and continued in hearty fashion, drinking steadily, draining the bottle dry and opening another secreted beneath his dressing table.

'Couldn't believe my eyes when I saw you out front. It's been what? Twenty years since we last met?'

'There or thereabouts.'

'My God, how time flies when you're having fun eh?' He laughed uproariously and Cream wondered how someone so obviously in thrall to alcohol could manage the subtle and skilful manipulations on stage that made his impersonation of the Chinese magician Wu Feng so flawless.

'So, tell me all. What have you been doing with yourself all this time, Creamy?'

'Oh, you know. Medicine.'

'Medicine! So you qualified then?'

'Yes.'

'Good for you. Never bothered to stay the course myself. Well, you know that. Had other fish to fry if you get my drift?'

Cream had no idea what he might mean by that and was not inclined to pursue the matter, but common politeness made him ask anyway. 'And what fish might they be?' he said.

It was then that the floodgates opened. Tumblety sank back in his chair, a sad, deflated figure of a man in grubby long johns, his face still smeared with the residue of his masquerade, the hearty build of youth transformed to a withered husk of middle age. The transformation was so swift, so complete that Cream was momentarily stunned.

'Ah, Creamy,' Tumblety whispered. 'If only you knew?' He sat forward suddenly, his eyes boring into Cream's. 'We've always been friends, haven't we, Creamy?'

The idea of friendship between the two of them was so absurd that Cream almost laughed out loud, but instead he said: 'Well … I suppose so.'

'Of course we have. I could always talk to you, Creamy, you know that don't you?'

Cream knew no such thing but simply nodded dumbly.

'Yes, of course we have,' Tumblety continued. 'It's been so long since I had someone to talk to. Really talk to I mean. Confide in, you might say. Now, I feel a need to unburden my soul as it were and it occurred to me tonight, when I saw you in the stalls that here was the answer to my prayers. My old friend Creamy, come to hear my confession.'

'If it's confession you need, maybe a priest … ?'

'Priest wouldn't understand, Creamy. Not men of the world, priests, not like you and me. Here, let me top up your glass and I'll tell you a tale the like of which you've never heard.'

13

'Always been a bit of a restless soul. Never could find anything that caught my attention for more than a fleeting instant. Nothing 'cept drink, gambling and the ladies eh? Pater despaired of me, I know that. Mater had died when I was just two and Pater was always so damned busy. Nannies just ain't the same as a mother's calming influence, wouldn't you agree? 'Course you would. Anyway, Pater indulged me, probably too much and when he died, well, there was nothing to hold me back. I chucked my hand in at medical school. Not my cup of tea at all and went travelling. Saw some sights, I can tell you. Made some chums with a like-minded way about them and we formed a sort of club. Called ourselves the New Reformed Paladins. No idea why. Think it was Nicoli's idea. Nicoli Wassili that is. Funny chap. Rich as Midas. Very interested in the occult, that sort of thing. Anyway, we teamed up with a few others and really let rip I can tell you. Tore a swathe through most of Europe. Carousing and deflowering maidens left right and centre. Couldn't go on of course. All good things and all that. Truth is, I was practically on my uppers. No head for business so I sold everything up and spent the lot. Never regretted a moment of it. Then, when we came back to England we all met up for what was meant to be a last hurrah. They all had careers beckoning, you see. Druitt was about to become a barrister, Maybrick had his cotton mills to attend to. Isenschmid was poised to take over the family meat business and Ostrog always had some sort of scheme in the works. Bury and Deeming had more pedestrian matters to attend to and Wassili had more money than the rest of us put together. Anyway, all I had left was a small place in town and the country house out in Hampshire. That and old Taxil, of course. You remember Taxil?

Family retainer sort. Pater had tried to get him to keep an eye on me, but the old scoundrel was more depraved than I was! Anyway, I telegrammed him to open up the Manor and we all trooped off there to round off a successful season. Eight of us. Nine if you count Taxil. Might have gone off as a very sedate gathering if it hadn't been for the girl. Taxil hired her. Gypsy girl she was. Very good looking. Meant to serve us our meal and help Taxil with the clearing up. The drink began to flow and one thing led to another and then someone, Wassili I think it was, he was always the ringleader I seem to recall, suggested we have some fun with her. That's all it was meant to be. Just a bit of fun. I mean, what peasant girl would object to being serviced by eight strapping young bucks, eh? Well, seven anyway. Druitt had other preferences if you know what I mean. Anyway, this girl gets a bit uppity. Slapped poor old Maybrick right across the chops she did! Well we couldn't have that. Had to put her in her place. Several of us held her down and by God didn't she put up a fight! Maybrick soon knocked the fight out of her, he was good at that sort of thing, and then Nicoli cut off all her clothes with a bloody great dagger! Prime piece of flesh she was too. After that we all took our turn, two or three times in some cases and that soon quietened her down. That was when Isenschmid decided he wanted her to perform one last service before we let her go. He got her on her knees and stuck his todger into her mouth. Seemed to be going all right, I mean, it's probably nothing she hadn't done a hundred times before. But then, I swear something happened. A look in her eyes. They seemed to glow. Hellish frightening I can tell you, but Isenschmid was enjoying himself too much to notice. Then I saw her do it. She opened her mouth just a fraction and then she clamped her jaws down tight on Isenschmid's todger! He screamed, as any man would, but the wretched girl wouldn't

45

let go. He was beating her about the head but she just growled at him! Growled like a dog, I swear, and tossed her head from side to side. Everyone was laughing. They thought it was a rare old joke, but then there was a terrible ripping sound. I can hear it to this day. A terrible ripping sound and she tore Isenschmid's todger right off. Tore it off and spat it out like a bit of gristle. Blood everywhere. Isenschmid fell down and everyone just looked, frozen in place. Everyone but the girl. She was up and off out of the French windows, naked as the day she was born and poor old Isenschmid lying there moaning and bleeding. I called for Taxil to take care of him and then we got dressed as quick as we could and took up arms. Well, we couldn't let her get away with that. We grabbed whatever guns and swords and cudgels that were lying about the place and took off after her.

'It was a rare old chase, I can tell you. Through the woods. Through bushes and brambles. Bad enough for us, but the girl must have been cut to ribbons, naked as she was. Anyway, eventually we came to a clearing. That was where she was heading. Where the caravans were set up. Her family I suppose. Man and woman. Ma and pa presumably and some old crone who came staggering down the steps of one caravan shouting curses in some heathen tongue. I think it was Maybrick who fired the first shot. It may have been Ostrog. No, no, more likely Maybrick. Anyway, the shot was true. Took the girl in the back and fair catapulted her into the arms of her mother. The father turned on us then, bold as brass. I mean to say, he had no case, none at all. No flippertygibbet little whore could expect to get away with inflicting that sort of grievous wound on an Englishman and get away with it. Didn't know it at the time, but she'd done more than that. When we got back to the house we found out that poor old Isenschmid was dead. Bled out right there on the floor. Not that that would have made any difference. The girl's father was screaming in our faces, calling us all sorts. Damned insulting it was when we were completely within our rights to exact retribution. It was Maybrick who struck the first blow. Again. Volatile sort of chap was Maybrick. Anyway, he knocked the man to the ground. And that's when it happened. The change. Now I know you won't believe this, but the gypsy vagabond began to change, right there in front of our eyes. Began with a sort of growling and a twitching. His bones looked ripe to burst out of his skin. Hair began to sprout all over his body and his eyes turned red as the devil's. And his teeth! My God, his teeth. Never seen the like. And he was growing. His clothes fairly exploded from him and when he was done he wasn't a man any more. He was a bloody great wolf! Black as Hades. Slavering and growling. We were frozen to start with. Mesmerised you might say. But that didn't last long. Not once he turned towards us making to leap upon us and rip out our throats. We fired. All at once. Deafening roar. Pretty much every shot hit him and he flopped to the ground bleeding and twitching, but he wasn't done yet. The bounder tried to get up and have at us once more. That's when the swords and the knives came into play. Flesh, blood and fur fair flew I can tell you. And it didn't stop there. The girl who had started all this was dead but her mother and even the old crone came at us then and we just kept on hacking and slashing until there was nothing left to slash. Covered head to foot in blood we were. Our constitutions shattered by what we had just seen. Damned devils in England! That's what they were. We were justified in putting them to the sword, that's for certain, but it was a hell of a thing to witness. Fair broke our nerve I can tell you. When we got back to the house and found out Isenschmid had died, well, that was the end of the Paladins. Next day we went our separate ways. It was a few years later that I heard the news. Bury, Deeming and Wasilli. All dead. All torn to pieces by some unknown brute. Fair put the fear of God into me, I can tell you. Someone or something knows what we did, Creamy. Knows and doesn't like it one bit. Making us pay for our sins. That's when I took up the guise of Wu Feng. Hiding in plain sight you might say. Never go out in public now if I can help it, less it's in disguise. Seems to work, but for how long? That's the question. A man can't live his whole life hiding behind a mask, Creamy, but what choice to I have? There's a hound from hell out there somewhere, Creamy and it's after me next.'

14

The drink and the emotional trauma of his tale had taken their toll on Francis Tumblety. He slumped in his chair, snoring loudly, his face streaked with tears that had been waiting to be shed for many years. Cream watched his former tormentor sleep and felt sorry for him. True, he had made Cream's life a misery but fate had exacted a far more damaging vengeance than Cream ever could. He quietly left the room shutting the door behind him.

Could his preposterous tale be true? Unlikely. The girl and the rape sounded plausible enough. Even her inflicting a grievous wound seemed possible. But the rest? The ravings of a madman, his senses addled by a lifetime of drink and overindulgence. Cream was glad to get away from his presence and out into the cool night air.

15

Abberline closed his own front door with the heavy sigh of a man who wanted to shut out the troubles of the world. How could one city spawn such a multitude of evil? he wondered. Killings, beatings, poisonings, robberies, vice; was there no end to the panoply of human degradation? Abberline was not a religious man, but had he been of that inclination, it would be tempting to ascribe the accumulated sins of his manor to the will of a vengeful God. Maybe this truly was the end of days. Well, not if Frederick George Abberline had any say in the matter it wasn't, even if that same capricious deity had relegated him to unmasking spurious spiritualists. Abberline shook his head and pushed such thoughts to the back of his mind.

He hung his coat on a hook in the hallway and sat on the stairs to remove his clumsy, policeman's boots as quietly as possible. The hour was late and Emma would be asleep by now. Abberline had promised faithfully to be home in time to take a late supper with his wife, but he knew that she would stoically forgive him for yet another missed meal. Despite the depravity that surrounded him on a daily basis, Abberline counted himself a lucky man. Seldom does one man have the good fortune to meet one woman in his entire life who so understands and supports her husband's endeavours, much less two. When he had lost Martha, Abberline had drunk deep from the cup of misery but after meeting Emma, he had learned how to smile again and did so now as he entered his kitchen to see a plate on the table covered with a cloth. Beneath the cloth was bread, cheese and ham. Not the meal he had intended to share with his wife but its very existence evidence of the bond between them. Realising he was famished, Abberline attacked the food with gusto, washing it down with a glass of beer before creeping softly upstairs in his stocking feet. Undressing as quickly and as quietly as he could, Abberline eased himself beneath the covers. Emma murmured and turned towards him, throwing an arm across his chest.

'You smell of beer,' she muttered.

Abberline chuckled. 'A policeman's smell,' he said softly.

'Did you catch him?' Emma asked sleepily.

Abberline thought about correcting Emma's assumption that the target of his evening's activities was male but decided it didn't matter.

'Yes,' he whispered. 'I did. Now go back to sleep, my love.' He kissed her on the forehead and she snuggled deeper into his side.

'Good,' she said. 'I knew you would. You always do.'

Abberline smiled into the darkness. He was indeed a lucky man.

16

'COLVERSON!' Sergeant Thicke's voice had the timbre and the volume of a canon blast and he liked to exercise it at every opportunity. Colverson appeared at his elbow. 'You called, Sarge?'

'Yes, Colverson, I did. If Inspector Abberline can spare you, I have a little job for you.'

'Actually, Sarge, I was just putting together some files for Chief Inspector Abberline's perusal, but I've just seen Inspector Reid go into his office, so I'm free to assist at the moment.' Colverson suppressed a smile. His subtle correction of Abberline's rank had hit the mark but Thicke was too wary to make an issue of it. 'Good,' he said. 'Then perhaps you could deal with "this"?' He pointed a stubby finger at a small, dishevelled figure who barely topped the counter.

'Hello, Nobby,' Colverson grinned. 'What is it this time?'

Nobby rolled his eyes and twisted his battered hat in his hands. 'It was 'orrible Mr C,' he said. ''Orrible it was,' he said.

'Get him out of my sight,' Thicke growled. 'Take his statement and get him out of here before he gives us all fleas.'

'Come on, Nobby,' Colverson said. 'Let's go in the muster room and you can tell me all about it. I'll even see if I can rustle up a cup of tea.'

Thicke watched them go. What is the force coming to, he mused, when an officer is on first name terms with filth like that? Knocking heads and kicking down doors, that's what policing is all about, not making cups of tea for dregs like that. He shook his head and turned his attention back to the racing form in front of him.

'It was 'orrible Mr C, 'orrible it was.'

'You already said that Nobby. What was "'orrible"? Just take it slow and start from the beginning.'

Nobby took a slurp of tea and wiped his mouth on his sleeve. 'Well,' he said, 'it was a couple of nights back. I was down on the embankment lookin' for a nice doorway to curl up in when I sees 'im.'

'Who did you see, Nobby?'

'Don't know his name. Nice dressed fella. Not a toff but respectable.'

'Go on.'

'Well, there was no-one about, it bein' so late but he weren't out for a late night stroll. He was runnin'. Runnin' like his life depended on it. Looked like he'd been at it for a while too because he pulled up and bent over coughing and wheezing like he was on his last breath. That's when I heard it.'

'Heard what?'

'A sort of rumblin', growlin' sort of noise.'

'Growling?'

'That's right. Then I seen it. 'Orrible it was. Black as the devil. And those eyes. Red they was and blazing like the fires of hell itself.'

'What are you talking about, Nobby?'

'A dog. That's what it was. A dog.'

'A dog?'

'But not just a dog. Massive it was. Big as a horse.'

'A horse?'

'Well, a donkey at least. Bigger than any dog you've ever seen.'

'And then what happened?'

'Well, this dog, it comes padding towards this geezer. Takes it's time it does. Like it knows this bloke ain't likely to outrun it.

53

Playin' wiv 'im it is. Well, he goes white as a sheet. I thought he was goin' to pass out on the spot. Then he sort of gathers himself for one last effort, but he doesn't run.'

'What did he do?'

'Jumped right over the side and into the river!'

'He jumped?'

'That's right. And the dog didn't like it neither. Took to howling something awful it did. Ran to the wall and put his paws up on it. Thought he was going to jump in after him I did. But he didn't.'

'Didn't he?'

'No. Because the lady called him back.'

'A lady you say?'

'Oh, aye, it was a lady all right, although she weren't dressed like one.

'What was she dressed like?'

'All in black she was. A bowler hat pulled down over her eyes, black jacket and breeches and high-top boots.'

'Dressed as a man, all in black at night. Are you sure it was a woman, Nobby?'

Nobby chuckled. 'Oh, aye, Mr Colverson. I may be old but I can still appreciate a fine female figure when I sees one and when she climbed up into the driver's seat she had as shapely a backside as I ever did see!' Nobby dissolved into peals of laughter.

Colverson grinned. 'And you're sure she was in charge of this black dog?' he said.

'Positive, Mr Colverson. She was standin' by the open door of a cab and she was whistling to the dog. It turned its head towards her and growled. First, I thought he was goin' to do for her, but he never. She started talkin' to it, real soft. Couldn't make out what she was sayin' but the dog seemed to understand. After a bit he trotted towards her and jumped into the cab nice as pie.

Then she climbed up and drove off. I swear to God that's what 'appened Mr C. 'Orrible it was'

'And what happened to the man who jumped?'

Nobby shrugged. 'Dunno. I went and had a look but it was too dark to see anything.'

'And this was two nights ago?'

'Yes.'

'Why didn't you report it sooner?'

'It was the shock, Mr C. The shock. Had to have a nip or two to steady me nerves and before I knew it ...'

'A whole day had gone by?'

'Knew you'd understand, Mr C. You do believe me don't ya?'

'Course I do, Nobby. Now, how about another cuppa?'

17

Edmund Reid was young to be a Detective Inspector. Even so, he recognised an opportunity when it was handed to him on a silver platter despite the fact that the caseload he had inherited was staggering in both number and variety. Robberies, murders, assaults, missing persons. All human depravity was there. To be put in charge of such a caseload could be the making of him. Or the finish.

Chief Inspector Abberline would have been the natural choice to handle the investigations. But not now. Reid stood in front of Abberline's desk like a nervous schoolboy summoned to the headmaster's office.

'I'd just like you to know, sir, that I never asked for this assignment,' Reid said.

'Sir Charles Warren rarely asks for permission in these matters I find,' Abberline replied. The younger man's discomfort was evidence in his stance, the way he avoided eye contact, the shuffling of his feet and the way he held his hands firmly clamped behind his back to prevent them betraying him by the slightest tremble.

Reid cleared his throat. 'Quite so, sir. And despite the … unfortunate reversal of the natural order, I hope I may still rely on you for advice should I require it?'

Abberline gave a small nod. 'My door is always open, Edmund.' Reid visibly relaxed at the use of his first name. 'But it's been my experience,' Abberline continued, 'that there are two types of investigator. The first seeks nothing but the outcome that will reflect well upon himself, regardless of any other factor. The second follows the course of law and seeks justice in all cases whilst shouldering the responsibility that such action results in, regardless of their own welfare. How broad are your shoulders, Edmund?'

Reid looked Abberline in the eye and nodded. 'Broad enough I think, sir.'

'Splendid. Then I doubt you'll have need of my advice, but it is always available should you do so. Now, off you go, Edmund. I'm sure you have much more important things to do.'

18

After writing up Nobby's statement, Colverson found himself ensconced in Abberline's office with a large pile of folders as requested. For the next hour, Abberline and Colverson combed through the written documents. The complaints, the accusations, the wild rumours. They segregated them into different piles in order of relevance and potential accuracy in relation to the many ongoing investigations that vied for police attention.

'In a perfect world,' Abberline said, 'we would have the resources to follow up on all of these leads regardless of how futile much of it may seem. Being able to rule out a suspect is just as important as finding a likely culprit. Given our current status, we may well be asked to shed some light on the more fanciful or time consuming reports that we have here,'

Colverson smiled. 'Something to keep us busy, you mean, sir?'

'Precisely. But it would do no harm to suggest a pecking order to Inspector Reid of those cases that may have even a glimmer of validity, do you think?'

'Absolutely, sir.'

'Splendid. So, let's see what would best use our expertise, shall we?'

A further half hour's work and a much smaller pile of folders lay in the centre of Abberline's desk. Though each one had a sliver of merit, only one such case rose to the top of this unsavoury pile. Abberline tapped the file. 'The Lambeth Poisoner,' he said.

'That's what the Gazette are calling him, sir. Four bodies so far. All working girls, all found dead in alleys or the like. All poisoned.'

'Hmmm.' Abberline steepled his fingers and mused for a second or two. 'The esteemed editor of the Pall Mall Gazette, Mr Stead, has deemed him worthy of banner headlines, but little progress seems to have been made in the case.'

'Accidental poisoning isn't unusual, sir. Inspector Reid didn't think it worth the manpower to follow up.'

'Four random deaths in a relatively short space of time, all disposed of in the same manner? Speaks of a certain modus operandi wouldn't you say, Colverson?'

'Could be, sir.'

'Get me what you can on the victims and I'll speak to Inspector Reid about letting us dabble in these particular murky waters. The rest seem fairly straightforward. Nothing that merits immediate attention at any rate, wouldn't you agree, Colverson?'

Colverson hesitated. 'Well, sir,' he said, 'there's something that has just come to my attention. It's not an official case as yet, but ...'

'But you think it bears investigating?'

'Yes, sir, I do.'

'Then let's hear it, Colverson. A good copper always trusts his instincts.'

Basking in the glow of his superior's compliment, Colverson outlined Nobby's account of the black dog and the victim who had consigned himself to the embrace of the Thames. When he had finished, Abberline sat back and steepled his fingers in thought.

'And what makes you think this wasn't just a fantasy brought on by drink or the possibility of a free cup of tea?' he asked.

'I took the liberty of going through the missing persons reports, sir,' Colverson replied. 'Nobby reckoned the victim was some sort of gentleman so it stood to reason that if he went missing someone would have reported it.'

'And did they?'

'I think so, sir, yes.' Colverson passed one last file across the desk. Abberline read the single sheet of paper therein. When he had finished, he closed the file.

'Add it to the pile, Colverson,' he said. 'Your instinct may prove right or wrong, but it is definitely worth investigating. Good work.'

19

In the still, small hours of the night when even London sleeps, Patrick Reilly stands on the roof of his warehouse headquarters surveying the city, listening to the diverse, small sounds that carry so well on the night air, smelling the many odours, malodourous and otherwise, that suffuse the atmosphere. This night has a rare, clear sky and a ripe full moon. Most would shiver in its dark embrace but Reilly welcomes it even though he is completely naked. He enjoys the feel of the chill against his skin, every inch of his body alive and sensitive to the vibrations in the air. He hears footsteps behind him. He does not turn. He knows who it is – knows that heartbeat as well as he knows his own, that scent so special and arousing, that light tread on the harsh surface of the roof. Siobhan. His wife. His love. The mother of his son. She comes to stand behind him and slips her hand into his. Like him, she is naked. She breathes deeply. 'Isn't she beautiful?' she says, gazing at the moon.

'Aye, she is that. But even her beauty pales next to your own,' he tells her.

She laughs quietly and nudges him with her shoulder. 'Go on with you,' she says.

''Tis nothing but the truth,' he says. 'You were beautiful the day I met you and you've become more so every day since.'

She takes the compliment and rests her head on his shoulder.

'How's the lad?' he asks her. She looks up at him and he can see the moonlit tears reflected in her yes. 'He sleeps peacefully. For now at least.'

Reilly nods. The malady that threatens to take their son's life tears the hearts out of his parent's breasts as it does so.

'We'll not lose him. I swear it,' Reilly says, his voice gruff with unshed tears. Siobhan nods and says nothing. After a long silence, she says: 'Do you not want to run, my love? Do you not want to shake off this skin and howl at the moon?'

He tightens his grip upon her hand. 'More than ever,' he tells her. 'But now is not the time. One day we will. One day when we are free and far from here. Back in the forest where we belong. For now, it would be too dangerous.'

He turned to her, taking her in his arms, her flesh cool against his, stoking a fire within.

'I swear we will be free one day soon, I can feel it in my bones. This final piece of business is already begun, and then …'

She stopped him by placing a finger across his lips. 'Don't talk of such things,' she said. 'Not now. Not when we have the moon and each other.'

He kissed her lips. Tenderly at first, then more fiercely. She laughed as she felt him grow against her, then he swept her off her feet and laid her down on the rooftop. Their coupling was not gentle. It was raw, passionate and overpowering. And then they did howl. In unison at their completion as the moon gazed down upon their naked writhings and gave them her blessing.

It was later, as they lay in bed together, that Patrick Reilly's dreams descended into nightmare. Once, they had lived such an ideal existence as he had promised Siobhan they would have again. The Pack. That was what they called themselves. An ancient name for an ancient clan. Just a few families, last descendants of the great packs that once ravaged the land before disease and mankind had driven them almost to extinction. Safely hidden, or so they thought, in one of the great forests of England, they kept to themselves and only hunted game when the moon was full, venturing into the local villages rarely and briefly.

The dream was always the same. Patrick was young, just

thirteen years old, but already the moon had called to him and the change had taken him over. How he had exulted in the sounds, the scents, the feelings that had consumed him that first time. The raw, savage ecstasy as he had rampaged through the woods in search of his first kill. Seeking, finding, rending with tooth and claw, the blood warm in his mouth, the flesh and bones snapping beneath his jaws. His father had watched over him that night, making sure he did not stray too close to so-called civilisation, keeping him safe until the killing madness had passed. And it *had* been a kind of madness. One that with time, patience and tutoring, he came to control. It was Granny Kelly, his mother's mother's mother, or so they said, who had taken him to one side after the blood lust had calmed. She took him back to the place of his first kill and told him of the old ways. Showed him how those with the skill could look into the entrails of an animal, or even a human being, and foretell the future.

'And what is my future?' he had asked. Granny Kelly had looked deep into his eyes, her wrinkled face grave and serious.

'You will serve our clan mightily,' she had said. 'But you will have a hard road to walk. If you are willing, I can teach you the old ways. Show you how to be wise as well as mighty.'

Patrick had considered that. The thrill of the kill was still singing in his blood, but something about the old woman's words stirred something else deep within him. 'Yes,' he had said. 'I would like that.' And so, it had begun. Granny Kelly had taught him the knowledge of the clan going back through history. Not just how to read entrails to divine portents, but herbs and cures and much, much more. 'You will be a chieftain one day,' she had told him, 'and you must be ready to make whatever sacrifice is needed to uphold the honour of the clan.'

Patrick's father had uttered a word of caution. 'Granny is old,' he had said. 'Don't put too much store in the old tales she tells. It's true enough that we are part of an ancient bloodline,' he said. 'Not all of our kind can make the change. Time has dulled their instincts. The call of the moon is not strong in them. Your sister, Eveline is one who finds it hard to answer the call, but you are blood pure and must remain so.'

That summer under the trees was a time of peace and discovery for the young Patrick. His sister, Eveline, found work as a housemaid in the big house and his father toured the local fairs selling his intricate carvings of forest creatures. Patrick spent his days wandering the woodland paths, not hunting but observing, watching nature in all its glory. On that one fateful day he had spent many long hours lost in the magic of nature. As the sun began to set he lay beneath a venerable oak and closed his eyes. With the last rays of the setting sun playing games upon his eyelids he drifted off to sleep.

How long he slept he didn't know but he was woken by screams. Screams and the sound of gunfire. Springing to his feet, Patrick raced back to their encampment only to be greeted by a scene of devastation. Bodies lay sprawled, bloodied, mutilated. Caravans overturned and wrecked. His mother and father, Eveline. All dead.

All except one.

Granny Kelly stood amidst the carnage, her bright, dark eyes fixed on Patrick. With a strangled cry, he ran towards her. He ran to Granny Kelly and fell at her feet, tears streaming from his eyes, his heart bursting, unable to speak. It was only as she reached down and placed her hand upon his head that he realised. Her touch was soft as a sigh with no more substance than a summer's breeze. With overwhelming horror, Patrick realised that the mangled remains beside which Granny stood were her own.

'Read, child,' she whispered. 'Read and know and give us our due.'

When Patrick looked up, the vision was gone, but the mortal remains still had a story to tell. He stared at the mutilated flesh that had once been Granny Kelly and he saw. Saw as clearly as if he had witnessed the awful events for himself.

There were eight of them. Eight distinct, individual scents. They were chasing their prey with wild abandon. Screaming and whooping. Their prey he realised was Eveline. Naked and blood spattered she charged heedlessly trough the undergrowth, thorns and brambles ripping cruelly at her bare flesh. As she burst into the clearing where their caravans stood, a blast from a rifle took her in the back and she fell. His father and mother rushed to her side, cradling her head as she died in their arms. The men, if such they can be called, entered the clearing. Patrick saw his father rise, spring forward, a growl upon his lips, the change already beginning to take him. In any fair fight, the interlopers would have been gristle and bone in seconds, such was his father's fury, such was the power of the Pack. But this was no fair fight. At first with rifle fire and then with blades, the murdering mob attacked, hacking and slashing until no-one was left standing. All fell beneath their fury. And through it all, they laughed.

When the initial bloodlust was over, they took their leave, laughing and joking as they retreated. Patrick felt the uncontained rage build inside him and he howled at the moon. If those who had desecrated his pack heard that sound it would have sent shivers down their cowardly spines as Patrick turned and made to track them down then and there and exact his revenge.

It was the shade of Granny Kelly who held him back. What could he do against those that had already slaughtered his family? He was strong, but he was still a lone boy against guns and swords. Better to wait, she argued, to plan, to stalk, to hunt and take revenge at a time and place of your own choosing. Slowly, unwillingly, grieving in the depths of his soul, Patrick had bowed to her logic as he would do so many times over the years and had never regretted it for an instant. Over the next day a boy not yet a man buried all those he held dear. Saying ancient prayers over their graves. When, at last he was finished, he harnessed their horse and rode away. A quest had begun and he would see it through to the bitter end.

Eventually, Patrick had been taken in by another clan. The Chieftan agreed to his presence grudgingly. He saw in the boy a potential rival, but his wife and daughter took pity on him and he found a home of sorts for several years. All that time his need for vengeance burned like a fallen star within his breast. The only thing that made his life bearable was Siobhan. Daughter of the clan Chieftan, she soothed his rage and dried his tears when he could hold them in no longer. On long, cold nights he told her of his quest and how he yearned to fulfil his destiny. She held him in her arms and whispered comforting words.

'You'll not have to do it alone,' she would whisper. 'Wherever you go and whatever you do, I shall always be with you.'

She was true to her word. Just a few days before his eighteenth birthday, Patrick and Siobhan left the clan and the hunt truly began. It was not to be easy. To track down such influential men, Patrick needed power and influence of his own. How could an orphaned gypsy boy acquire such power? The answer was simple.

Crime.

Quick of wit and ruthless in execution of daring plans, Patrick soon became a force to be reckoned with in the big city. As his power grew, so too did his influence, his knowledge. One by one, the killers of his family were identified. One by one he had hunted and killed and each had known the terror visited upon his own family before he gave them their release. Now, just three remained. Three amongst the thousands who resided in this city that he now called home. He had them in his sights. He could smell them. He could sense them. It was just a matter of time. With their deaths, Patrick hoped the dreams would subside. He had made a life for himself. A criminal life, it is true, but a life he intended to enjoy without encumbrance. A wife he loved more than anything in this world or the next. And a son ... The only sorrow that threatened to mar his triumph. Sick. Fading. But not without hope. Patrick Reilly had resources and he intended to use every one of them to return his son to health. And God help anyone who stood in his way.

20

Lady Constance Barlow. Society hostess. Widow of Sir Terrence Barlow, property baron and staunch Christian moralist who, during his lifetime, had supported many campaigns aimed at ridding the streets of London of all forms of licentiousness and lewd behaviours. The fact that his efforts had largely been futile did not diminish his ardour in this respect and had, instead, inspired him to renew his efforts. All the while, his wife had stood steadfastly by his side, presiding over many social gatherings of the good and influential who may have been persuaded to join his crusade. The fact that many of these individuals took full advantage on the immoral activities pervading the nation's capital, and whose worthy contributions were nothing more than conscience salving exercises, and whose support was nothing more than lip service, escaped Sir Terrence's attention but not his wife who had a much keener sense for these things.

With Sir Terrence reposing serenely for all eternity in Highgate Cemetery, Lady Constance saw no reason to continue with this particular charade and herself began to indulge hitherto repressed desires of the more erotic and carnal variety, albeit in a most discrete manner.

It was in this endeavour that she had first met Michael Ostrog. A handsome gentleman of means, he had recently returned to England after selling his overseas mining operations for a considerable fortune and was now deliberating over his next project and would Lady Constance perhaps be willing to join him in whatever venture he decided upon for a small financial investment? Flattered by the younger man's attention, Lady Constance agreed to give his proposal her utmost consideration. In the meantime, they began to socialise both in public and in private. It was the nature of these private associations that weighed heavily in his favour when deciding to commit to a financial relationship in addition to a more intimate sort.

Ostrog, for his part, seldom played the gigolo, but the size of Lady Constance's fortune quickly overcame any scruples he might have. His overseas sojourn had coincided with his stay in a French prison for fraud and any mining operation he may have had resided firmly in the realms of fantasy. In truth, he was a confidence trickster suffering from a spate of ill-timed misfortunes that had left him almost penniless. It was not a situation that he was unfamiliar with and had every confidence that his fortunes would take a significant upturn as they always had. If only he could persuade Lady Constance to part with the promised funds he would be free to depart for pastures new with his pockets full. But she was proving a tougher nut to crack than anticipated and her physical demands were becoming increasingly more onerous.

Today, for instance, he was forced to sit through her interpretation of the legend of Salome and the seven veils before, he was sure, she would demand a most vigorous servicing, and he was beginning to find it more and more difficult to rise to her expectations as time went on. True professional that he was, he sat on the expensive embroidered chaise and smiled and applauded enthusiastically as veil after veil was discarded with elephantine grace. At sixty years of age and with a girth that could only be described as ample bordering upon gross, Lady Constance finally disposed of the final flimsy covering to stand displayed in all her considerable glory for her lover to admire.

'Bravo!' Ostrog shouted. 'Bravo!' He clapped and blew kisses at this outstanding vision of womanly charm, who, in appreciation, simpered like a schoolgirl but made no attempt to cover her blushes or her nakedness, preferring to parade her charms for his closer inspection.

Ostrog attempted to rise, hoping to plead that he had been so enraptured by Lady Constance's erotic display that he had quite forgotten the time and an urgent business meeting would drag him away from her company forthwith with the promise of a return later in the day when he had had time to fortify himself for the labours still to come.

But he was too late.

With an enthusiastic lunge, Lady Constance threw herself upon him with enough force to drive the air from his lungs and to slide the chaise upon which they now both reposed back a foot or so across the floor.

'Oh, Michael!' she whispered. 'I'm so glad you enjoyed my performance.'

'You were magnificent my dear,' he whispered, finding no breath for any more forceful conversation.

Taking his breathlessness for passion, Lady Constance began to smother his face with wet kisses even as she fumbled with the buttons of his trousers.

Trapped as he was, Ostrog feared that escape was to be impossible and was about to surrender to the inevitable when he heard a noise. It was the sound of heavy footfalls and the click-clack of something hard on the polished floor of the hallway.

'What was that noise?' he asked.

'Just the beating of my heart, my darling,' Lady Constance sighed.

'No, not that. Something else. Is there someone in the house?'

Ostrog tried to push his enamorata away but realised it was a futile effort.

'There is no-one, my love,' Lady Constance told him. 'We are quite alone.'

'No!' he gasped. 'I don't think we are.'

As he spoke, the drawing room door swung open to reveal an apparition the like of which Ostrog had never seen. A huge canine. Hellish black with coal red eyes and open, slavering jaws. He watched over Lady Constance's shoulder, aghast, as this demonic vision padded slowly across the carpet to stand next to their entwined forms.

Engrossed in her endeavours, Lady Constance had no idea they had been joined by a third party until she felt hot breath upon her bare shoulder. Thinking it was the passionate exhalations of her erstwhile paramour, she giggled happily. When the hot breath was followed by a low growl, she took it as a sign of imminent carnality and whispered: 'Oh, Michael, you animal, you!'

How truly she spoke was revealed in the next second when sharp fangs sank into her naked buttocks. She screamed and sprang up from Ostrog's prone form with an alacrity he did not know she possessed.

Glimpsing the beast, Lady Constance continued to scream and scramble back on all fours until she collided with an armchair from where she had a ringside seat as the beast took her place on the chaise atop Michael Ostrog whose throat the hell hound commenced to rend and tear into bloody strips. Her screams diminished to a whimper as the beast, satisfied that his task was complete, turned from his prey and padded slowly from the room.

It was some time before Lady Constance could rouse herself from her position on the floor. She had wet and soiled herself but this seemed a small matter compared with the sight of Ostrog's mutilated corpse.

Small, whining noises escalated once more into full-blown

screams as her neighbours in this most sedate neighbourhood were treated to the sight of a naked Lady Constance running for her life.

21

Jacob Crow was a big man, an inch over six feet, solidly built and muscular with a square face that bore the marks of a hard life and hands as broad as shovel blades. His physique was most appropriate for his former occupation of prize-fighter. At one time the South of England Heavyweight Champion, many a betting man would have laid odds that Jacob Crow could even have beaten the legendary Tom Cribb had the two men been contemporaries.

For Crow, his former life came to an end one August night as he made his way up the stairs to his first floor room above the Black Swan Inn where he also served as a barrel man and general keeper of the peace. He had just returned from an exhibition match at Exeter fair; a long trip but a fruitful one and he was glad to return home a good two days earlier than expected due to unseasonal inclement weather that had led the fair's owner to move on to their next location sooner than expected. On his way through the bar, the landlord had attempted to impede his progress by imploring him to regale his customers with tales of his latest exploits in the ring. Crow declined the invitation, promising to tell all the following day. For now he was tired, wet and hungry and wanted nothing more than the company of his wife, Flora. It was as Crow reached the door to his room that he realised that Flora was entertaining some company of her own.

Two voices, a man and a woman's, came clearly through the wooden barricade. Voices tainted with laughter and low moans. Crow knew those sounds and what they denoted all too well. How often had he heard Flora make those same sounds as she lay with him? Too often for them to be mistaken for anything other than what they were. A pulse began to beat in Crow's temple and a red mist veiled his vision as he turned the handle and opened the door.

Jacob and Flora Crow lived in one large room with a single, grubby, window. Flora kept the room clean and the furnishings, though far from new, were in good repair. A table, two wooden chairs, an armchair, a closet and a bed comprised their meagre possessions. It was the bed which now commanded Crow's attention. Unlike the spic and span nature of the rest of the room, the bed was unkempt, the covers thrown onto the floor in disarray the better to accommodate the bed's occupants and to remove any hindrance to their activities.

Flora screamed when she saw him, grabbing a pillow to hide her nakedness. Her companion, a skinny whippet of a man called Honest John whom Crow recognised as a bookmaker from many of his contests, was equally naked and made a grab for his clothes that lay scattered on the floor. His quest for modesty ended when Crow's boot took him square in the stomach with a force that lifted him off the floor and slammed him into the wall. With scarce a glance at his dishevelled wife, Crow closed in on the man who had made him a cuckold, lifted him by the throat to a standing position and began raining blows to his face and body until bones cracked and blood flowed. At some point in his rage, Crow was aware of Flora screaming in his ear to stop and beating her fists against his broad back. Her blows may as well have been the beating of butterfly wings for all their effectiveness. Crow's opponent, who had yet to raise a single hand in self-defence, became a human punching bag upon which Crow unloaded his anger. Finally, the red mist that flooded Crow's mind began to recede. He was aware of Flora sitting on the bed that had so recently been besmirched by her betrayal, sobbing helplessly. He was dimly aware also of a group of people standing in the doorway, the landlord and some patrons from the bar, watching, both appalled and fascinated by this unexpected turn of events. Crow looked down at his bruised and bloodied fists and took a step back. Honest John, no longer held pinned to the wall by Crow's relentless pummelling, slid to his knees and would have fallen flat upon his face had Crow not taken a handful of his hair to keep him upright. Crow took a long, slow look about the room, at Flora, at his familiar possessions that now held no meaning or attraction for him and at the small crowd of onlookers and finally at his victim.

Crow was a pugilist of remarkable strength and ability. He knew what damage the human body could take and still recover. He knew how and where to hit to ensure that maximum pain and injury would be inflicted. His perusal of the sack of meat and bones that had previously been Honest John was a precise as any medical man. There was no hope of resuscitation, no means of undoing or mending the damage Crow had inflicted and so, he did the one compassionate act he was capable of; he put Honest John out of both their miseries. With one hand on the top of Honest John's head and the other beneath his jaw, Crow tilted his head up so that he could stare into the rapidly swelling eyes. Then, with a sharp twist, he snapped the man's neck with a sound like a single gunshot.

Flora let out one more piercing, ululating scream. Crow let the dead body fall. Then he moved to the door, the group of onlookers parting as swiftly and as irrevocably as the Red Sea had done for Moses to let Crow stride down the stairs where he helped himself to some ale, sat at a table and waited for the police to arrive.

Crow could have run. He had his fee from the fair in his pocket. He could have made his way north, Scotland maybe, even overseas where no-one knew him. He could have taken labouring jobs until the hue and cry had died down, then, maybe returned to the only trade he knew, fighting in booths at travelling fairs, always on the move. It would have been a hard life, but a change of name and a little patience may even have seen his fortunes return to a more reasonable level. Crow could have done any of those things but chose not to. Without Flora, life did not seem worth living and so he decided to let the fates decide his future. He expected the drop. So many witnesses, including his wife. He was too well-known for there to be any question of mistaken identity. Crow knew he would die for what he had done and said not a single word in his own defence.

It was Judge Blackstone who presided over his case. Blackstone was known to be a hard man with no ounce of mercy in his soul. Crow barely took any notice of the proceedings. He expected a long line of witnesses from the pub, all denouncing his act as one of brutal murder and he waited patiently for Blackstone to reach for the black cap that would send him to the rope. It did not happen.

Before a single witness had been called, before the jury had heard one shred of evidence, Judge Blackstone made an announcement.

'I have had significant petitions made to me in regard to this case and have reviewed all the salient facts in minute detail. In my opinion it would be a waste of the court's time to proceed with a trial and I am prepared to pronounce judgement immediately.'

Crow's barrister protested vociferously, but Blackstone silenced him by application of his gavel and his booming voice, not to mention the threat of six months hard labour for disrupting his court. The man remained silent and Crow waited for his death sentence to be delivered.

'Jacob Crow,' Blackstone continued, 'you are a man to whom violence is a way of life. It is your natural recourse when events occur that vex you beyond all reason. In this instance, I have several witness statements that verify that such an event did occur on the night in question. The victim of cuckolding by your wife, a woman to whom you had shown nothing but respect, who you had provided for in all material ways, and who had betrayed you in the most blatant fashion would be enough to put any man into a justifiable rage. It is my opinion that the crime of murder of which you are accused was nothing more than a faithful husband's attempt to save his wife from what you no doubt perceived at the time as the most unwanted attentions of a scoundrel and a cad. The fact that your wife freely admits that this liaison was of her own making was not known to you at the time and has put irrevocable strain on your relationship leading to her wish that said marriage be annulled forthwith. I concur with that wish and will draw up a document that states you are now legally divorced one from the other. The demise of the aforementioned scoundrel is therefore nothing more than an accident of her betrayal and, as you had no previous desire to be freed from the matrimonial bonds, I feel that this is punishment enough. The charge of murder is therefore dismissed and you are free to go without a stain upon your reputation.'

The uproar in the packed courthouse was almost enough to drown out Blackstone's gavel as he called for order.

Crow was led away and found himself sitting on a bench outside the court bemused and unbelieving. It was then that a man approached him. A smiling, dark haired Irishman, as his accent soon declared him to be. He sat down next to Crow as though they had been acquaintances for many years and began to speak.

77

'Well, me bucko, there's a turn-up for the books and no mistake, eh?'

Crow shook his head. 'Leave me alone,' he said.

'Now is that any way to talk to the man who just saved you from the noose,' the stranger said.

Crow looked at him. 'You?' he said. 'How did you save me from the noose?'

Patrick Reilly tapped the side of his nose. 'That would be telling,' he said. 'Let's just say Judge Blackstone owes me more than a few favours and I persuaded him that sending you into the arms of Jack Ketch would be terrible waste of prime horseflesh that could be better utilised in other ways.'

'I'm not a horse.'

'True. But you are a thoroughbred. Think of it as my way of saying thank you for all the wagers I've won over the years betting on your fights. The name's Reilly by the way. Patrick Reilly.'

He held out his hand.

Crow looked at it. 'I've never heard of you,' he said.

'Not many people have, and that's the way I like it. Come on, shake my hand. I have a proposition for you that you'll not want to refuse. One that's much better than dangling from a noose I can tell you that.'

Crow considered for a moment and then reached out to shake Reilly's hand.

'That's better,' Reilly said. 'Now, what say we get out of here and celebrate your first night as a free man?'

22

When the celebrating was over, Crow wondered just what it was that Reilly wanted with him that made him worth all this effort. It didn't take him long to deduce that Reilly's business interests did not always fall within the letter of the law. True, he did own drinking establishments, bawdy houses, pawn shops and the like, but, without exception they were simply a mask for many and varied criminal activities.

Reilly lived in a townhouse situated near the docks. At the rear of the house was a warehouse which was a veritable Aladdin's cave of stolen goods. Crow was given quarters at the back of the warehouse and afforded every courtesy by Reilly and his men, but as to his actual role in the grand scheme of things? That soon became apparent.

At first it was quite simple. A series of private exhibition bouts for an invited audience of rich, influential members of the aristocracy who would pay a pretty penny to see the former South of England Heavyweight Champion in action. Some of them would even pay considerably more to spar for a single, three minute, round with the man whose lethal fists had almost sent him to the gallows. For those bouts Crow was more akin to a dancing partner, ensuring that his opponent didn't inadvertently trip and hurt himself, allowing them to get in a couple of solid punches whilst delivering the gentlest of rejoinders for the sake of verisimilitude. During these matches, Reilly and his wife, a fiery redhead called Siobhan "worked the room" making contacts and cementing business arrangements and soliciting information or the promise thereof in return for various illicit favours.

'These men are in the know,' Reilly told him. 'They are of a kind and they know others of their kind. It's that knowledge I desire. I seek names, you see. Names and locations. By promising favours and exerting leverage I will get those names and locations and then my real mission will begin.'

When Crow expressed his confusion over this information, Reilly sat him down with a glass of brandy and told him a tale. He told him about his family. About his sister. About how eight men from the upper classes that thronged to see Crow's bouts had massacred them all. He told him that it was his sacred duty to find each and every one of them and avenge the wrong that had been done to his kin. Over many years, four of those men had already fallen like wheat before the scythe of his vengeance. Four more remained, their fate inevitable, before his mission was complete.

'You can understand that, can't you?' Reilly asked.

Crow considered for a while and then nodded his head.

'Good man,' Reilly beamed. 'And that is why you are so important to me Jacob. You are my ticket into the company of such men who can supply me with the names of those I seek.'

Reilly deliberately left out any information pertaining to his and Siobhan's true nature. He was unsure how such a revelation would go down.

That issue was settled some six months after Crow had commenced his employment in the Reilly household.

23

Florence Maybrick was a mousy woman in her mid-thirties. She had been one of Cream's patients for some time now. He had treated her for a number of minor injuries. Cuts, bruises, cracked ribs and, on one occasion, a broken finger. Not given to over-sentimentality about his patients, Cream felt an overwhelming sympathy for the thin, washed-out woman who sat in his consulting room and gingerly rolled up her sleeve to reveal a forearm mottled black and yellow with bruises. She reminded him of his mother. Her explanation for her ongoing injuries, like Florence Maybrick, was an inordinate level of clumsiness. In his mother's case, Cream knew different. His father had been the administrator of such clumsiness to his two sons as well as his wife, thinking that his wealth as a respected draper endowed him with impunity when it came to using his fists to underpin his arguments. At least the old devil had the decency to pay for James' medical school tuition and his death had led Cream to believe that his inheritance would be substantial enough to finance his own career. Alas, he was disappointed in that regard when it was revealed that his father's cavalier attitude towards the physical well-being of his family extended also to his business affairs. Cream's inheritance amounted to a pile of debts that the sale of his father's business had been barely enough to cover. James, having not yet attained his current level of success was barely able to keep their mother in genteel poverty which left Cream the younger to fend for himself. It was then that Cream's own decline had really begun and, seeing Florence Maybrick's pathetic condition brought all the unpleasantness that had infested Cream's life back to the surface.

Cream probed gently at her injured arm and she winced. 'My

apologies, Mrs Maybrick,' he said. 'I do not think it is broken, just badly bruised.'

'That is a blessing, doctor,' she murmured. 'I really don't know how I would cope if it had to be put into plaster. My husband is a prominent businessman and would be most vexed if I were not able to see that his clothes were washed and ironed and his food prepared on time and to his liking.'

Cream made a reflective "hmmm" sound. He could well imagine the form Mr Maybrick's vexation would take were his creature comforts not available. 'I will give you something for the pain,' he said, 'but you must be careful. How did you say you came by this injury, Mrs Maybrick?'

A flush suffused Florence Maybrick's sallow cheeks. 'I foolishly trapped it in a door,' she said.

Cream reviewed his notes. 'You do seem to have a surfeit of awkward doors, Mrs Maybrick. Likewise obstructive stairs, pernicious gas lamps and vicious lengths of loose carpeting.' Florence blushed deeper and said nothing. 'It would lead me to believe that there may be some other cause for these injuries,' Cream said mildly. 'One might almost suppose that some hidden malady of the brain were causing you to have such mishaps. Or maybe, that some outside agent was visiting these misfortunes upon you.'

'I'm sure I don't know what you mean, Dr Cream,' she said softly.

'Then let me speak more plainly, Mrs Maybrick. Have you been the victim of beatings that result in this conglomeration of injuries? Or someone mistreating you to the point where it may endanger your life? Your husband perhaps?'

Florence Maybrick regarded him with the wide eyes of a startled rabbit. She opened her mouth to reply, but no sound was forthcoming. Then, her lower lip began to tremble and she began to sob. For a second, Cream was most discomfited. As the level of her sobbing increased, he moved to awkwardly to comfort her although such close contact with a woman who was still breathing , whose flesh was still warm to the touch, was alien to his nature unless it was strictly within the bounds of his medical duties. At last, her sobbing subsided.

'He's not a bad man,' she told him. 'He provides well enough in every other way. It was his most sincere wish to have a family, but I have been unable to provide such a service.' She bowed her head. 'It is my failing that drives him to such anguish and he has no other way to express his frustration. No other way, that is, except one. And I do not blame him for that. He has needs and his revulsion at my inability to satisfy his deepest wish leads him to seek succour in certain quarters where more fulfilling consorts may take his mind off my failings, if you know whereof I speak.'

Cream nodded. He knew only too well what she was saying. Her husband was a brute and a fornicator. A frequenter of brothels who took his foul temper out on his defenceless mouse of a wife.

'He beats you for his own pleasure, 'Cream said acidly. 'That much is self-evident regardless of any spurious reason he may ascribe to the act.'

'Please don't tell him I told you!' she pleaded.

'I have no intention of doing so,' Cream said. 'Whatever you reveal to me here remains strictly confidential. However, I feel I would be derelict in my medical duty if I did not suggest some remedy for the malady that afflicts you.'

'A remedy?' she asked, startled.

Cream considered for a second and then reached a decision. He moved back to his desk and removed a nondescript packet from a bottom drawer. 'Take this,' he said. 'Put one spoonful into your husband's drink on a regular basis. I think you will find it improves his temperament significantly. Once a day should suffice, but if that proves insufficient to effect a beneficial change, increase the regularity of the dosage. Make sure you keep the packet in a secure place where your husband is not likely to come across it and be sure not to take any yourself. Do you understand?' he asked

She nodded dumbly and reached for the packet. 'What is it?' she asked.

Cream smiled. 'A cure for what ails you, my dear,' he said. 'Fear not, I have employed it myself on many occasions and found it to be most effective.'

24

Cream cursed himself for a fool a hundred times over for using Reilly's services but his gambling debts had left him bereft and the meagre pittance from his practice barely kept a roof over his head. Just enough to see me through to my next big win he had told himself. But his next win, big or otherwise, was taking its own precious time in materialising.

Tumblety, of course, had ample funds, but the thought of putting himself once again in the thrall of his one-time nemesis appalled him. No, it would have to be another source that saved him from a mauling. A source that Cream hated to approach and would never have done so if circumstances had not been so dire. He made his way now to that wellspring of humiliation and misery that was sure to come his way and, by mid-afternoon, found himself outside the Methodist Community Hall in Old Compton Street. A billboard outside proclaimed that on this very day a lunchtime talk would be given on the subject of mesmerism and its beneficial effects on the female disposition. The lecturer was heralded as being the world famous expert on that topic: Dr James Cream.

Cream's lips curled as he saw his brother's name emblazoned in glory for what Cream considered to be nothing but quackery and parlour tricks. That his elder brother had wasted his medical training in favour of such nonsense incensed Cream intensely even as he had to admit that the financial rewards of such flim-flammery were copious and consistent. He checked his watch. With any luck he would just be able to catch James before he departed. Straightening his tie and giving his coat a cursory brush so as to present as respectable an appearance as possible, Cream hurried into the hall.

A large crowd of ladies, all a-twitter and flushed with excitement impeded his progress. As he made his way through the exiting throng and into the main hall, he saw his brother, smiling benignly at an attractive young woman who seemed reluctant to follow her sisters in delusion into the street and, instead, hung upon his every word.

Time being of the essence if his wellbeing was to be assured, Cream approached the pair. James held the young woman's gloved hand in his, their heads close together as they spoke in soft tones of endearment no doubt, each smiling insipidly into each other's eyes.

Cream gave a discrete cough. James looked up, his smile transforming into a scowl of disapproval at sight of his sibling. That the two men were brothers was obvious from the cast of their features. The older sibling was taller, more solidly built with a fuller face which may be accounted for by the deprivations of Cream the younger's lifestyle but a similarity of colouring and bone structure marked them out as brothers to anyone who cared to look.

'Thomas,' James said. 'What are you doing here?'

Cream affected a light-hearted tone. 'Heard you were giving one of your little talks. Thought I'd come along and lend moral support.'

James gave a snort of disbelief. 'And did you enjoy it?'

'Unfortunately I was detained on other business and missed all but the denouement, but I'm sure it was ripping stuff. Your audience seemed to enjoy it anyway.' He gave a small nod to James' lady friend as he said this and James jerked his head around as if he had almost forgotten she was there.

'I beg your pardon, my dear,' he said. 'Forgive my ill-manners. Let me introduce you to my brother, Dr Thomas Cream. Thomas, this is my intended, Miss Matilda Clover.'

Miss Clover held out her hand and Cream took it politely in his. 'A pleasure,' he said. 'And please accept my congratulations.'

'It's not official,' James warned him, 'but we have hopes that Matilda's father will soon give us his blessing.'

'And you are also a doctor?' Matilda said.

'I am,' Cream replied. 'But not of the elevated status of your future fiancé.'

'Your modesty does you credit, Dr Cream.'

'Thank you Miss Clover. If I could, may I beg your indulgence whilst I have a quiet word with my brother on a matter of some delicacy?'

'Oh, of course. I must be going anyway. Mother is expecting me. I will see you later, James. Goodbye Dr Cream.'

The brothers Cream watched Miss Clover exit the hall. When she was finally out of earshot Cream said: 'It seems you have done rather well for yourself there James, if I'm not mistaken.'

James Cream scowled. 'Miss Matilda Clover comes from a good family and, if I can convince her curmudgeon of a father to agree to our betrothal, we shall be wed. If I thought you capable of such finer feelings I would ask that you be happy for me since Miss Clover is everything I could hope and dream for in a wife, but as I know you are incapable of such generosity I will not waste my breath. Now, what is it you really want?'

'How you do wound me, James. Can't I simply show support for your endeavours without my motives becoming suspect?'

James Cream let out a weary sigh. 'Given that you have made no secret of your opinion regarding my field of research, I find that hard to believe,' he said. 'Did you actually hear any of my lecture?'

'Circumstances prevented me from attending all but the exodus of your admirers I'm afraid.'

'Pity. You might have learnt something. Now, what is the real reason for your presence?'

'I need your advice, James. As an older and wiser hand as it were.'

'Advice? On what topic?'

'Financial management.'

'Ah-ha! So, the purpose of this visit is to ask for money. Again'

'A short-term loan only. If I could borrow a sum sufficient to overcome my present difficulties …'

'To "borrow" implies you have the future means and intention to pay back the sum borrowed, does it not?'

'You are, as ever, pedantically correct, James.'

'Given that you have never repaid a single penny of any of my previous loans, what would induce me to give you even more money that I will never recoup?'

'Perhaps the impending arrival of two gentlemen whose intentions are less than honourable towards my health and well-being might sway you to generosity this one last time?'

'You borrowed from a money lender and now that you have defaulted he has set his dogs on you, is that it?'

'In a nutshell.'

'Thomas, you are utterly irredeemable. How much do you owe?'

Cream named a sum and James flinched. 'Good God man, are you mad?' he said. 'To borrow such a sum when you knew you had not the slightest chance of repaying it.'

'James, I beg you,' Cream replied. 'If you wish to lecture me on my many shortcomings, financial and otherwise, I will present myself for my scolding at a date and time of your choosing, but time is pressing. Will you advance me a loan or not?'

'No, Thomas, I will not.'

Cream started to protest but his brother held up an imperious hand to forestall his words. 'You have squandered every penny ever given to you with no regard for anything but your own pleasure. It's time you learned that your actions have consequences. I shall not waste another penny on such a lost cause as yourself. Whatever penalty this moneylender extracts from you, you have brought upon yourself. As far as I am concerned we are brothers no more and I thank you to respect my wish that we have no further contact. Good day, Thomas and good luck.'

25

Sanctimonious, self-righteous, pompous ass! Not content with sucking the coffers dry when father's business fell into decline to finance his own career, leaving me to look after our ailing mother until her death and then to scrape by on a pittance as I attempted to make my own way in the world, he has the audacity to belittle my lifestyle and leave me penniless and at the mercy of those barbarians! When has the almighty James Cream ever known hardship? Known humiliation? Ever known loss? Well, maybe it's time he learned all those lessons in no uncertain terms. Thus did Cream's thoughts run as he fumed following his summary dismissal from his brother's company. Such coldness, such hostility he had never expected. It turned sour in his guts and an idea surfaced in his mind that would be a just retribution for James' rebuff.

26

It was all ridiculously easy when it came to it. Cream had spent a sleepless night finalising his plan. The wretched girl had seen him, and James had no doubt dripped poison in her ear about his dissolute younger brother, so the chances of persuading her to share food or drink with him were slim to non-existent. Luckily, Miss Matilda Clover was well known in society circles for her many good works. So many good deeds must not go unpunished and it was her much publicised public schedule that led to her undoing. The Gentlewoman's League for Social Reform met once a month in a church hall. Nothing but a bunch of gossiping do-gooders who ought to leave such things to their fathers and husbands, but it gave Cream the opportunity he had been waiting for. A row of carriages lined up outside the hall, waiting to ferry the good ladies back to their homes replete with pious notions and good intentions.

How to cull Miss Clover from the herd? That was the problem. Once she reached her carriage she would be out of reach. A simple enough solution suggested itself. His features hidden by a cap pulled low over his face and a muffler masking the lower half, Cream procured the services of a passing urchin for a sixpence. He gave the boy a note with strict instructions to deliver it to Miss Matilda Clover in person and no-one else. The note, purporting to be from James, beseeched his beloved to leave the hall alone by the rear exit where he would be waiting with a wonderful surprise that he could not wait to share with her.

Cream was confident that he could manufacture a realistic facsimile of his brother's handwriting but if that was not enough to ensure her compliance it mattered little. There would be other opportunities and vengeance was a dish best served cold after all.

As he waited in the shadows, Cream could envision the giggling and envious glances his note would garner from the clucking hens of the Gentlewomen's League if Miss Clover shared his correspondence with them. Women were ever fools where matters of the heart were concerned and Cream relied on their unwitting support to persuade Miss Clover to agree to his request. The door to the hall swung open letting out a sliver of light. A figure momentarily blotted out the light and then the door closed. There was silence for a second or two and then a tentative footstep. A girlish giggle. A soft voice whispered: 'James? Are you there, James?'

Just a few more feet and the trap would be sprung. 'James? Stop teasing. I must be getting home or father will worry.'

Now!

Cream sprang forward. His left hand circled her throat as his right clamped a chloroform soaked rag over her mouth and nose. She half turned at his first movement but even if she caught a glimpse of his face, his hat and muffler would prevent her identifying him. If she intended to scream it never elevated itself beyond a mild squeak. She struggled but fear made her inhale deeply and within seconds she slumped against him all senses numbed into unconsciousness.

Cream picked her up and scurried into the maze of back alleys that his predilection caused him to know so well. She was a slim little thing but even so, Cream was panting hard before he felt far enough removed from the scene of her abduction to move on to the remainder of his plan. He placed her carefully on the ground amongst the filth and refuge that would become her bed. He removed his hat and muffler and took several deep breaths to restore his heart to its normal rhythm. He listened intently for any sounds that might indicate he could be interrupted. Distant voices and the sound of horses' hooves rose and faded. When he judged the silence to be his friend, Cream produced a bottle of smelling salts and waved them under Miss Clover's nose. She groaned and coughed and then her eyes flew open.

It was tempting, so tempting, to take her back to his rooms before administering the poison. There he could strip her and take his time pleasuring himself on her lifeless body. More pleasure than this stuck-up bitch had ever allowed his brother he'd wager. He could never admit it of course, but just that knowledge would warm his heart when he met James in the future. But in the end he decided against it. It would take too long. The physical effort of carrying her all that way was beyond him. He would need her to be conscious to accompany him on such a journey and she would, no doubt, insist on being taken home, or worse, to James. He needed to get the lethal dose into her as quickly as possible whilst she was still groggy from the chloroform and not thinking straight.

'Miss Clover! Miss Clover! Are you unharmed?' Cream put every ounce of sincerity he could muster into his question. Miss Clover focused on him with difficulty.

'Dr Cream?' she ventured. 'What happened? Where am I?'

'Thank Heavens you seem unharmed. Such an ordeal for a lady like yourself. I thank the Lord that I was on hand to prevent you from coming to any serious harm.'

'But what ...' she shook her head and groaned softly.

'Do not distress yourself dear lady. Do not try to rise just yet. You will feel better soon.'

'But how did I get to be in this predicament? Please, Dr Cream, you must tell me.'

'Very well, although in truth I know little more than you. I was taking the evening air when I heard the sounds of some sort of altercation. Naturally, I investigated and saw some ruffian snatch up a young lady and make off with her into the shadows. I had no idea at that time that you were the victim of whatever crime this miscreant had in mind, but I pursued him nonetheless, calling upon him to halt and lay down his burden. He cursed me soundly but, when he realised he could not escape me and continue to carry his burden he abandoned his victim here and ran off into the night. Imagine my surprise when I found his intended victim to be yourself. That, I am afraid is all I know.'

Of course she believed him. Why shouldn't she? He was her saviour. A respected medical man and the brother of her beloved James.

'How can I ever thank you, Dr Cream?'

'Think nothing of it, dear lady. Now, I implore you to rest a moment longer.' He reached inside his coat and produced a silver flask and two white tablets. 'Take a small sip of this tincture and these tablets. They will aid you in restoring your strength. I would not ordinarily offer such to a lady of your breeding but in emergencies I feel such a thing is permissible.'

Miss Clover seemed to consider this for a moment before nodding ascent. On his urging she took the tablets with several small sips and then it was just a matter of time. So very little time. In a matter of minutes it was all over and Matilda Clover lay dead at his feet.

Cream contemplated his usual denouement to the evening's activities. Up with the skirt, down with the drawers and have at it, but something prevented him. This was not just for his own sexual gratification. This was something different. Something more. Vengeance.

James would be distraught, no doubt, but that was the aim. Now perhaps he would know the pain of loss. The desperation of failure. The destruction of all his hopes and dreams and ambitions by another's callous hand. Yes. That was much better.

Cream left her there in the filth and strolled into the night, whistling as he went.

27

It was as Cream was returning to his lodgings that he heard a low whistle from behind him. He turned instinctively towards the source of the noise and that was when something hard hit him on the back of his head. There was one moment of searing, blinding pain and then blackness.

Cream opened his eyes slowly. He realised with a vague certainty that he was sitting upright in an armchair, his head lolling forward onto his chest. He tried raising his head but the blinding pain invaded his skull once again and he abandoned the attempt with a low moan. A voice steeped in Irish peat spoke next to his ear.

'Well, well, I do believe the good doctor is about to join us once again.'

The terror invoked by that voice vied with the nausea in Cream's stomach but he gritted his teeth against the pain, opened his eyes once more and slowly, very slowly, raised his head.

'There we are,' the voice said. 'You had me worried for a while so you did. I thought Mr Crow had tapped you a wee bit too hard and I was going to lose one of my best sources of income.' He laughed with no trace of humour.

Patrick Reilly was a muscular, black-haired, dark eyed Irishman with a thick stubble clinging to his pointed chin. Cream had met him in person only once, on the occasion of his first loan. Thereafter, his dealings had been solely with intermediaries such as the thuggish Jacob Crow, who, it seems, was the author of his present discomfort. To have been summoned into Reilly's presence in such a manner could only bode ill. Cream took in his surroundings. It was a comfortably furnished sitting room although none of the furnishings seemed to match. Not a pair of chairs bore the slightest relationship to each other, the floor was covered with rugs of assorted sizes and patterns and the paintings on the walls were an ill-assorted collection of styles and subject matter. If he had cause to think about it at all, Cream would have realised that the entire contents of the room were no doubt the proceeds of various robberies carried out under Reilly's auspices and chosen, magpie-like, because they appealed to a passing fancy and not for any aesthetic reason. Cream whetted his dry lips and tried to speak. Failed, cleared his throat and tried again.

'I have your money,' he rasped.

'Really?' Reilly replied. 'Then why didn't we find it when you were brought in?'

'To carry such a large sum would surely invite robbers and thieves to relieve me of it. I have it safe and sound, believe me.'

Reilly laughed again, a hollow sound with no real warmth or humour. 'Don't kid a kidder, Dr Cream,' he said. 'Until they close down all the card schools and gaming establishments in the whole country, I'm never going to see a brass farthing of what I'm owed. Am I right?'

Cream tried to protest his innocence but he well knew the lure of the cards were nigh on impossible to resist. He said nothing.

'It's not that I'm ungrateful for all the coins you put in my pocket, doctor,' Reilly continued, 'but you are the most tardy fellow when it comes to paying your debts. You're a blessed nuisance to be honest with you. Regular as clockwork each month I have to send a couple of my associates out to remind you of your obligations when they could be more usefully employed on other tasks. I'm a mite fed up with you to be honest.'

Cream squeezed his eyes shut against the pounding in his head. He felt the blood drain from his face.

'I swear,' he muttered, 'from now on, I will pay you back every penny without delay, just please, please don't …'

'There, there, don't take on so, doctor. It's like I always say, dead men can't pay their debts, so I'm not going to do anything drastic. Of course, there are many and varied methods of persuasion that can be employed to make sure you remember your obligations short of death, but let's not dwell on such unpleasantness. No, what I'm suggesting is an arrangement that may have significant benefits for both of us.'

Reilly took a seat behind his desk. Cream waited, sweat trickling down his face and seeping into his collar.

'How would you like the slate wiped clean?' Reilly asked.

'W … what?' Cream stammered, believing that his hearing had betrayed him.

'Wiped clean,' Reilly repeated. 'All debts cancelled. Would you like that?'

'Yes. Of course. But how? Why?'

When Reilly spoke it was in a voice so soft Cream could hardly make out the words.

'I have a son,' Reilly said. 'Fin. A fine boy, just six years old. These past weeks he's taken ill. We've tried remedies from the old country. Nothing works. I'm afraid he's not long for this world.'

Reilly rose and paced around the table. 'Despite your obvious lack of skill at cards, you are, are you not, a more than competent medical man, Dr Cream?'

'I like to think so.'

'Good. Then here's the deal. I want you to take a look at Fin. Cure him if you can. If you can, I will wipe out all your existing debts and, in addition, I'll owe you a favour, how does that sound?'

Cream considered his options, then said: 'And if I can't cure him?'

'Then it's business as usual Dr Cream. And before you think my generous offer means I'm getting soft in my old age, you and I both know that even with the slate wiped clean, it won't be long before lady luck turns her back on you again and you're back at my door with your hand out. If that happens and Fin is alive and well thanks to you, I might see my way clear to going a bit lenient on the interest. But, if my son lies under the sod at that point, the interest may well be harsh indeed. So, what do you say Dr Cream? Do we have a deal?'

'What choice do I have?'

'None.'

'Then we have a deal.'

'Good man. Come, I'll take you to see the patient.'

Reilly snapped his fingers and two figures appeared from the shadows. They hoisted Cream up between them, one under each arm, and made his reluctant feet follow Reilly down a long, bare, corridor. At the end of the corridor, Reilly gently opened a door and ushered Cream into the boy's sick room. The room was dimly lit by candles and there, on the bed, lay Fin Reilly. Pale, sweating and muttering incoherently. A red haired woman sat at his bedside, bathing his fevered brow with a damp cloth. Cream took her to be the boy's mother, a view confirmed by Reilly's next words.

'Siobhan, my love,' he whispered. 'This is Dr Cream. He's come to take a look at our boy.'

Siobhan Reilly looked at Cream with flashing emerald eyes and obvious distaste.

'He looks like a raggedy man,' she said.

'Looks can be deceiving my love,' Reilly told her. 'Dr Cream had a bit of a trying journey to get here, but, come, let him see the patient. What harm can it do, eh?'

Siobhan Reilly looked as though she was seriously considering several possible replies to that question but reluctantly relinquished her place at her son's bedside.

Cream examined the boy for form's sake; one glance was really all it took. 'How long has he been like this?' he asked.

'More than a week now,' Reilly told him.

'And you waited this long before seeking medical advice?' Cream's voice came out more harshly than he had intended.

'You'll take that tone out of your voice, doctor,' Reilly commanded.

Cream backtracked. 'I'm sorry, it's just, his condition is so advanced, I'm amazed he's still alive.'

'He's a strong wee lad, doctor.'

'Do you know what's wrong with him or not?' Siobhan demanded.

'Yes, I do,' Cream said. 'It should be obvious to anyone that he has tuberculosis.'

'Mother Mary, save us,' Siobhan said and crossed herself.

'Can you cure him?' Reilly wanted to know.

'I can try,' Cream told him, 'but really he should have had medical attention long ago.'

'There are reasons as to why we didn't want any doctor treating our son,' Reilly growled.

'Patrick,' Siobhan whispered and clutched at Reilly's arm. 'It's happening again.'

'Watch closely, doctor,' Reilly said, 'and you'll see why we chose to keep this to ourselves.'

Perplexed, Cream observed the child as he moaned and sweated and twisted upon his sickbed. 'Distressing, I know,' he said, 'but these symptoms are only to be expected.'

'Keep watching,' Reilly told him. Cream did as he was told. The child's thrashings became more violent, his moans lower and increasingly guttural, his hands clenched at the bedclothes with such ferocity that the material tore in his grasp and sweat cascaded down his brow. With a huge, convulsive, shudder, Fin Reilly sat bolt upright. His eyes flew open wide and Cream stepped back in fright at the sight of the boy's bright yellow pupils. Fin opened his mouth to emit a full-throated roar, the teeth protruding over his lips were pointed and feral. The skin of his face began to move as though the very bones of his skull were moving, readjusting to another shape altogether. Cream himself emitted a shriek of terror and would have fled from the room had Reilly not clamped a vice-like grip upon his arm.

The spasm, the fit, whatever it was, for Cream had no name for it, passed within the space of a minute and the small figure, his features once more those of a normal young boy, collapsed back onto the bed in a state of exhaustion. His mother moved to his side and began bathing his brow with a damp cloth.

'That …'Cream began and found he had no more words. 'That,' he finally managed, 'is not tuberculosis.'

'No, doctor, it isn't,' Reilly told him. 'But it's the consumption that triggers the change.'

'The change?'

'Ay, doctor, the change. It wasn't due for a good few years yet. I figure it's his way of fighting this disease. The change makes him stronger, but it's a losing battle sure enough, unless you can help him.'

'You know what this "change" is?' Cream asked incredulously.

'Of course we know,' Reilly told him. 'You might say, it runs in the family.'

'I don't understand.'

'No, and why should you? Tell me, doctor, have you ever heard of werewolves?'

28

Reilly told the story and told it well. A natural raconteur, his Irish lilt lending the tale a lyrical quality that, had Cream not seen evidence of the truth of it with his own eyes, he would have ascribed to myth and legend.

'Now you know,' Reilly said. 'The whole truth and nothing but.'

'It's … incredible,' Cream managed.

'It's that right enough, but can you cure him?' Siobhan demanded.

'I believe so,' Cream said with a confidence he did not truly feel.

'You better had, doctor,' Siobhan told him. 'Or you'll have me to answer to.'

Reilly gave a low chuckle. 'You see, doctor,' he said, 'it's not me you have to worry about. Sure, don't they say the female of the species is more deadly than the male? Now, what do you need? Tell us and we will provide it.'

Cream nodded and gave a list of chemicals and medications as well as a course of action to be taken to give the boy the best possible chance. A change of bed linen and clothing every day, lots of fresh air in the room, cold compresses to keep the fever at bay and the burning of certain herbs and potions to help the congestion in his lungs.

It was well after midnight before Cream was deposited outside his dwelling. He leant against the wall, gulping in the cold night air. Tomorrow they would come for him again and all he wanted to do was take a draught of something to quell the pounding in his head and to sleep. He knew that sleep would still be some hours away. His medical library was not extensive but within its confines there must surely be something to support his diagnosis. For the first time since medical school, Thomas Cream would have to study.

29

'Gentleman to see you, Inspector. Waiting in your office.'

'What gentleman would that be, Sergeant Thicke?'

'An American gentleman.' Seemingly satisfied with narrowing the options down to an entire continent, Thicke returned his attention to "minding the desk", an occupation of such mysterious significance that it seemed to absorb all his attention and time without producing one tangible result. Abberline shook his head in exasperation and continued to his office. As he opened the door, his visitor rose to greet him. He wore a finely tailored tweed suit and offered Abberline a broad, engaging smile and his hand.

'Inspector Abberline' he said. 'So pleased to meet you again.'

'Mr Pinkerton. What an unexpected pleasure. What can I do for you?' Abberline waved Pinkerton to resume his seat as he settled into his chair behind his desk.

'I believe I intimated to you the other evening the purpose for my visit to your fine city?' Pinkerton began.

'I believe you said you were here on Pinkerton business, is that correct?'

'You take it correctly, sir.'

Pinkerton withdrew a single sheet of folded paper from his inside pocket, unfolded it and passed it across to Abberline. It was a wanted poster that showed an artist's impression of a thick set man with wavy hair and a full moustache and notice of a reward of $500 payable on his capture. The name beneath the likeness was George Hutchinson.

'I'm on the trail of this man, Inspector. Been tracking him for some time now, but he's always managed to slip through the net. I now believe he took passage to Southampton and may have made his way here, to London.'

Abberline tapped the poster. 'It says here that he is wanted for murder,' he said.

'True enough. And more than one. Truth be told, that's just one of his crimes, but the only one we can prove. His victims are women of a low sort, if you get my meaning and his preferred method of dispatching his victims is by the knife.'

'Really?' Abberline raised an inquisitive eyebrow and absent-mindedly tugged at his earlobe. A light of interest sparked in Pinkerton's eyes as he leaned forward, smiling.

'Does that ring any bells with you, Inspector?' he asked.

'Perhaps. When do you think this George Hutchinson may have fled to this country?'

'We can't be sure, but no more than a few weeks ago perhaps.'

Abberline nodded. 'Just about the time Spring Heeled Jack made his presence felt again,' he murmured.

'Spring Heeled Jack?'

Abberline waved the enquiry away. 'A minor nuisance that we thought we had dealt with some time ago. Young women were being accosted by a mysterious figure described as a demonic manifestation. He cackled and waved a knife at them before cutting a piece of their clothing as a souvenir before running off into the night. It truth he was an actor named Lawrence Babcock with plans to mount a stage production based on the legend of Spring Heeled Jack, a succubus said to infiltrate ladies bedrooms at night and sit upon their chest as he drained the life from them. His escapades were his way of drumming up publicity for said production. It was a grievous error of judgement on his part that saw him incarcerated for six months. Recently there have been reports of another such person, although one without the demonic trappings employed by Mr Babcock, who mutters incoherent threats and brandishes a blade. Several times he has been heard to mutter the name Spring Heeled Jack, but no-one has been harmed, whereas your man seems to have a much more serious intent so I doubt there's a connection, but I will make enquiries of Mr Babcock just to be on the safe side. Do go on, Mr Pinkerton?'

'Please, call me William. And what may I call you?'

Abberline thought for a second. 'Inspector?' he offered.

Pinkerton roared in good-natured humour. 'Very well, Inspector,' he said. 'This fellow Hutchinson has a chequered history. A frequent inmate of the Elgin Illinois Lunatic Asylum, his whereabouts were unknown for quite some time after his most recent release. He only came to our notice again when he began his murder spree. It's quite possible that he spent the intervening period of time travelling. Not just in the United States either. It's further possible that he may have visited England during that period which would explain why he has now returned. I was hoping you may see some similarities between the crimes of this Hutchinson fellow and a certain Jack the Ripper and that you might be prepared to share any insights you may have that could assist me in my investigation. It did even cross my mind that Hutchinson and the Ripper might even be one and the same. The modus operandi being so similar and all.'

'What makes you think that, Mr Pinkerton?'

'Well, the Ripper murders ceased round about the same time that Hutchinson became active in the States.'

'A coincidence, I assure you.'

'Are you sure about that, Inspector?'

'Positive.'

Pinkerton looked up and there was a shrewd, calculating look in his eyes. 'Then you caught him, right? The Ripper I mean. How else could you be so positive that the Ripper and Hutchinson are not one and the same? You at least know who he is, right?'

Abberline paused, half tempted to say something he shouldn't, something dangerous. What is it about this man, he thought, that would make me behave in such an unprofessional way? In all but the case of the invaluable Constable Colverson, such trust was almost unheard of in Abberline's experience. He pushed the thought from his mind and said: 'I really couldn't say.'

Pinkerton guffawed loudly and slapped his knee in mirth. 'By gad I knew it! You cracked the case!'

Abberline opened his mouth to object, but Pinkerton held up his hands in a gesture of surrender. 'No, no,' he said, 'you don't have to explain, Inspector. Confidentiality and all that, but why on earth didn't you shout your triumph from the rooftops? Surely such a success would have put the fears of the populace to rest instead of leaving them waiting in trepidation for the fiend to return and painting Scotland Yard in a less than favourable light?'

Abberline shook his head. 'I'm really not at liberty to say, Mr Pinkerton, but I will pass your description of this Hutchinson fellow on to my superiors and request that all constables be asked to be on the lookout for him. Should he be sighted, we will, of course, inform you as a professional courtesy.'

'That sounds splendid, Inspector,' Pinkerton said. He paused and frowned. 'Pass it on? But Inspector, why would you need to do such a thing? Surely you have the authority to issue the relevant order yourself?'

Abberline cleared his throat, embarrassed. 'Our encounter the other evening may have given you a rather false impression of my position within Scotland Yard. I am, at present, on restricted duties and, unfortunately, am unable to take action without my superior's approval.'

Pinkerton rose up out of his chair, his face flushed with righteous indignation. 'What in tarnation is the matter with your Scotland Yard?' he boomed. 'I told you on our last encounter that I had been studying the methods of Scotland Yard and their detective division in some detail. In all my endeavours I have never encountered an investigator with a more outstanding record than Chief Inspector Frederick Abberline. Why, your work on the Ripper case alone ...'

Abberline waved his visitor back into his seat least he burst a blood vessel. 'I'm afraid I cannot go into details, but the result, or rather the lack of result, in that case and one other, has been the cause of my temporary situation. Unfortunate though it may be, there is nothing I can do about it.'

Pinkerton thought for a few seconds, the colour gradually fading from his cheeks. Abberline felt the change in mood as though a tide, whipped up by a storm, had receded and the waves of emotion lapping at the shore diminished into calm and placid waters once more.

'You cracked the Ripper case,' Pinkerton mused, waving aside Abberline's attempted interjection as he did so, 'but were prevented from glorying in your triumph by some force beyond your control. Am I right? No, don't answer that, you are far too discrete an individual and far too loyal to your superiors to do so with any honesty, but I know I'm right. There is only one reason that I can conceive of that would have put you in such an invidious position. Petty bureaucracy, am I right?'

'Well ...'

'I knew it! And this other case you spoke of, I take it that you received similar interference from petty fogging pen pushers more concerned with their own reputation than exposing the truth?'

'I wouldn't quite put it like that …'

'Don't get me wrong, Inspector. I hold Scotland Yard in the highest regard, but here, as in my own country, there are those who place protocol and red tape above the search for justice. But you and me, Inspector, we are not such men. Working for a private organisation such as Pinkerton's I have no such restrictions …' He paused. 'In fact,' he said, 'that has helped me come to a decision I had been mulling over ever since our previous encounter, but now is not the time to discuss it. Perhaps you would do me the honour of meeting with me this evening at my hotel. The Albion. Do you know it?'

'Of course.'

'Then shall we say eight o'clock?'

'I will do my best to be there.'

'Splendid. Just ask for me at the desk. They'll know me.'

Of that, Abberline had no doubt.

30

Upon his arrival at the Albion Hotel, Abberline asked for William Pinkerton's room and was somewhat confused to be directed to the top floor. 'And what room number?' he asked.

The desk clerk smiled a professional smile. 'Mr Pinkerton resides on the entire floor, sir,' he said.

'Really? How very convenient for him. Thank you.'

Still somewhat confused as to why one man should require an entire floor to himself, Abberline took the elevator to the top floor. As the doors opened onto a plushly carpeted corridor, Abberline saw Pinkerton in earnest conversation with a tall, bespectacled man. They were poring over several large sheets of paper that appeared to contain plans of some kind. Looking up as the elevator doors clanged open, Pinkerton's face lit up in a smile of welcome. 'Inspector!' he said. 'Allow me to introduce Mr Galsworthy of Galsworthy and Jones, Architects.'

Abberline and Galsworthy exchanged greetings. 'Architects?' Abberline asked.

Pinkerton grinned. 'Come, let's retire to my sitting room. I'll ring for some tea and fill you in.'

Abberline nodded. Giving a few parting instructions to Mr Galsworthy, Pinkerton led the detective into a lavishly furnished sitting room and rang for some tea and cakes as Abberline settled himself on a comfortable sofa.

'You're probably wondering what I'm doing taking up such extravagant lodgings, eh, Inspector?'

'It had crossed my mind.'

'Well, although my search for George Hutchinson is of primary importance, it fortuitously coincides with that business proposition I told you about. I thought it would be economical to combine the two.'

'A canny Scot when it comes to money, I'm sure, as befits your ancestry.'

'You got that right, Inspector. The truth is, the Pinkerton agency has been looking to expand our organisation into Europe for some time, and what better place for our European headquarters than here, in London.'

'You said as much on our last encounter. But I still don't see ...?'

Pinkerton spread his hands expansively. 'What better place for a discrete but well-appointed base of operations than the top floor of a well-respected hotel?'

'You plan to rent this entire floor as your office space?'

'Rent? Hell, no. We bought the whole thing. The entire hotel. The other floors will carry on as usual, bringing in a nice amount of capital I might add. And this floor will be for our exclusive use. Not just offices either. Living accommodation too. You see, whoever runs this operation needs to be on call at any time, day or night so it's only fair that we provide all the comforts of home. That's what I was discussing with Mr Galsworthy: how best to reconfigure the rooms and, of course, the elevator would be restricted for our use only. What do you think, Inspector?'

'An impressive plan. I wish you well with it.'

'Thank you. Of course, its success hinges on finding the right person to put in charge. I confess that tracking down Mr Hutchinson has eaten up much time that I had otherwise intended to spend selecting possible candidates.'

'I'm sure you will have no shortage of applicants.'

'Quantity does not always guarantee quality, Inspector. Fortunately, I have found someone who I believe will be the ideal candidate for such a responsible post.'

'I'm pleased for you.'

'Thank you, but you haven't said yes yet.'

'I haven't … ? You mean you are offering me the post?'

'I can think of no-one better suited and after the way Scotland Yard have treated you I do not believe you owe them any further loyalty. What say you, Inspector?'

Before Abberline could reply there was a discrete knock at the door. Pinkerton rose to open it. 'Ah, our tea has arrived. Let's enjoy some refreshment while you consider the proposition and I'll tell you more about our plans for Pinkerton's London operation.'

31

Over some excellent Darjeeling tea and the finest confectionary that Abberline had tasted in a long while, Pinkerton regaled him with many tales of his adventures in America. All the while Abberline had the distinct impression that the bluff American was taking a circuitous route to the main object of the conversation. Finally, he paused and, setting his tea cup down, adopted a more serious tone.

'All of that was most exhilarating, of course,' he said. 'But even the most hair-raising of escapades tend to pale in comparison with what I'm about to tell you next.' He paused as if uncertain of his territory. 'I can rely on your complete discretion, Inspector?' he asked.

Abberline nodded. 'Of course,' he said. 'Whatever you say will go no further than these four walls, you have my word.'

'Very well. You see, when I said that my presence at Madame Olga's was purely out of idle curiosity, I was not being entirely truthful. In fact, I was trying to ascertain if that charming lady did, indeed, possess any sort of psychic ability. Your own efforts disproved that theory, but it did not dissuade me from believing that such abilities do exist.' Pinkerton settled back in his chair and folded his hands across his stomach, taking up the position of a consummate raconteur as he continued with his tale. 'It was during the Civil War and its aftermath that I first encountered what you might call "supernatural phenomenon". I realise how that sounds, Inspector, and I freely admit that my father and brother regarded me as some sort of crank, but it is my belief that war, in fact, conflict of any kind, the violence, the killing, the process by which the goodness in the human spirit atrophies under excessive brutality, attracts malign forces and allows them to fester and grow. Pure evil, if you will. I have seen things, Inspector, that cannot be explained by the rational mind and I have made it my business to investigate such cases. I was on the trail of a bank robber in New Orleans when I first encountered what is commonly known as voodoo. Have you heard of such a thing?'

Abberline nodded. 'Voodoo is a well- documented phenomenon,' he said 'It has its roots in Africa many hundreds of years ago.'

'Quite so, but please do not let that mislead you into thinking that it is merely superstitious nonsense believed in only by the weak minded or primitive natives on that dark continent. In New Orleans I encountered a woman named Marie Laveau, who, I believe is the most powerful voodoo priestess alive today. I hope you will believe me when I say that, using nothing but a purloined handkerchief of mine, she cast a spell that incapacitated me and nearly led to my death. If it were not for the intervention of a Cree shaman, or medicine man if you will, named Jack Fiddler, I would not be sitting here today and that is the truth.'

Abberline shifted uncomfortably in his chair. 'Is it not possible,' he said, 'that some malady resulting from the unusual cuisine of that area simply laid you low and maybe induced a fever dream that fuelled your impressions of some supernatural agency?' he said.

'I appreciate your delicacy, Inspector, but I have reliable witnesses that have signed an affidavit to testify to the effects of this malady. To name but a few, I was seen to levitate myself from my sick bed, to vomit up a full grown and living frog, to howl like a tom cat and to exhibit such strength that I tore my room apart and it took three people to hold me still whilst Fiddler administered the cure. Now, I'm a strong man, Inspector, but even in the midst of delirium I would not be capable of such a feat. What say you, Inspector? Do you give credence to such a tale?'

Abberline tugged reflectively at his earlobe, a sure sign that his mind was processing myriad pieces of information despite his placid outward appearance.

'I am not a religious man, Mr Pinkerton,' he said. 'Rather, I view the world from the viewpoint of cold, hard, logic. The compilation of facts, information, the piecing together of fragments that, when put together, lead to an inescapable conclusion. It is a frame of mind that has served me well in my chosen career. That being said, I do not deny any man his beliefs, however unlikely they may seem when viewed through the lens of a logical mind.'

'Then you believe me?'

'I believe that you believe that what you say is true. I would require proof. I would need to witness with my own eyes those things you say that you have experienced and witnessed and if, after extensive investigation, should all forms of rational deductive reasoning fail to produce a satisfactory result I would be prepared to consider alternative explanations no matter how irrational they may seem.'

Pinkerton laughed heartily. 'By crickey I knew it! You've had dealings with supernatural elements before. I'm right aren't I?'

'I really couldn't say.'

'Of course, of course. Discretion and all that, but at least tell me what case it was. Was it the Mayfair Garrotter? The London Burkers, maybe?'

'You seem rather well informed as to my previous investigations if I may say so.'

'I do my homework, Inspector. Now, which one was it? Wait, it was Jack wasn't it?'

'I can neither confirm nor deny ...'

'I knew it. I knew there had to be something inhuman about that fiend to allow him to elude Scotland Yard's finest the way he did. That's if he did elude you.'

'I really ...'

'Can't say. I know, but promise me this. One day, when it is acceptable to do so, you'll tell me the whole story. Will you promise me that?'

'I give you my word.'

'And that's good enough for me, Inspector.'

'Interesting though this diversion into the realms of the supernatural may be, your primary mission in England is to apprehend a murderer of the common or garden variety I believe. Why then the interest in investigating psychic phenomenon? Did you hope that Madame Olga could use her psychic charms to locate the felon for you?'

Pinkerton chuckled. 'Now wouldn't that be a detective's dream come true? No, Inspector, I had no such hopes, but, as you may have gathered, this area of endeavour is of particular interest to me. It is my belief that such phenomenon are more prevalent that most people realise and that evil left unchecked will fester and grow until it is unstoppable. It is my desire to embed such beliefs into the very essence of the Pinkerton Detective Agency and, by spreading our influence throughout the world, act as a bulwark against such evil becoming epidemic in scope. I realise that may sound a trifle fanciful, Inspector, but it is my heartfelt belief. Naturally, any senior operative employed by Pinkerton's would, at least, have to be open to such scenarios of a supernatural sort that came their way. That may or may not have a bearing on your reaction to the post I have offered you. I sincerely hope it has not dissuaded you from considering my offer since I believe you would be invaluable to our cause.'

Abberline sat back and considered all that Pinkerton had said. Finally he said:

'I have only one question.'

'Only one? Fire away.'

'What happened to the bank robber?'

32

It wasn't the first time Polly Kettle had had to sing for her supper. And a sparse meal that would be tonight if the parsimonious generosity of the scurrying citizens of Whitechapel were anything to go by. True, it wasn't the best pitch in the world. Many had little enough to spare for their own needs but moving to a more salubrious neighbourhood brought its own problems. Polly was fairly certain the coppers would be on the lookout for her after Fanny's spiritualist scam had been wound up. Anyone working the streets in Regents Street or Oxford Circus were more likely to put rich noses out of joint and a sharp eyed copper might be called to move her on. And if he recognised her …

Polly dearly wanted to know how Fanny was getting on but had no safe way of finding out. The fact that they shared a surname was simply one of many gifts that Fanny had bestowed upon her over the years but it gave her no legal claim to demand information even if her own liberty would not be put in jeopardy by demanding such. As the day drew towards evening and the cold started to make Polly's voice quaver she decided it was time to give up for the day. She had enough, barely, for a meat pie that would be more gristle than meat, but, if she was careful, would do for supper and breakfast. If she was lucky there may be a bed at Sanguine House, a shelter for destitute women. Not only a bed, but, if she was lucky, they may have some soup on the go if the others hadn't scoffed it already.

'Hey, Poll!' a voice called out. 'How you doin' ducks?'

Polly turned and saw Ellen "Nellie" Donworth hurrying towards her. At nineteen, Nellie was five years older than Polly but they had struck up a friendship based on the fact that they both scraped a living on the cold streets of London. The two girls embraced and smiled at each other.

'Perishin', ain't it?' Nellie said.

'Too right,' Polly agreed. They linked arms and began strolling along the crowded streets. Polly dipped into her pocket and pulled out a silver flask. She intended to pawn it. When it was empty that is. It had been "dropped" by a toff who was slumming it and had impressed his two friends by offering a less that flattering critique of Polly's vocal ability. He'd never miss it and Polly felt it was only just recompense for his unkind words. She offered the flask to Nellie.

'Here,' she said. 'Have a nip of this. Keep the cold out.'

'No ta,' Nellie said. 'I don't drink.'

Polly raised her eyebrows. Here was something she didn't know about her new friend. Surely everybody had a nip now and then didn't they?

''S'true,' Nellie said, interpreting Polly's look of disbelief correctly. 'Never touched a drop in me life. I've seen what it does to you if you're not careful. My old man, now there was a drinker. We were starving and freezing and he was pouring what little money we had straight down his gullet. And if anyone said it weren't right to leave a wife and three kids hungry and cold, he used his fists to teach us otherwise.'

Polly slid the flask back into her pocket. 'Sorry, Nell. I didn't know.'

''S'all right, ducks. No reason why you should.'

A cold wind brought the first intimations of coming rain and both girls shivered as they bent into it. 'Thought I might try me luck up west tonight,' Nellie said. Maybe find a nice gent who's got a nice warm room for a change. You can come if you want. You'd do a good trade, nice looking girl like you. You'd be what? Fifteen? Sixteen?'

'Fourteen.'

'There's plenty younger. I started when I was your age. After me dad finally buggered off for good and we couldn't get by on what me mum made from takin' in laundry.'

'Doesn't she mind? Your mum I mean. What you do?'

Nellie shrugged. 'She don't like it but we needs the money. Me two bruvvers ain't old enough yet to bring in much. And it's not all bad. What do you say? Fancy a trip up west?'

Polly shook her head. 'No, I'll carry on singin' for my supper, thanks all the same.'

'You've got a good voice, I'll give you that. And it's better than what I have to use me mouth for sometimes, that's for sure.' Nellie gave a throaty laugh and Polly felt the colour rise to her cheeks. She hated that her friend had to demean herself in such a manner and vowed that if she ever came into real money she'd see to it that Nellie and all the other girls who worked the streets never had to do such a thing just to survive ever again. Something like Sanguine House she thought. Only bigger and better.

'You should try and get taken on at one of the Music Halls,' Nellie continued. 'Better than standin' on perishing street corners for a couple of pennies if you're lucky.'

'I might. Sometime. But right now I need to keep my head down. Know what I mean?'

'Are the coppers lookin' for you?' Don't you worry, gal, no-one round here's gonna snitch on you. So, if I can't tempt you …?'

'No. But thanks.'

'Stay safe, ducks.'

'Good luck finding a rich toff.'

Nellie laughed, the sound fading into the night.

33

Ellen "Nellie" Donworth never made it to the West End. Not ten minutes after leaving her friend Polly, she saw someone who she thought might be good for a bob or two, him being a professional man and all.

'Why, if it isn't Doctor Cream!'

Cream looked around, startled. It took him a few seconds to recognise the blonde haired young woman in the threadbare shawl and red hat. ''Why, yes, it is,' he faltered.

'Nellie,' she smiled.

'Yes, Nellie, of course.'

'We met a couple of months back when I brought Mary in so's you could sort out that little problem of hers. Remember?'

Yes. Now he remembered. A drunken slattern with child and the desire to be without. Butchers work, but if they can pay, who was he to criticise?

'Of course,' he said. 'How are you?'

Nellie linked her arm in is. 'Freezin', that's how I am,' she laughed. 'I bet you got a nice warm fire back at your lodgings, eh?'

'Well, yes, I suppose I have.'

'How about you show me then? I've always wanted to stretch out in front of a nice warm fire on a night like this. Why, I bet your rooms are so hot I wouldn't even need all these clothes. It would just be too warm, don't you think?'

Cream supressed a shudder. What she was suggesting was abhorrent to him, but when opportunity presents itself there are ways to adjust the scenario to his liking.

'Yes,' he said, 'I suppose it would. I might even be able to offer you some liquid refreshment to warm up your insides as well.'

Nellie smiled. 'No hard liquor for me, ducks. I don't touch a drop

I don't.'

'Oh! Well, maybe a cup of hot chocolate then? There's a little tea shop I know not far from here.'

Nellie laughed. 'That would be just fine.'

34

Annie Spruce and Doris Thistle had been friends since schooldays. Not that those days had lasted very long and were more years ago now than either of them cared to recall. Since then, they had seen off three husbands, raised, and quickly relinquished, seven children and been "over the cobbles", the common name for Cobblestones Prison, more times than either of them could count. Now, they rolled along together, arm in arm, cackling and singing, the better part of a bottle of gin keeping out the night chill. Annie had come into a spot of cash, courtesy of a toff who had no idea that he was contributing to the two friend's welfare when he bent down to retrieve his hat, knocked from his head by an urchin in Annie's employ. When Annie had bumped into him he had even apologised for his abrupt stop and they had exchanged commiserating words on the lamentable behaviour of the young. First to last, he had no idea that his pocket was lighter by three guineas until Annie and her accomplice were several streets away and laughing at his gullibility.

The night had been an uproarious one. Food and drink to excess and enough left over to buy a bed for the night in a respectable hostel. It was as the pair picked their way towards their chosen refuge for the night that they saw one of their more unfortunate sisters slumped in an alley.

'Poor cow,' Doris said. 'She'll freeze on a night like this.'

'Yea.' Annie paused, the drink and her good fortune moving her to largesse. 'Wot say we do the girl a favour, Dot? We've got enough for one more cot at the hostel, ain't we?'

'That we do, Annie, that we do, and a right Christian gesture it would be too.'

Thus moved onto the path of the Samaritan, they wandered

unsteadily towards the slumped figure.

''Ello, gal, 'ow's yer luck?' Annie asked.

When she received no reply, Doris nudged the girl's foot with the toe of her shoe, nearly overbalancing in the process. The figure didn't stir.

'Blimey! She must have had a skin-full,' Doris said.

Annie leaned unsteadily over the recumbent figure. 'Wake up, gal,' she said, loudly. 'We want to do you a favour, so we do.'

When this also received no response, Annie reached out and shook her by the shoulder. The girl toppled sideways and slumped to the ground. Annie and Doris jumped back and exchanged worried looks.

'Gawd!' said Doris. 'You don't think she's snuffed it, do yer?'

'Nah. Can't have. Just sozzled, that's all.'

'You sure?'

With a worried glance at her friend, Annie crept forward and reached out a hand to touch the girl's face. Her flesh had a clammy feel to it. Annie's nervous fingers lingered over her mouth and nose. She jumped back with a squeal. 'Lawd 'elp us, she ain't breathin'!' she said.

'Dead,' Doris decided. 'I knew it,' and began dragging her friend away. Annie hesitated.

'She's no more than a girl, really,' she said. 'Shouldn't we tell someone?'

'What!?' Doris shrieked. 'And get blamed for doin' her in? Not likely.'

Annie was still reluctant to leave. 'All the same,' she said, 'she looks like she's got a nice dress.'

Doris peered closer. 'And those shoes look hardly worn,' she said.

'And as she's already dead ...'

'She won't be needin' them anymore will she?' Doris finished for her.

With a final look around to make sure they were unobserved, the two friends set to and, within a few minutes had stripped Nellie Donworth naked. Their arms full of clothing, they toddled off into the night. 'I know a nice pawn shop who'll gives us a good price for this lot,' Annie said.

'Been a lucky day all round, ain't it?' Doris said.

'Very lucky,' Annie agreed. 'Very lucky indeed.'

An hour later, Police Constable Abel Perkins, new to the force and barely out of his teens, discovered the naked body of a young woman lying in an alley. As the light from his lantern played upon her flesh, he blushed, never having seen a fully naked adult female before. He prodded her thigh with his night stick and told her: 'You can't sleep here you know. And where are your clothes?'

When neither his prodding nor his admonishment produced any response, he plucked up courage to investigate further. Once realising there was no sign of life, he blew his whistle to summon reinforcements. As he waited for his colleagues to arrive, he played his lantern light once more over the body, just to that he could give a full and accurate report, then covered her with his cape out of respect.

35

Lawrence Babcock, noted thespian, actor manager and director at your service. That it has come to this. A once glittering career, well, a career at least, reduced to tatters by one ill-advised endeavour. That judge was obviously biased. Never been to a theatre in his life I'll wager. What was his name? Blackwell? Tombstone? Blackstone! That was it. Six months over the Cobbles for what was nothing more than a harmless prank. After that, no-one wanted to know. Couldn't get a legitimate acting job for love nor money. And so, I've been reduced to this. Handing out playbills for the efforts of lesser lights who aren't fit to shine my shoes. But I will survive. I will return to the footlights in a blaze of glory, you mark my words.

Lawrence Babcock's thoughts meandered along these lines as they were wont to do, when he heard a familiar voice.

'Good morning, Mr Babcock. Might I have a word?'

Abberline! Gawd, not him again!

'I'm frightfully busy at the moment, Inspector. Maybe later.' Babcock attempted to move smartly on, but Abberline's hand upon his arm prevented him.

'I'm sure your employer wouldn't object to you taking a short break for some liquid refreshment. After which you would be able to return to your lawful business with renewed vigour.'

Babcock licked his lips. 'Well,' he said, 'there is a certain persuasiveness to that argument.'

Abberline indicated a nearby hostelry and Babcock allowed himself to be led into its dusty confines. Like a lamb to the slaughter, he thought, a lamb to the slaughter.

Babcock finished his first tankard of ale at one gulp. 'Thirsty work this publicity business,' he said.

'So I see,' Abberline said and signalled for a refill. As they waited, Abberline said: 'Have you read the Gazette of late?'

'My duties keep me too occupied I'm afraid.'

'Then let me enlighten you.' Abberline pulled a copy of the Gazette from his pocket and passed it across to Babcock. The headline read:

IS JACK BACK?

Babcock's eyes bulged and his mouth made a silent "Oh!"

'Look familiar?' Abberline asked.

'It's what they said when I made my most unfortunate error of judgement.'

'Exactly.'

A muddled kind of certainty made its way to the forefront of Babcock's mind. 'But surely, you don't think that I ...'

Abberline held up his hand for silence as the barmaid delivered their drinks. When they were once again alone, Babcock continued in a much lower voice.

'Surely you don't think that I am this person?'

'There are certain similarities.'

'Plagiarism is rife in the theatrical world.'

'Then you think it likely that this person is executing the same plan that you, yourself, once set in motion?'

'Well, I don't know. I've not heard of anyone planning to mount such a production, but it's possible I suppose. And stealing my thunder into the bargain! The nerve of the fellow.'

Abberline suppressed a smile. 'Your outrage is understandable, but I suspect his motives may be less benign,'

'You mean he's attacking people in earnest?'

'No-one has been injured as yet. He seems to slash haphazardly at his victims. Ripping their clothing almost by accident before shuffling off into the shadows.'

'A coarse brute no doubt.'

'He has been described as such.' Abberline reached into his pocket and passed Babcock a copy of the wanted poster William Pinkerton had given him. 'An American colleague believes the perpetrator may be this man. George Hutchinson.'

Babcock studied the poster. 'A most dangerous individual it seems,' he said. 'Then I'd wager, if I had the means, that he is not a member of the theatrical profession. If you recall, my own performance was enhanced by the most accomplished of disguises and my incisions as precise as that of a skilled surgeon, cutting a mere snippet of fabric with a skill any seamstress would be proud of.'

'Quite. But with this sort of publicity …' Abberline tapped the paper, ' … others who are aware of your escapades in the past may take a different view.'

'You mean I could be in danger?'

'Conceivably, but if this person is emulating your activities he may feel inclined to make contact with the person who might be regarded as his mentor.'

Babcock smiled. 'Yes, yes. I take your point. He may seek out the master to learn the subtle arts of performance that he seems so clearly lacking.'

'Something along those lines. As it is, you may be in a position to aid us in our investigations should such a contact be made or if you should hear of such an individual through your professional activities.'

'Yes, yes,' Babcock said, but the far-away expression on his face led Abberline to believe that inside his mind he had already embarked upon a triumphant return to theatrical success. It was a line of enquiry that had to be followed but Abberline was convinced that this latest Spring Heeled Jack had nothing to do with Lawrence Babcock. Indeed, he felt sorry for the man. He may have been foolish, but he had paid a hard price for his stupidity. Abberline left a few coins on the table to fuel his afternoon fantasies and left him to it.

36

Dr Eugene Pettifer presided over a kingdom of the dead. It was not a kingship which offered the monarch much in the way of comfort or satisfaction. His was a dark, dank, cold, subterranean realm, but the position of Coroner suited Dr Pettifer's temperament perfectly. The company of his fellow man had ever lacked appeal and what companionship he may occasionally desire could be bought for a handful of coins and a tot of gin. The ability to imbibe whilst working was also satisfactory, for who among his patients would complain if his hand slipped a trifle with the scalpel?

Only two things disrupted Dr Pettifer's carefully ordered world. The first was the sheer number of cadavers that passed through his emporium of the deceased. That many of them were the victims of violent ends led Dr Pettifer to the conclusion that, sooner or later, the entire population of London would arrive upon his tables. He had thought about agitating for an assistant, but that might disrupt his sovereign right to rule as he saw fit and so he soldiered on in solitude apart from one attendant whose sole responsibility was to ferry his clientele to and from the mortuary.

The second thorn in his side was Detective Chief Inspector Frederick George Abberline. A busybody who, unlike his predecessors who were content to let Dr Pettifer carry out his duties in his own good time, insisted upon regular visits to the morgue to harry and cajole Dr Pettifer into unseemly haste. The dead are not going anywhere, he had told him, but that had earned him the stern rebuke that where apprehending the perpetrators of violent crime is concerned, time was of the essence. With the Lambeth Poisoner on the rampage, Inspector

Abberline's visits had become more frequent. Although the activities of that perverse gentleman dominated the newspapers, he was by no means the only purveyor of violent death in the city, and, from all the deceased that crossed his threshold, Dr Pettifer was supposed to differentiate which ones were the victims of the Poisoner and which ones were simple casualties of numerous other, less celebrated, lunatics.

Damn the man. Dr Pettifer could hear his footfalls on the stairs to his subterranean lair even now. He surveyed the six new inhabitants that had come in overnight, each laid out and covered by a sheet that he had barely had time to inspect, let alone decide upon a cause of death that may be attributed to a specific individual.

'Good morning, Dr Pettifer.'

'Good morning, Inspector.'

'What news do you have for me?'

Dr Pettifer moved along the row of tables, whipping back each sheet in turn, like a magician revealing a particularly pleasing effect meant to dazzle and delight his audience.

'A labourer who fell from a roof, breaking his back. A foreign seaman fished out of the docks, drowned. A butcher who mistook his hand for a lamb chop and died of acute blood loss. Two male lotharios who argued over a lady of easy virtue and came to blows, the one dying of a knife wound, the other from a blow to the head. One unknown female ...' he pulled back the sheet. He had yet to examine her properly but what difference would one more or less victim of the Poisoner make? It wasn't as if Abberline was any closer to catching him. 'Alcohol poisoning,' he concluded. 'Found in an alley, stark naked,' he supplied. 'Shame. She's a pretty little thing.' He pulled the sheet further back so that Abberline could more fully appreciate the attributes of the shapely cadaver and was pleased to see the Inspector avert his gaze. As well as being a blessed nuisance, the man was also a prude!

'Nothing that would point to a victim of the Poisoner then?' he asked.

'Nothing whatsoever,' Dr Pettifer replied.

Abberline began to retrace his steps, up towards daylight. 'Good,' he said. 'Keep me informed, if you would, particularly on any cases that bear the hallmarks of the Poisoner.'

'As always, Inspector, it will be my pleasure.' If Abberline detected the sarcasm in Dr Pettifer's tone, he chose to ignore it.

'Until tomorrow, doctor,' he said. 'Until tomorrow.'

37

Hetty Donworth was in a fighting mood. Henry Moody's black eye and split lip bore testimony to that fact. 'I want her arrested!' he shouted. 'She assaulted me in my own shop!'

'Ask him what he's done with my Nellie!' Hetty demanded. 'Then tell me I didn't have a mother's right to lump him one.'

Sergeant Thicke bowed his head and sighed. Domestics. He hated domestics. He did what he always did in these situations.

'Colverson!' he bellowed. 'Come and sort this lot out, quick as you like.'

With the help of two other constables, Colverson persuaded Hetty to release her grip on Henry Moody. Sequestering each in separate cells, Colverson flitted between one and the other, piecing together a more or less coherent story. Moody's line was that he had been attacked by a mad woman in his place of work for no good reason. Hetty Donworth claimed that Moody had committed some nefarious deed on her innocent daughter and wanted him hanged for it.

Piece by piece, bit by bit, a few critical facts began to surface. Hetty Donworth's daughter, Nellie, had gone missing. Henry Moody ran a pawn shop. Hetty Donworth, whilst scouring the streets for her missing child had seen Nellie's dress and shoes for sale in Moody's window. Fearing the worst, Hetty Donworth had confronted Henry Moody, demanding to know Nellie's whereabouts. Henry Moody denied all knowledge, whereupon Hetty Donworth had assaulted him and marched him straight to the police station. When asked where the incriminating garments had come from, Henry Moody had named two well known pickpockets, Annie Spruce and Doris Thistle.

PC Colverson began to see the light. A quick check in the ledger detailing the previous night's activities revealed that a young woman had been found naked and dead in an alley just off Baker's Row. The police surgeon had recorded the death as alcoholic poisoning.

Requesting the two combatants to behave themselves, Colverson went in search of Annie and Doris. They were not hard to find. They were enjoying a mid-morning snifter outside the Crown with the last of the money Henry Moody had given them for Nellie's clothes. Hoping an invitation to join Colverson at Whitechapel Station may result in a cup of tea and a bite to eat and, if they were lucky, a warm cell for the night, they came along willingly enough.

Annie and Doris. Doris and Annie. As inseparable in the public consciousness as they had been all their lives. Most people couldn't tell who was who, their shared lives had given them a similarity in both appearance and manner. Colverson sat opposite them in the duty room and prepared to take their statement.

'I believe you recently visited a shop owned by Mr Henry Moody,' he began.

Annie and Doris looked at each other. 'Did we?' said Annie.

'We may have done,' said Doris. 'We visit so many shops in our walks, don't we, Annie.'

'That we do, Doris, that we do.'

Colverson sighed. 'He knows who you are, ladies, so there's no point denying it. You sold him some items of female clothing. Isn't that so?'

The two women looked at each other. 'Might be,' said Annie.

'Might be,' said Doris.

'Now you come to mention it, we did find some clothes the other night didn't we?'

'Yes. I think we did. Just lying there in the street. Seemed a shame to let them go to waste. No crime in that is there?'

'Was anyone wearing them at the time?' Colverson asked.

Annie looked at Doris and Doris looked at Annie. 'All right, yes,' said Doris. 'But it's not like we robbed her.'

'No,' chimed in Annie. 'She was already dead, poor cow.'

'She didn't need 'em no more,' explained Doris. 'It's not like she'd feel the cold without them. So we helped ourselves.'

'And you didn't think to report finding a dead body to the police?' Colverson asked.

Annie looked at Doris and Doris looked at Annie. 'No,' they both chorused.

After a few more minutes of pointless interrogation as to whether or not the two biddies had seen anyone else in the vicinity at the time – no, not a soul – Colverson escorted them to a cell and gave instructions they were to be fed and watered and then released when they had sobered up. He had more important things to do.

The viewing of the deceased in order to establish identity was a grim affair. Hetty Donworth collapsed in a fit of hysterics and needed to be helped from the morgue.

''Ow did she die?' Hetty wanted to know. Reluctantly, Colverson told her an excess of alcohol had been the root cause of Nellie's demise. Hetty Donworth screamed that it was murder most foul and renewed her request that someone be hanged for it. Several minutes later she vouchsafed her reason for her accusation.

'My Nellie never drank. Not a drop. 'E killed her he did and I want him charged.'

'Mr Moody was safely tucked up in bed at the time of Nellie's demise,' Colverson told her quietly. 'His wife and children can testify to that effect.'

'Well someone did for her, and I want them to pay for it,' Hetty demanded.

With the lack of any physical injury, only one other cause of death seemed likely. PC Colverson went straight to Chief Inspector Abberline's office.

'I think we've another poisoner victim, sir.'

'You want me to do what?' Dr Pettifer was peeved and out of sorts. Abberline noticed no discernible difference in his demeanour or attitude.

'I want you to examine Nellie Donworth again. This time, look specifically for signs of poisoning.'

'She drank herself to death, Inspector, pure and simple.'

'Her family would beg to differ. They maintain she was as close to tea-total as makes no difference.'

Pettifer made a dismissive noise. 'Her family may believe what they will if it soothes their conscience. My conclusion is that she was a drunk and a slut and that's the end of it. I have more than enough to do without going over old ground on a whim.'

Abberline's voice dropped to a low, cold rumble barely above a whisper. 'You will be good enough to indulge my "whim" doctor and present me with a detailed report before the end of the day or I will find a Coroner who will.'

38

The Mudlarks found him. Human scavengers who scoured the waterfront for anything of value. He was lying on the shingles. Tentative and then fierce prods and kicks ascertained that he was unconscious at the very least. The pallor of his skin and the rents and tears in his flesh told of a more permanent state of affairs. Having taken whatever they could find from his pockets after Father Thames had taken his toll they shambled away. It was no business of theirs after all. Some hours later a police constable was alerted to his presence by a passing fisherman. The constable's initial inspection differed only slightly from that of the Mudlarks. Satisfied that the individual was indeed deceased, he blew lustily on his whistle to summon aid in transporting the poor unfortunate to the morgue.

In due course, for nothing grinds as slowly as the wheels of justice, the report found its way onto Detective Chief Inspector Abberline's desk. Among the many injuries listen by the medical examiner was the fact that the poor unfortunate seemed to have suffered numerous bites and rips as though from some predator as yet undetermined, but probably rats he thought. Violent damage to those washed up on the shores of the Thames was not uncommon but Abberline had an aversion to coincidences – it led to shoddy police work.

'Colverson!' he called. 'I think we may have Nobby's black dog victim.'

39

Ledderman and Fitch were a well-respected firm of lawyers dealing with clients from the highest echelons of society. The presence of two policemen in their front office caused some consternation. A prim young woman asked them rather frostily what their business might be. Abberline explained it was in connection with a missing persons report filed by the senior partner Mr Ledderman. The young woman hastily ushered them into a small side room explaining that Mr Ledderman was with a client and would summon them into his presence when it was convenient.

'As Mr Ledderman himself requested our involvement in this matter,' Abberline said, 'and since we have reason to believe there is cause for some concern over the welfare of the individual concerned, maybe you could advise him of our presence and inform him that, in cases like this, time is of the essence?'

The young woman raised her nose in the air for the express purpose of looking down it. 'Mr Ledderman is in conference with the Duke of Richmond,' she informed him. 'The Duke does not like to be rushed.'

'Of course, but perhaps in this instance …'

'I will call you when Mr Ledderman is ready to see you.' And on that final note, she left them to their own devices.

Abberline and Colverson looked at each other. 'That told us and no mistake,' Colverson muttered.

'Indeed,' Abberline agreed. 'We'll give him five minutes, then, Duke or no Duke, the forces of the law will have their way.'

40

In a voice loud enough to carry to anyone within earshot, even through closed doors, Abberline announced: 'I am Detective Chief Inspector Abberline of Scotland Yard and I would like to interview Mr Ledderman about his connection to the events in Cleveland Street. At once,' he added for good measure.

The prim young woman gave a squeal and several of those good gentlemen waiting their turn to be summoned to some inner chamber squirmed uneasily in their seats.

Doors opened and inquisitive faces peered out. Surprisingly, the prim young woman seemed lost for words and, in the ensuing silence a rumble of voices could be heard emanating from one particular door that had remained closed. Seconds later, this door too opened and a robust figure in tweeds emerged in somewhat of a hurry. The Duke of Richmond tugged his hat down over his eyes and hurried to the door, pointedly ignoring Abberline and Colverson's presence. Leonard Ledderman, a short, rotund individual with wispy grey hair trailed helplessly in the Duke's wake. As the door to his chambers slammed shut behind the scurrying aristocrat, Ledderman turned hostile eyes on Abberline.

'What the devil do you mean by coming in here ...' he began.

Abberline cut him short, taking his arm and leading him back into his office. 'So good of you to see us at such short notice Mr Ledderman,' he said. 'I can see you're busy so we will make this as brief as possible.'

As Colverson followed Abberline into the office, he paused at the door and turned back to address the prim young woman on reception duties. 'Cuppa tea would be nice,' he said. 'And maybe a biscuit.' With a grin he closed the door on her startled expression.

41

'Damned irregular,' Ledderman fumed. 'I've a good mind to complain to the Commissioner about your behaviour.'

'I'm sure the Commissioner would be pleased to add it to a rather cumbersome file,' Abberline said mildly. 'But I am sure you will understand that a missing person is a serious matter, especially one who may have access to sensitive information concerning influential clients.'

'Is that what that nonsense about Cleveland Street was all about?'

'It's possible there may be a connection, but right now I am more concerned with the gentleman in question. Mr Druitt?'

There came a discrete knock at the door. Ledderman barked: 'What?' and the door opened. The prim young woman entered carrying a tray of tea and a plate of biscuits.

'What is the meaning of this Miss Jones?' Ledderman spluttered. 'I didn't ask for tea. This isn't a social occasion.'

A pink flush suffused her alabaster cheeks. 'No, sir,' she stammered. 'These gentlemen …'

'All right, all right.' Ledderman waved away her explanation. 'Just leave it and go,' he said.

Miss Jones set the tray down on a small side table. Colverson gave her a broad wink. 'It's all right, luv,' he said. 'I'll be mother.' She gave a small squeak, her blush deepening to a positive scarlet and hurried from the room. As Colverson handed out the tea and biscuits, Ledderman began to explain the circumstances of Montague John Druitt's disappearance.

'Three days ago he was due in court. Blasted man just didn't turn up. I sent one of the clerks around to his lodgings to roust him out of bed, but there was no sign of him. Damned nuisance all round. The judge was not pleased I can tell you, nor was the client.'

'Did Mr Druitt make a habit of being unreliable?'

'No. That's the thing. Most reliable usually. That's what made me think there may be something wrong. Maybe he had been in an accident or taken ill or something. When there was still no sign of him the next day, that's when I notified the police. Do you think he may have come to some harm?'

'We haven't ruled anything out at the moment, but we are concerned with his welfare. Tell me, did Mr Druitt have a habit of taking an evening stroll along the Embankment?'

'Couldn't tell you. Never really disclosed much about his private life. Bit of a cold fish if you want my opinion, but damned good at his job.'

Abberline exchanged a glance with Colverson and the two men reached an unspoken agreement. 'Mr Ledderman, we have reason to believe that a body discovered washed up on the shore yesterday may be that of Montague Druitt.'

Leddernan blanched. 'Good Lord!' he said.

'Foul play is suspected, I'm afraid, but we do need someone to make a positive identification. As the person who filed the missing person's report, would you be willing to do that for us?'

Ledderman's face turned an even whiter shade. 'Identify a corpse!? No, no, I don't think I have the constitution for that sort of thing.'

'Is there anyone else who might be willing to undertake such a task?'

Ledderman nodded. 'Yes. Makepeace. Charles Makepeace. One of my clerks. He always seemed to get on well with Druitt. He's out on an errand at present but as soon as he returns I'll tell him to report to the station as soon as possible.'

'That would be most helpful Mr Ledderman.'

'Of course, of course. And that business about Cleveland Street …?'

Abberline smiled. 'You can rely on our discretion Mr Ledderman. Now, come along Colverson. If you've quite finished with the biscuits.'

42

When Abberline returned to his office, the Coroner's report was waiting for him. In it, in rather shamefaced phrases, was a revised opinion that Nelly Donworth's cause of death was strychnine poisoning. The same as in all the other Lambeth Poisoner's victims. It could be a coincidence, of course, but Abberline was disinclined to believe in such things.

As he pondered this latest turn of events, there was a knock at the door and Colverson entered.

'Mr Makepeace is here, sir,' he said.

'Good. Bring him in. I'd like a quick word before we go to the morgue, see if we can glean any useful information about this latest victim.'

43

'Monty, that is, Mr Druitt, was a complicated man.' Charles Makepeace sat in Abberline's office. He gave every evidence of being in a state of high nervousness. His eyes flitted here, there and everywhere. Never once did he look Abberline in the face and his hands twisted themselves into knots in his lap.

'In what way "complicated"?' Abberline asked.

'He was prone to moods. Most of the time he was a kind, affectionate, caring person, but at others …' His voice trailed off.

'You think that these other times may have placed him in harm's way?'

'It's possible. When I heard you mention Cleveland Street I wondered …' At this point his nerve seemed to break and he rose from his chair. 'I know nothing that can help you. I'm sorry. Can we not just get this wretched business over with?'

'On the contrary, Mr Makepeace. I think you may have valuable information that may shed some light on the movements of your friend, if indeed it is Mr Druitt who has come to this most unfortunate end. If it is not, then any such information may aid our efforts in finding your friend. I take it my assumption is correct,' Abberline continued. 'You and Mr Druitt were friends and not just work colleagues, were you not? Maybe more than just friends?'

Makepece turned his pale face towards the detective. He affected a haughty manner, but his voice cracked and came out sounding thin and uncertain. 'I'm sure I have no idea to what you refer, Inspector.'

Abberline sighed. 'Please sit down, Mr Makepeace.' He waited as Makepeace shuffled nervously and then did as he was asked. 'Good,' Abberline continued. 'Now, let me put a hypothetical situation to you. Two gentlemen of good standing in the community have formed an attachment to each other that provides mutual comfort and happiness. Their happiness is marred only because a stringent and, some might say, blinkered society, has decided that such an attachment is not suitable for polite society. Of necessity then, these two gentlemen must keep their relationship secret for fear of censure or worse. When one of these gentlemen goes missing, the other is naturally concerned, but is afraid to come forward lest their secret be revealed with disastrous consequences. As an officer of the law, it is my duty to prosecute such behaviour should it become less than discrete or be traded for financial reward as in the case of Cleveland Street. However, my primary concern is to safeguard every member of the public regardless of their personal inclinations or my own feelings on the matter. A missing person who may have come to harm is far more important than the fact that they may have broken some artificially constructed social taboo. Any and every piece of information concerning the missing person will be invaluable and, in this hypothetical situation, I would encourage his friend to come forward with the assurance that any information disclosed will be treated in the strictest confidence and not disclosed to any other individual including that person's employer.' Abberline sat back and waited silently. After a few seconds, Makepeace nodded. 'Thank you,' he said. 'That is very reassuring.'

'Good,' said Abberline. 'Now, in your own time, tell me what you know about Montague John Druitt.'

44

'Monty and I were friends. Good friends, unlikely as that might seem. He was a good few years older than I and a successful barrister whereas I am simply a minor clerk. But there was something in our natures that drew us to each other. Something that blossomed outside of the working environment. Discretion, of course, was our watchword, but in private, Monty felt able to unburden himself to me and disclosed many secrets about his past that I feel may have contributed to his current plight.' He paused, glancing up briefly to assure himself that his words were not falling on deaf ears.

'Go on, Mr Makepeace,' Abberline prompted gently.

'Well, Monty had led a tempestuous youth. Falling in with bad company. He felt unable to tell me many of the details, but one particular group of associates from that period in his life seems to have left deep emotional scars. He was a member of a group that called themselves the New Reformed Paladins. Young men of ample means to whom the normal rules of behaviour meant nothing. It was in their company that Monty became infected, and I use that word deliberately for I fear it was a pernicious disease that entered his system at that time and has never let him be ever since. Nor am I talking about a medical infection. No, this was instead an infection of the mind that led to ever more abnormal and aberrant behaviour based solely on the fact that they held themselves above the laws of God and man. He never burdened me with specifics but there was one defining incident that led to the dissolution of that particular group. Something so abhorrent and extreme that even they could not tolerate each other's company any more. Something that left all of them mentally and emotionally scarred for the rest of their lives. For

Monty, those scars took the form of violent outbursts where he would rage against the world. Not that he ever took his anger out against me, you understand. No. He would always treat me with the greatest respect and consideration. Many a night I've held him as he wept in the aftermath of such an episode. For the sake of his career he knew he had to do something to assuage the effect that these fits of anger produced in him. I am ashamed to say that his only release was to unleash his torment in the most physical of ways on those women who degraded themselves for money.' Here he paused, breathing hard as though the mere act of speaking those words had imposed physical hardship upon his system.

'Are you saying, Mr Makepeace, that Montague John Druitt frequented brothels where he would brutalise the women who worked there?'

Makepeace nodded.

'Any particular brothel? One that may have led to him being present on the Thames Embankment on the night he disappeared?'

Makepeace nodded again. 'One in particular, yes. In Minnows Walk.

'I know the one. And do you believe that this ... predilection, led in some way to his eventual fate, whatever that may be?'

'How can it not? I warned him how dangerous this activity was, but he claimed it was the only thing that calmed his troubled soul. After such visits he would be calm, cheerful, happy. It was most perverse and I begged him to stop. I even volunteered myself as the object of his violent outpourings but he would not have it. He cared for me too much to sully our relationship with such diabolical actions. I fear I should have been more insistent for now he may well have paid the ultimate price for his past sins.'

Abberline let the silence accumulate for a few seconds, hoping that it may provide a modicum of solace to the young man before the trauma he had no choice but to inflict upon him next.

'Mr Makepeace,' he said. 'I believe I may have a solution to Mr Druitt's disappearance but I need someone to provide definite confirmation of the facts as we know them. As someone who shared a deep and genuine affection for Mr Druitt, I hope that you may have the strength to provide that confirmation if you are willing.'

45

Charles Makepeace was shaking. The chill atmosphere of the city morgue was not solely to blame for his condition. The grim surroundings, the smell of disinfectant and other less identifiable odours, the perspiration that beaded the walls and the mere fact that he was here in this house of the dead was enough to un-nerve him. His limbs trembled and his face twitched. Abberline stood on one side of him and only his stalwart presence prevented him from turning tail and running.

'Are you ready?' Abberline asked.

Makepeace could find no voice to reply and simply nodded. Abberline gave the morgue attendant a brief signal and the man peeled back the shroud that was covering the body that lay on the slab before them. Only the man's face was revealed. Pale, discoloured and bloated. Makepeace gave a small cry. His knees buckled and Abberline stepped in to keep him on his feet.

'Is this Montague Druitt?' Abberline asked.

Makepeace nodded. Through teeth chattering so hard they threatened to break he said: 'Yes. Dear God, yes.' And then he began to weep.

46

After securing the services of a cab to take the sobbing Charles Makepeace back to his lodgings Abberline returned to Whitechapel and found Colverson in the duty office.

Colverson looked up from the file he was reading. 'Did Mr Makepeace have anything useful to say, sir?' he asked.

Abberline nodded. 'He did indeed, Colverson, although I fear it may scar that young man for the rest of his life,' he said. 'We have a positive identification at least and we certainly have a more complete picture of the life and times of Montague John Druitt. How relevant it may turn out to be I can't say.'

'Is there anything I can do to help, sir?'

'You can take yourself off home, Colverson and get some rest. Tomorrow will be a busy day. After a visit to Minnow's Walk, I want you to find out all you can about a gentleman's club known as the New Reformed Paladins.'

47

Miss Violet Carew had a position that might charitably be described as "medical adjacent". As Dr James Cream's secretary/receptionist she often found that this proximity led his patients to confide in her in ways disproportionate to her actual knowledge or station. Mrs Dolores Huxtable of the banking Huxtables was a case in point. She entered Dr Cream's waiting room with all the elegance of a perfumed and bejewelled tug boat towing a thin, pale girl, her daughter Annabelle, in her wake.

'Do you really think Dr James will be able to help?' Mrs Huxtable asked. Dr Cream liked everyone to call him "Dr James" because, he said, it created the right sort of ambience. Violet wasn't so sure that such familiarity was appropriate but had no choice but to acquiesce.

'Dr James has achieved some remarkable results,' Violet said, truthfully.

Mrs Huxtable indicated her daughter who wandered listlessly about the room admiring the framed portraits on the wall. 'Only I do despair of Annabelle ever finding a suitable husband. She has no social skills, refuses to enhance her appearance by the application of anything more than soap and water, seems incapable of learning even the simplest of dances and prefers fashion that is "functional".' Mrs Huxtable laced the word with venom enough to fell an ox. 'Lord knows I've tried but she's almost twenty-one years old and I fear she will remain a spinster forever. She does have good bone structure,' she added by way of some small recompense for her daughter's many flaws.

Violet looked at the girl. She had large, chestnut eyes and straight black hair. Her expression, rather than sullen as her mother's recitation of transgressions and character deficits would suggest, bespoke of a quiet, introverted nature. Was there even a glimmer of fear in those eyes? Hardly surprising if there was, Violet thought, with a mother like that. Had she known it, that fear was likely to be well founded. She was, indeed, an ideal patient for Dr James and his techniques. Whether those techniques benefitted Annabelle Huxtable more than Dr James himself was a matter of debate. Violet silently chastised herself for such uncharitable thoughts about her employer who gave her a reliable salary with which she was able to support her family after her father's death, but every good deed exacts a price. In truth, Violet had no real idea how much of a price Dr James exacted for his largesse. She only knew she had come to dread being summoned into his private office. When no patients were due, the summons would come on some pretext such as reviewing the diary for the next week or the need to write to certain clients on some trivial matter. The thing was, Violet could never remember the details of such meetings. Her work had never been criticised so she assumed she had completed the tasks assigned to her successfully, and yet … It was small things she noticed. The buttons on her blouse misaligned, a stray lock of hair that had hitherto been held firmly in place, a stocking twisted or a shoelace untied. Puzzling. More importantly, there were sometimes marks. A slight bruise or small scratch on her upper arm or stomach. Even more intimately, a reddening about her nipples which were unaccountably sore. And inside. In areas most personal she felt bruised and tender. Inexplicable as they were it had created a feeling of creeping dread in Violet that she could not explain to herself and was too embarrassed to admit to anyone else.

'I'm sure Dr James will be able to bring her out of herself,' she said.

At that moment, the man himself threw open the double doors to his inner sanctum with a theatrical flourish and descended upon Mrs Huxtable with a charming smile. He took up her hand and patted it comfortingly.

'My dear Mrs Huxtable,' he said. 'Such a pleasure to see you again. And this must be your charming daughter Annabelle that you have told me so much about.'

'I do hope you can help her Dr James. I really am at my wits end.'

'Have no fear, dear lady. I feel sure that Annabelle and I will become the closest of friends. Now, as I explained, my methods require solitude and quiet, so I must ask you to leave Annabelle in my hands and return for her in, say, two hours. Would that be convenient?'

'Of course, Dr James.' Turning to her, thus far silent, daughter, she said: 'Annabelle, you do what Dr James tells you and I will see you soon.'

Amidst much maternal clucking, Dr James ushered Mrs Huxtable out of the door which he closed, with a barely audible sigh Violet noticed.

Turning to Violet, he said: 'No interruptions whilst I am with Miss Huxtable, Violet.'

'Of course Dr James.'

Smiling, he turned to Annabelle and beckoned her to precede him into his office. He followed her inside and closed the door. Violet waited and heard the subtle click of the well- oiled lock being turned. She sighed. 'Better you than me,' she thought and buried her face in her hands in shame.

48

Dr James Cream. How proud father had been when he had passed his exams with flying colours and was able to take up his professional duties with that most salubrious prefix "Doctor". Of course, the old fool had promptly squandered the family fortune on drinking and gambling and disastrous financial investments. Not hard to see where Thomas gets his wastrel characteristics from. But not Dr James Cream. He was a man above such petty inclinations. Nor was he the sort to waste his talents toiling on the wards of those insanitary cesspits they call hospitals, tending to the smelly ailments of the poor and worthless, most of whom brought their situation upon themselves and deserved no better and probably much worse. No, Dr James Cream was more interested in those ailments of the mind rather than the body. A brief sojourn in a discrete mental institution catering for the better class of lunatic led him to believe that the sphere of mesmerism was where his fortune lay. And he had not been wrong. As a private practitioner he had access to the upper echelons of society who were willing and able to pay to keep their mental aberrations secret or to indulge their own imaginary ailments with the most personal and expensive treatment they could find. To heal the mind, you had to enter the mind. To take control of it and adjust its function and focus. Of course, there were beneficial side effects to James Cream's skill. To implant a word in a man's mind that, when heard, would give him the impulse to cluck like a chicken never ceased to amuse. Better yet, the same technique could persuade buxom young debutants to disrobe completely and disport themselves in the manner of the most wanton harlot and then to remember nothing at all about it. The Huxtable girl had been a prime example and a pleasing

155

diversion. She could do with a little more meat on her bones but being able to coax such a timid little mouse into behaving like the most debauched whore had been most satisfactory. It chaffed that he would have to wait until his wedding night before he could enjoy Miss Matilda Clover in a similar manner and he had often toyed with the idea of using his powers to expedite matters in that regard but his nerve had always failed him. Inconceivable though it was, should something go wrong in that endeavour then it would spell ruin for him. No, better to play that game with a straight bat.

Aside from a mild trance to cure headaches and the most trivial of gastric pains, his relationship with Miss Clover was pure and unsullied. It was a situation that James Cream was unused to. The feeling that he cared for another more than himself. It baffled him for some time until he was, at last, able to diagnose his condition. He was in love. The fact that her family was worth a fortune didn't hurt, but James Cream could almost swear that he would feel the same if the girl was a pauper. It was his avowed intention to ask Miss Clover to do him the honour of becoming his wife thus merging true love with immense wealth in that most happy of endings. Her father – always the father – was a small stumbling block. He had less regard for the efficacy of mesmerism that Miss Clover and her mother. It was a stumbling block that James Cream would have to overcome before the intransigent old goat would give his permission for them to be wed. In the meantime, there were plenty of other ways to pass the time. His next patient would not provide the same level of physical satisfaction as the Huxtable girl but was even more vital in securing his reputation forevermore and would give the irascible Mr Clover no reason to refuse his request to marry his daughter.

It was on a lecture tour of the United States that James Cream hit upon the ideal way to cement his reputation, improve his own financial status beyond all recognition and claim the love of his life into the bargain.

After one of his successful demonstrations an individual approached him and requested, nay, begged him to aid him in his own mental dilemma. James Cream was, at first, inclined to send him on his way, but something about the man piqued his curiosity. He asked the man to tell him his story and quite a story it was. From spells of absolute normality this individual plunged into the depth of mania that required frequent stays in a mental institution where they were totally unable to fathom his problem and discharged him as soon as his moods became docile once more. As time passed, his moods became more aggressive until his violent outbursts led him to commit unspeakable acts of violence on women for which he was now wanted by the law.

Logic dictated that James Cream should turn this person over to the proper authorities but after one brief mesmeric examination he became convinced that the mental affliction that presented itself was so complex, so intriguing, that any medical man able to unravel and maybe even cure the condition would become world famous overnight.

Subsequently, James Cream arranged for the man to accompany him on his return to England, whereupon he arranged lodgings and a modicum of financial support as he began an exhaustive series of mesmeric treatments that would secure his future, his fortune and the love of his life.

The man's name was George Hutchinson.

49

'Just relax. Focus on my watch. See it swing. Follow its movement and let your eyes grow heavy. Think of nothing. You are sleepy. Your eyes are closing. Open your mind to me.'

It was remarkably easy the way some people succumbed to hypnotic suggestion. James doubted that George Hutchinson even needed the swinging pocket watch. A few soothing words would be enough. A mind so fragmented, so roiling with suppressed emotion might have been more resistant. The fact that he was not made James suspect that the surface personality that masqueraded as George Hutchinson was desperate for some sort of solace, some sort of cure. James had little intention of providing such a release from the inner demons that tormented his patient. Not until he had mined all the deep, dark secrets that his mind had to offer at any rate. Nor was it the surface George Hutchinson that interested him. No. The source of James's fascination with this nondescript and rather scruffy individual lay beneath the layers of civilisation that kept him cloaked and hidden from view. This was a personality as distinct from George Hutchinson as an ant is from a buffalo. The one, tiny and insignificant, easily trodden on and forgotten. The other huge, muscular and ferocious and unmissable. It was this personality that James wanted to mine for the golden career he felt he so rightly deserved.

The personality that fascinated him was christened by James Cream as Spring Heeled Jack.

'Good evening Doctor Cream.'

It always sent a shiver up James Cream's spine when Jack first spoke. His voice, husky and sibilant in nature was markedly different from George Hutchinson's normal bass growl. The tone and speech patterns also differed significantly. George was a simple man from a poor, uneducated background, his speech redolent of rural farms and rough poverty. Jack was educated, at least on the surface. Erudite and skilled with words and phrases that would be completely alien to George. James had detailed minutely every aspect of this vocal transformation. If such a small thing could be so completely anomalous, what else might this divergent personality be capable of?

'Hello Jack,' he said.

'Are you going to let me out of my box today?'

'Is that what you want?'

'What creature doesn't want to be free from captivity?'

'Is that how you regard yourself, Jack? A creature?'

Jack laughed. The sound of a highly amused rattlesnake. 'That is how everyone sees me isn't it? How you see me at least. That's why you have locked me up in here and taken away the key.'

'I'm flattered that you think I have such power over you.'

'Don't try and flatter me, James.' The voice a snarl now, filaments of anger filtering through the polite façade. 'You know damn well you've placed a barrier between myself and George. It was you, was it not, who taught him that ridiculous rhyme? You who christened me after a child's game? How it must delight you "Doctor" Cream to see little girls skipping in the street, chanting that puerile mantra, knowing that it, and it alone, keeps me enslaved. Remind me if you will, how does it go?'

'You know the rhyme, Jack.'

'Humour me if you will.'

James cleared his throat and began to recite:

'Incubus Succubus
Sitting round a table

Lucifer is watching you
Stick him if you're able

All around this great big town
Goes Spring Heeled Jack and Mabel
Takes his coat of wasted dreams
And lays it on the table

Twelve plus one the devil's sons
Are gathered round a fire
Lay him down inside a box
And pile the dirt up higher

Bend the knee and bow your head
And go to church on Sunday
Say the words and praise the Lord
And dig him up on Monday'

Jack's voice slid down the emotional scale almost like music. 'Ah, yes. How appropriate. How pleased you must be with yourself. You have certainly shut me up inside a box, haven't you?'

'I simply gave George a means to resist your influence. By reciting this rhyme whenever he feels your presence, George is able to retain control of his own mind, his own spirit.'

'By reducing me to a mere fantasy?' Jack's voice rose again to almost a shout.

'Isn't that what you are, Jack? A fantasy? A diseased part of George's damaged mind? A canker that cannot be cut out with a surgeon's knife, but, nonetheless needs to be exorcised for the greater good?'

There was silence for a few seconds and then Jack chuckled, a cold, inhuman sound. 'It matters not,' he said. 'It won't last forever. You have sown the seeds of your own defeat, for, does the rhyme not also state that I will be "Dug up on Monday?"'

'No-one is going to dig you up, Jack.'

'Really? Isn't that what you are doing right now James? Digging me up so you can delve into my soul to further your own ends?'

James said nothing. Jack chuckled. 'Ask George about his dreams,' he said 'You may have temporarily prevented me from entering the real world, but I still rule in the realm of dreams.'

'You think this situation is temporary?'

'Of course. Even the mightiest boulder can be worn away by a single constant drip of water. I am that drip of water and I am inexhaustible. It is only a matter of time before I am free again.'

'And what will you do with this freedom you crave?'

'You know what I will do, James.'

'I'd still like you to tell me.'

Jack sniggered, an ugly, triumphant sound. 'Of course you would, James. I've noticed that about you. You like it when I talk to you about my desires. My urges. My passions. We are very much alike in some ways. Would you not agree?'

'So, will you tell me?'

'Of course. Now, where shall I begin …?'

And Jack began to speak. James Cream wrote furiously to keep up with the sinister monologue. He carried on writing even after his wrist ached and a cold sweat ran down his brow, wiping an impatient hand across his eyes as his vision blurred. Continued writing into the night until even he could take no more and, regretfully, consigned the demon called Jack back to its prison of flesh and blood. The creature's departing words echoed inside his skull and made him shiver with fear.

'Soon, James. I will be with you very soon.'

161

50

George Hutchinson was a desert creature. Used to the arid, sand-choked landscapes of his homeland he found the damp, foggy streets of London injurious to his health. He had a constant, nagging cough and runny nose. His rooms were of little comfort. Cold and damp, but, as his room and board were being paid for by Dr James Cream in return for his co-operation in the doctor's investigation into his unfortunate problem he could not afford to complain. Especially as the only alternative was to return to his native climes where a warrant for his arrest had been issued and which the agents of the Pinkerton Detective Agency were all too keen to foreclose upon. If the doctor's efforts resulted in a cure, that would, indeed, make all his discomfort worthwhile.

As the English climate so ill-suited him, you may wonder why he chose to venture forth on a chilly, damp and foggy night. The answer was simple. Despite Dr James Cream's efforts, the results they had produced, and, in fairness, they had significantly improved George's condition, they were not fool-proof. The plain fact was that on this night as on so many others, George Hutchinson was not in control of his actions. Someone else was in the driver's cab of this particular locomotive and it was all George could do to keep it from jumping the rails. George knew all too well the consequences if that should happen. He'd seen it often enough in his homeland and it sickened him to his core. At least now he had a name for that reckless engineer. Dr Cream had at least been able to give him that.

Jack.

A name and a means to make him pull back on the throttle when things began to get out of hand. But it was hard. So damned hard. And sometimes, like tonight, George just didn't have the strength.

As his footsteps took him through the dark back alleys of Whitechapel, George viewed the unravelling scenery as a helpless passenger. A voyeur to his own downfall. The house that had once housed George Hutchinson in splendid isolation now had another tenant. One who was happy in his work. George felt the vibrations in his vocal chords as Jack hummed a merry tune but could not remember having heard it before. The scent of prey was strong in Jack's nostrils and George experienced it as a sour taste that burned the back of his throat. He knew what would happen next. Unlike the mysterious tune of which he had no recollection, other memories concerning Jack remained long after Jack himself had departed. It was those memories that had prompted George Hutchinson to attempt to take his own life on more than one occasion. Each time, Jack had intervened. Before the blade could draw sufficient blood, before George's finger could squeeze the trigger, Jack would be there to thwart him. Many doctors had tried to beat Jack into submission but they had all failed. Only Dr James Cream had achieved any modicum of success, but it required strength of will and determination and George was so tired.

For a while, the streets were so empty, so inhospitable that George dared to hope that Jack's intentions would be thwarted with no interference from himself. But then, up ahead, he saw her. A pale figure moving through the gloom. He felt himself move towards her. Felt his hand grip the knife in his pocket. If he could not muster the strength, George knew what would happen next.

The woman was young. Pretty beneath the grime. She carried a basket of wilting blooms. A flower seller then. Plying her trade outside the theatres and on street corners of the more well to do areas. Drooping now like her wares, wending her weary way homeward, chased from the streets by the inclement weather. The thing that motivated George Hutchinson's body quickened its pace.

No more than three paces distant now, George felt the surge of anticipation flood his body. The hand holding the knife came up. Feebly George began to recite the rhyme Dr James Cream had taught him.

'Incubus Succubus
Sitting round a table
Lucifer is watching you
Stick him if you're able'

He felt Jack growl his displeasure. He stumbled, almost tripped, but his determination saw him follow through with his intention. The knife flashed down as George screamed out the words.

'All around this great big town
Goes Spring Heeled Jack and Mabel
Takes his coat of wasted dreams
And lays it on the table

It was little enough, but it was sufficient. This time. The blade snagged the back of the girl's dress, ripping the fabric but leaving the flesh unblemished. She turned angrily.

''Ere, wots your game?' And then she saw the knife in George's hand and realised it was no game at all. Temporarily stymied, Jack retreated, leaving George once more the master of his own destiny. A profound weakness overcame him and he staggered against the wall for support. Raising his head with an effort he said: 'Run. For God's sake, run!'

Seeing the wisdom of his words, the girl did just that, screaming as she did so. Panting and on the point of exhaustion, George forced himself to move. He stumbled blindly, quickening his pace as much as he was able only when he heard the distant call of a police whistle. By the grace of God he made it back to his lodgings and collapsed onto his bed. He felt momentarily elated. Triumphant even, but he knew his victory would come at a terrible price. His night would be filled with dreams of abominations and vile images, but he didn't care. He had proved himself Jack's master and that was a most prodigious step forward.

51

Limehouse Lil ran a respectable establishment. A place where gentlemen of taste and refinement could come to indulge their passions, be they of the liquid, female or game of chance variety. Whilst her girls plied their trade in the parlour and upstairs, the downstairs back room played host to card and dice enthusiasts.

Although Lil prided herself on catering for a superior type of client, it was not always possible to keep the riff-raff out, nor would it be desirable if they were particularly flush and intent on parting with most of it. The last thing she needed was a visit from the police, but that was what she got. Two of them. One of them in full uniform as well! What would the neighbours think? Mind you, it wasn't the first time her establishment had been graced by the representatives of law and order. But that was usually after dark, with their hats pulled down over their face. These two walked in bold as brass in broad daylight. The cheek of it! She took some solace in the fact that most of her girls were still slumbering after a hard night's work and her clientele wouldn't be seen dead anywhere near her establishment before the hours of nightfall. Still, word gets around. Best to nip this in the bud.

'I run a respectable establishment,' she told them. The one in normal clothes smiled at her. It was a nice smile she decided, open and friendly, but she had learned the hard way over the years that appearances cannot always be trusted.

'I'm sure you do,' he said. 'We're not here about your business practices, I assure you.'

'Good,' she said. 'My …' she sought for the right word, '…patron would not be happy about that.'

'Oh? A patron. Who might that gentleman be? Maybe he should be the one we need to talk to, eh, Colverson?'

'Always pays to go straight to the top, sir,' the uniformed one replied.

'No!' said Lil, a little too loudly and a little too quickly. 'He don't like to be disturbed. I'm sure I can answer any questions you might have.'

'Splendid. In that case, we need to ask you about one of your clients.'

'Can't tell you anything about them,' Lil declared. 'We operate a strict confidential policy here. We have some very important gentlemen who come here to take their ease after a hard day's work and they would be most upset if I were to go about giving their details to all and sundry.'

'Quite. But we are not "all and sundry". We are officers of the law and it is your duty as a respectable citizen to co-operate with us in the furtherance of our duty.'

His voice was still mild, his smile beguiling, but Lil detected a steel beneath the meek façade. Watch yourself, gal, she told herself. He's not one you want to mess with.

'Besides,' Abberline continued. 'This particular client will have no objections to you answering our questions I'm sure. He's dead,'

'Lawd!' Lil visibly paled and reached behind her to find the succour of an overstuffed armchair into which she sank with a soft "whump!" sound and a cloud of dust, housework not being high on her agenda.

'Dead you say?'

'I'm afraid so.'

'It wasn't while he was here, I can tell you that. No-one ever died on these premises. All my clients leave here upright even if a little bandy legged on some occasions.'

'Indeed. This particular client died on the embankment. His

167

body received by the Thames until he was washed up on the shore some days later.'

'That's terrible, but what's it got to do with me?'

'We believe he was a regular client of yours and that he may have let slip to some of his "companions" information that may lead us to identify his killer.'

'Does he have a name?' *Not that that will tell me anything. A lot of our gentlemen don't like to give their real names. They prefer privacy in their leisure pursuits, you understand?*'

'I understand perfectly.' *That smile again. Like a cat just about to close his jaws on a mouse,* Lil thought. 'This particular gentleman,' Abberline continued, 'was a lawyer. He would be well dressed, possibly carrying a briefcase as I believe it was his habit to visit you on his way home from his work. Medium height with dark hair. His name was Montague Druitt.'

'Can't say I've ever heard of him,' Lil said, smoothly.

Abberline paused, his smile hardening into a frown. 'Perhaps,' he said, 'you may like to take a moment to re-consider that name. Montague Druitt. Think carefully.'

Lil felt a chill run up her spine. *Oh, my Gawd, he knows I'm lying! But how can he? He may suspect, but that's not the same thing.* Lil considered her options for a moment. *What would be the cost of lying to this man compared to the cost of telling him the truth and risking the wrath of her "patron" Patrick Reilly? And that wife of his. She was even more frightening if truth be told. Either way lay potential ruin.*

'I believe, on further consideration,' Lil said, 'that the name does ring a bell.'

Abberline's smile reasserted itself. 'I thought it might,' he said. 'Now, what can you tell us about him?'

'A regular, like you say. A good tipper. Had particular tastes if you get my meaning. I only ever exchanged pleasantries with him

'Did he have any particular favourites among your employees?'

'One or two that catered to his special needs, yes.'

There was that smile again. 'Then perhaps we could speak to them?' Abberline said. 'Now would be a good time, don't you think?'

Sally and Jenny were none too pleased about being dragged out of bed at some unearthly hour before noon. They appeared for questioning yawning and blinking, clad in nightgowns that left little to the imagination of even the most dull-witted individual.

'Good morning, ladies,' Abberline greeted them.

'Ooooh, ladies is it,' said Jenny. 'You must be a right toff and no mistake.' She ran a hand over Abberline's arm before a short, sharp cough from Lil pulled her up short. 'These gentlemen are policemen,' she told them

'Police?' said Sally, giving Colverson a puzzled look. 'You mean that uniform is real?'

'It is indeed, madam,' said Colverson.

'Does it come off?' Jenny asked. And both girls dissolved into fits of giggles until Lil clapped her hands and restored a modicum of silence.

'They want to ask you some questions and you'll answer them with no back-chat or you'll have me to answer to.'

Both girls stood, shuffling their feet, their eyes downcast like naughty schoolchildren but each wore a grin that belied their compliance.

'Thank you,' said Abberline. 'I believe both of you have had dealings with a client called Montague Druitt. Is that correct?'

'Never heard of him,' Sally said.

Lil sighed. 'The one who likes special treatment,' she said.

'Always carries a leather bag.'

'That one!' Sally frowned

'Gawd, tell me you've got him locked up and I'll give you one for free,' Jenny offered.

'Most generous,' Abberline replied, 'but locking up Mr Druitt would be rather pointless as he is deceased.'

'Good riddance,' Sally said.

'I take it you did not hold Mr Druitt in high esteem?'

'Would you hold someone in high esteem who did this?' she said, turning her back on the two policemen, bending down and flicking up her nightgown to reveal her naked buttocks and thighs were criss-crossed in red welts.

Jenny began to giggle again.

'Girls, girls,' Lil said. 'Some decorum, please.'

'Quite all right,' Abberline said. 'I have seen much worse sights in the course of my duties.'

Colverson looked less accepting of the circumstances, although it was no-less true that he had also seen much worse sights, and turned bright red.

Sally re-adjusted her clothing and turned to face them once more, a look of sullen defiance on her face. 'Sorry,' she muttered, 'but he was an evil one that one and no mistake.'

'That's true,' said Jenny. 'He had to pay double just to get anyone to put up with that.'

'The gentlemen don't need to know about our financial dealings,' Lil reminded them.

'Indeed not,' Abberline said. 'I'm more interested to know if he ever spoke to you about anything during your acquaintance.'

'Apart from calling us all the vile names under the sun you mean?'

'Yes. I take it you had dealings with him separately.'

170

'Sometimes. Sometimes both together. He really enjoyed those sessions.'

'And apart from insulting your good names, did he tell you anything about himself? His life, his past, any friends or acquaintances he might have had? The smallest thing could be important.'

Sally shook her head. 'Nuffing that I remember. I was hurting too much to take much notice anyway.'

Jenny remained quiet.

'Miss?' Abberline prompted. 'Do you have anything to tell us?'

'Well, she said, 'there was one thing.'

'Yes, go on.'

'Well, he seemed in a rare old mood. Gave me a right going over. I was in bed for a week.'

'You always are,' Sally laughed.

'Cow.'

'Bitch.'

'Ladies, please. Go on, Miss. He told you something?'

'More like talking to himself. Said I reminded him of a gypsy girl he once knew and how Jacob would have enjoyed giving me a good going over just like he did to her before she spoiled it all by biting off his todger. Pardon my French.'

'No apology needed. Did he mention any other names or a surname for this Jacob person?'

'No, but I was in so much pain, he may have done for all I know. Sorry.'

'Not at all. You have been most helpful. If you think of anything else, anything at all, you can contact me at Whitechapel Station. Thank you for your time ladies. Come Colverson, we must be off.'

'Come back soon,' Sally called after them. 'I like a man in uniform I do.'

It was during his investigation into the Jack the Ripper murders that Detective Chief Inspector Abberline received a potentially fatal wound. His life was saved by the timely intervention of Sir Francis Varney, a self-confessed vampire, who gave Abberline an infusion of his own, vampire, blood. True, Abberline's recovery had been quite remarkable, but, ever the paragmatist, the Inspector doubted Sir Francis's claims to vampirism. The medical journals had been trumpeting the efficacious properties of blood transfusions for some time now and, despite the unorthodox method of delivery, this was what Abberline attributed his continued existence to.

Subsequent events in the Ripper case gave him cause to doubt his scepticism and his improved health and vigour ever since gave credence to the fact that some vampire essence still circulated in his veins.

Abberline's abiding fear, once he had accepted that possibility was:

Am I now a vampire?

Sir Francis was a great pains to assure him that this was not the case and that his infusion should be looked upon as nothing more than a most superior tonic of sorts.

Unconvinced, Abberline was prompted to have a singular conversation with PC Colverson on the subject.

'If it transpires that I develop vampiric tendencies that I cannot control, I want you to promise me something, Colveson. I want you to promise me that you will put an end to me. Sir Francis seems to cope well enough, but he is, by all accounts a natural born vampire. I have no wish to endure such a transformation into an un-natural state. I know this is much to ask and, if it is more than you can commit to, you must say and I will make other arrangements. The only other person who knows of these events is my wife and this is hardly something I can ask of her, so I hope, I pray, that you will be willing to carry out my wishes should the need arise.'

Colverson thought the request over for barely a heartbeat before replying. 'It is true that during that case I witnessed things that I never thought I would see. The fact that such a thing as vampirism is real I have no doubt and how anyone can contemplate living with such a curse is beyond me. Should it come about that that you develop that condition in full, I would be honoured to carry out your wish though it would pain me sorely to have to do so.'

'I thank you Colverson. I knew I could rely on you.'

And that was the last time the two men spoke of such matters, but it was the memory of that conversation that now prompted PC Colverson to ask:

'How did you know she was lying when she said she didn't know Druitt?'

'Other than the fact that persons in her line of business habitually lie to policemen?'

'Apart from that, yes sir.'

'Just a hunch, Colverson. Call it my "coppers nose".'

'There is something else I could call it, sir. Something that seems to be happening a lot more since our meeting with a certain Sir Francis Varney.'

Abberline gave a wry smile. 'You have the instincts of a bloodhound, Colverson. I confess that my own instincts have become sharper since that incident. Nothing untoward, just an ability to sense small things, the quickening of a suspects breathing, the smallest flicker of an eyelid, a raising of the tone when speaking, a tendency to speak too quickly and too much.

Sometimes I swear that I can hear the very blood coursing more robustly through their veins when their agitation peaks. Or it could just be a co-incidence. A figment of my imagination. I confess I am not entirely sure myself as to cause and effect. I just know it is proving to be most useful, most useful indeed.'

'Nothing that need concern us then, sir?'

'No, Colverson. Nothing of any undue concern, but your vigilance is noted and appreciated. But I'm curious. How did you know I was employing something other than a "copper's nose"?'

'You have a look about you, sir. An expression that comes over your face when you employ means other than those normally open to the rest of us.'

'Really? I must be careful of that. Your powers of observation are, as ever, razor sharp Colverson. Thank you for pointing it out.'

'You're welcome, sir. As to the rest, was that any use to us, sir?'

'I believe so, Colverson.'

'But who's this Jacob character? And a gypsy girl who goes around biting off men's parts. It all sounds a bit far-fetched to me, sir.'

'Maybe so, but it's a start at least. If we can find corroborating evidence that such an attack took place we may be on to something.'

'By "we" I take it you mean me, sir?'

Abberline smiled. 'Once again you have the instincts of a bloodhound, Colverson. Once you've been set on a trail I have every confidence you will produce the required results.'

52

'You're a damned disgrace and I curse the day Matilda ever laid eyes on you!'

Sir Edward Clover had a booming, foghorn of a voice and he was using it to full effect. His wife, Lady Elspeth Clover was a mewling, lachrymose wisp of a woman forever, as now, cringing in her husband's shadow.

Dr James Cream hastily closed his office door on the avid eyes of his receptionist and the two clients patiently waiting to be summoned into his sanctum. That Sir Edward had "jumped the queue" was of little importance compared to the slur on James's character he was taking such pains to make known to anyone within earshot. Given the volume of his voice, that could include half the street if not half of London.

'Sir Edward, I really don't know what I have done to deserve such a description. I have nothing but the noblest intentions towards your daughter. Why, the last time I saw her ...'

'The last time you saw her!' thundered Sir Edward. 'I'll tell you the last time I saw her shall I?' Less than an hour ago at the Whitechapel Morgue!'

'The Morgue? I don't understand. What was she doing there? She doesn't know anyone at the Morgue.'

Sir Edward gave an inarticulate roar and advanced upon James, raising his silver-topped cane above his head. Shocked, James stumbled backwards, raising his arms to protect himself, tripped and went sprawling. Sir Edward loomed over him.

'She was at the Morgue because she is dead, you imbecile!' he screamed.

'Dead? I don't ... no ... she can't be!'

Sir Edward stepped back, his face puce. 'Dead I tell you!' he said.

'We have just identified her body. And it's all your fault!'

'Mine?' James scrambled to his feet, his mind awhirl. How can it be my fault?'

'You associate with the lowest of the low,' Sir Edward told him. 'Before she met you and got caught up in your hypnosis nonsense she barely knew such a world existed. She was safe. Cosseted. Protected. You undid all that with your mindless blathering and now look at the result.'

'But how did she die?' James asked. 'Was it an accident?'

'No,' Sir Edward growled. 'It was deliberate. My angel girl was murdered. Poisoned by the sort of low-life miscreant whose fantasies you indulge every day.'

'I can assure you, my clientele are sophisticated, if troubled, individuals who would not harm a living soul.'

'Your assurances be damned!' Sir Edward snarled. 'Your assurances won't bring Matilda back. I've a good mind to sue. And if you have one shred of decency left in your misbegotten soul, you will keep well away from the funeral and do not seek to contact us in any way from this moment on. Leave us to grieve in peace. Come Elspeth.'

Sir Edward turned on his heel and made for the door. James approached the weeping edifice that was Lady Clover, his hands spread like a penitent seeking forgiveness.

'Lady Clover,' he began, 'I beseech you …'

He never got to finish his sentence because Lady Clover spat full in his face. He felt the spittle trickle down his cheek as she turned and followed her husband through the now empty waiting room.

53

The night-time alleys and back streets of Whitechapel were not the sort of places that respectable young ladies would be advised to frequent. It was, however, exactly the sort of place where Miss Ambrosine Philpott, faded blossom of the music hall stage, wronged in love and over fond of a gin or two would likely be found. Or so Lawrence Babcock decided.

'An actor must inhabit his creation,' he used to tell his adoring acolytes when his theatrical star was in the ascendance. 'One must invest oneself in the smallest detail of their lives in order to give a meaningful and memorable performance however small the role might be.'

And so it was that Miss Ambrosine Philpott took shape in his mind as exactly the sort of young woman who might, if she was not careful, fall prey to this most recent incarnation of Spring Heeled Jack.

Miss Ambrosine Philpott's physical appearance owed much to the efforts of Babcock's former dresser, Rupert, who had managed to "borrow" a suitably shabby, but not too shabby, dress and a bedraggled wig from the costume store of the Alhambra Theatre where he was currently employed. Babcock's expertise with powder and paint created a visage that a mother may love but others would rarely give a second glance.

'How do I look, Rupe?' Babcock asked once the outward accoutrements of Miss Ambrosine Philpott had eclipsed his own persona to his satisfaction.

Rupert eyed him critically. 'Ask for a shilling and you might get tuppence,' was his verdict.

'Cheek!' Babcock said. 'I'm not hawking my wares like some common trollop.'

'Then what are you doing?'

Babcock smiled, revealing two lipstick reddened front teeth. 'I'm what you might call "taking the show on the road". If this works, I shall not only have retrieved my reputation, I will have a whole new career ahead of me as a cause celebre.'

'Just remember I need the frock back by the end of the week or there'll be hell to pay.'

If things went according to plan, Babcock thought, there will be hell to pay long before then.

His plan was elegant in its simplicity. The three victims thus far of Spring Heeled Jack had been young, working class women, not doxies, not upper class. All had had legitimate reasons for frequenting the byways of Whitechapel at night. Miss Ambrosine Philpott was one of their sisterhood and, with luck and persistence, her presence would be noted by the perpetrator of the assaults upon their persons that bore only a crude relationship to Babcock's own interpretation of the Whitechapel Demon. That, he decided, would be the name of his play, the masterpiece that would see him take his rightful place amongst the likes of Henry Irving as the man who not only played Spring Heeled Jack but who also brought the real life miscreant to justice when the police had failed.

So great was Babcock's desire for restitution of character that he relegated as negligent the actual danger he may be putting himself in. Such a prize was worth a little risk. Besides, he had two things the other victims did not. Firstly, he knew who he was looking for thanks to the sketch so thoughtfully provided by Inspector Abberline. The second was a small derringer pistol which he kept in a purse, ready to discourage and detain the culprit who was besmirching his reputation. What, he argued, could possibly go wrong?

By his third night on patrol, Babcock was beginning to think that any number of things could go wrong. The first night it had poured with rain, driving even the most determined assailant indoors. The second had been dry and had attracted a certain amount of interest from various individuals but none came close to the likeness he sought. Too short, too fat, too pock marked and Babcock had been lucky to preserve his maidenly state. Third time lucky he reasoned. A dry night, the streets not too populated as to be a deterrent, but not quiet either.

Babcock promenaded along the more frequented thoroughfares so as to attract attention before diverting off down more secluded routes. After his fourth pass his feet were hurting and he was about to admit defeat when the sound of footsteps behind him gave him pause. He stopped, pretending to search for something in his purse. A masculine voice from behind him said:

''Ello, lovely. Wot you doin' all by yourself, eh?'

Babcock turned, his heart thudding. Could this be the one he was seeking? The light wasn't good, but he had the same coarse features. His hair was somewhat lank and he sported a scrappy beard whereas the sketch was clean-shaven save for a full moustache, but even so, these details could be changed easily enough.

Babcock cleared his throat and spoke in a high, lilting voice. 'Why, just going about my lawful business good sir.'

'Lookin' for business, eh? That's good coz so am I.'

'You misunderstand me, sir. I am simply on my way home.'

'And where might that be?' He moved closer, crowding Babcock. This was all going wrong. Not at all as he had planned. Spring Heeled Jack or not, this man was a different sort of threat. With nervous fingers, Babcock opened his purse, reaching inside for the derringer. Where the hell was the damned thing?

'Wot you lookin' for in there, gal?' the man said.

'Nothing. Nothing at all,' Babcock muttered.

'Let's have a look, shall we?' he said and snatched Babcock's purse in one meaty hand.

'No!' Babcock almost screamed. 'It's mine. Give it back.'

'I'm just havin' a butchers. No need to get riled now is there? Well, well, what have we got here?'

His hand emerged from the purse holding the derringer. It looked so small and pathetic in his massive palm that Babcock almost cried. How could he have thought that something so puny could provide adequate protection?

The thug leered in the half light, showing brown and broken teeth.

'Wot say I keep this until we've had our fun, eh?'

He took a step forward. Babcock cringed back against the wall, expecting the worst and resigned to his fate, when something quite remarkable happened.

The sound of a gunshot and a shower of brick dust where the bullet had impacted with the wall. At first, Babcock thought his assailant had pulled the trigger of the derringer by accident, but the pistol was still in the man's hand, pointing away from where the bullet had hit. The look on his face indicated that he was as bemuse by this turn of events as Babcock.

A tall figure stepped from the shadows and spoke with an American accent.

'The next one goes between your eyes, friend,' he said in a voice that was both steady and deceptively friendly.

The thug looked down at his own hand where the derringer resided. The newcomer chuckled.

'Don't even think about it,' he said, glancing down at his own hand where a weapon of a much more considerable size and

180

power lay comfortably pointed steadily in the thug's direction. 'If that little toy could even reach me from over there,' he continued, 'do you think you'd be able to aim and fire before I got off a shot? You might. Stranger things have happened so they say. But I doubt it. Want to try your luck, fella?'

Preferring to answer with actions rather than words, the shabby man tossed the derringer on the ground and took to his heels. The stranger watched him go then holstered his Colt .45 and moved to pick up the discarded derringer which he held out to Babcock.

'Here you go, ma'am,' he said. 'Next time, keep it handy so you can get to it before they do.'

Babcock swallowed hard. 'Thank you,' he said. 'How can I ever thank you?'

'No thanks needed, ma'am. But if it would help, I'd be pleased to accompany you to your door, just to make sure you don't meet up with any more unpleasantness.'

'I … I'd like that, but please, let me at least buy you a drink by way of showing my gratitude. I know a nice little place not far from here.'

The stranger thought for a second and then smiled. 'Thank you, ma'am. I'd like that very much.'

'My name is George. George Hutchinson,' he said.

'Ambrosine Philpott,' Babcock said.

George smiled. 'Pleased to meet you, formally, as it were.'

He had a nice smile, Babcock/Ambrosine decided. And was much better looking than his sketch indicated. The artist hasn't caught his rugged handsomeness or the twinkle in his eyes. There's sadness there too he/she decided. Something deep and haunting. It wasn't until they had entered the Gown and Taffeta

181

that the light had been good enough to tell for sure, but now, Babcock/Ambrosine was positive and a great conflict assailed his/her senses.

His/her plan had worked, but not exactly as expected. His/her ploy had certainly drawn the new Spring Heeled Jack but even if it were still possible to capture him, would that be fair? He had, after all, saved Babcock/Ambrosine's life, albeit with a very large gun that he seemed to be all too familiar with, but then, weren't all Americans versed in such things? Babcock/Ambrosine found it hard to believe that the person sitting opposite could be one and the same as the miscreant who went about slashing innocent young women.

Before making a final decision, Babcock/Ambrosine decided he/she needed to know more about his/her mysterious saviour.

'Tell me about yourself,' he/she said.

Was there a fleeting glimpse of panic in his eyes? There and then gone?

'Not much to tell,' he murmured. 'Grew up in Texas.' A far-away expression came over his features. 'God's own country,' he said. 'Great rolling plains, hills and forests. Beautiful.'

'It sounds glorious.'

'It is.'

'So, what brings you to England?'

A definite downward cast to his expression now. 'I got in some trouble back home.'

'Haven't we all, dear, at one time or another.'

Babcock/Ambrosine's attempt at levity fell flat.

'This was serious trouble,' George said. 'More than I could rightly handle.'

'Would it help to talk about it?'

He gave a short laugh. 'Seems I ain't done nothing but talk about it these last months, but it ain't nothin' I care to burden a lady with. Let's just say I met someone, a doctor, who reckoned he could help me. He was headed back home to London and he took me with him to continue my treatment.'

'Is it helping?'

'Some.'

'Good. I'm glad.'

Babcock/Ambrosine reached out and laid his/her hand on top of George's.

'You have a lovely nature ma'am,' he said.

'I try.'

George cast a quick glance about the rest of the clientele that populated the Gown and Taffeta. 'Say,' he said. 'Do some of these folks look a mite strange to you?'

Babcock/Ambrosine surveyed the congregation. Nary a one was what they purported to be. Men dressed as women. Women posing as men. He/she sighed. 'I doubt there's anything quite like this on the open prairies,' he/she said. 'Maybe this was not the best choice of watering hole. Should we take a stroll instead?'

'If you're feeling sufficiently recovered,' he said.

'I'm tickety-boo, thanks to you. Come, let us promenade.'

It occurred to Babcock/Ambrosine that George may still be under the impression that he/she was a bona-fide female. That could prove a handicap if the romantic notions fermenting in his/her breast should find release in reality. Still, he/she reasoned, stranger things have happened.

Cloaked in night-time shadows with only a lambent moon for company, the mismatched pair strolled with impunity. Babcock/Ambrosine regaled George with tales from his/her theatrical past, suitably amended of course in order to preserve

183

anonymity. He, in turn, recited tales of the wild west and the picturesque rolling plains with their attendant tranquillity that soothed a troubled soul like his own.

'I guess I ain't never felt really like myself,' he confessed. 'There was always something, someone, inside of me trying to get out and I just don't know how to handle that.'

Babcock/Ambrosine patted his arm. 'I know that feeling,' he/she said. 'Sometimes one immerses oneself in a role so deeply it completely consumes you.'

'But at the end of the show you put that to one side and go back to being yourself, right?'

'Yes,' said Babcock/Ambrosine, a touch hesitantly, well aware of the dual role he/she was inhabiting at this very moment.

'Well, it ain't like that for me,' George said. 'I don't get to take off the paint and the costume. This "other" person is inside of me all the time, just waiting for the right moment to come out and I can't rightly stop him and then all hell breaks loose.'

Babcock/Ambrosine felt a sudden chill run up his/her spine. 'The right time?' he/she said. 'What would be the right time, do you suppose?'

George stopped walking and looked him/her in the eyes. It may just have been the reflection of the moon, but Babcock/Ambrosine could have sworn his eyes glowed and the soft mouth hardened into a cruel smile. Moreover, their meandering had taken them into a desolate area of back streets and alleyways far from the passage of humanity.

'I think now would be the perfect time,' George said, but his voice had changed. It was lighter, more clipped, the words more precise in place of the comforting western drawl.

Babcock/Ambrosine gasped and drew back, finding only a solid brick wall at his/her back. Encumbered as he/she was by female garments he/she doubted if running would be a viable option. Despite the certain futility of such an action, Babcock/Ambrosine opened his/her mouth to scream for help but was forestalled in that action when George gave a muffled groan and doubled over.

'No,' he said in the more familiar tones of his normal voice. 'Not now. I won't let you.'

This was followed by a peal of laughter in that other voice that had supplanted George's own, gentler tones, just a moment before. 'You think you can stop me?' the voice said. 'You never have before and you won't now. I am in control and you know it.'

'No!' George screamed the word and then began to recite a litany that Babcock/Ambrosine recognised as a child's rhyme, the very rhyme in fact that had inspired him/her to resurrect the legend of Spring Heeled Jack for theatrical purposes.

'All around this great big town
Went Spring Heeled Jack and Mabel…'

The words made Babcock/Ambrosine's bowels turn to ice. His/her plan, it seemed, had worked only too well and now he/she would pay the price.

George screamed again in abject agony and fell to his knees. Babcock/Ambrosine watched as he wrapped his arms around himself and shook and shivered as though plagued by chills of the most violent sort. In hindsight, Babcock/Ambrosine realised that this would have been the ideal time to affect an escape. To run for his/her life, but something rooted him/her to the spot. Was it fear? Yes, but not fear alone. Something inside resonated with compassion for this poor wretch and maybe something more than compassion alone. Dear God, what a time to fall in love!

A length, George's seizures passed and he became still, huddled on the ground. Fearing he was dead or, hope against hope, had regained his former senses, Babcock/Ambrosine took a hesitant step forward and reached out a hand.

'George?' he/she said. 'Are you all right?'

Suddenly, the crouching figure sprang to its feet, all vigour restored it seemed. Babcock/Ambrosine cringed away from his looming presence.

'George is not here,' the voice said. 'He won't be back for quite some time. Maybe not at all. What shall we do whilst we wait, hmmm?'

The creature formerly known as George reached a hand inside his coat. Babcock/Ambrosine gave a small squeak of terror and raised his/her hands in supplication. 'Please,' he/she said. 'Don't shoot me.'

The creature laughed but there was no humour in the sound. 'Shoot you? Why ever should I do that my dear? Guns are George's toys. Nasty, loud, messy things. I prefer something much more subtle.' He withdrew from some secreted scabbard inside his coat a large, flat bladed knife with a wicked gleam to its edge.

Babcock/Ambrosine wanted to scream but the breath would not enter his/her lungs. It was as his/ her certain death advanced upon him/her that he/she saw a shadowy figure appear from the blackness of the night. A dizzying sense of déjà vu encompassed him/her as the events of earlier in the evening replayed in his/her head. The menacing bulk of the assailant intent on violence foiled by the sudden arrival of a mysterious stranger. Can I be so lucky again? he/she thought.

The newcomer spoke in a strong American accent and Babcock/Ambrosine almost laughed at the co-incidence. 'Hello, George,' he said. 'Long time no see.'

The man who used to be George spun at the sound of the voice. 'Pinkerton!' he snarled.

'Drop the knife, George,' Pinkerton said calmly. 'I have you bang to rights and I'm taking you in.'

George slowly shook his head and then, looking up from hooded eyes, gave a feral grin.

'I suppose I have no choice,' he said. He opened his hand and let the knife fall to the ground. 'Come and get me,' he said.

As Pinkerton took a step forward, George's hand moved under his coat.

'He has a gun!' Babcock/Ambrosine shouted.

Pinkerton's hand was a blur of motion as he too reached beneath his coat. Two weapons were drawn but only one was fired. Twice. Babcock/Ambrosine closed his/her eyes and when he/ she dared to open them again, the body of the man he/she had known as George lay on the ground, two neat holes in his chest, seeping blood.

In the fullness of time, Lawrence Babcock would write a successful stage play about the events of that night. About his encounter with a mysterious stranger who could very well have been the love of his life had his tortured soul not been split in twain by an uncaring world. For the sake of propriety, the leading "lady" would be played by an actual woman and Babcock himself would take the role of the tortured Spring Heeled Jack in the initial run. Critics would say that his performance was an astounding and emotional piece of theatre and the play received standing ovations every night.

All that would come in time, but in the immediate aftermath of those events, Babcock was a quivering wreck, his wig abandoned, his make-up smudged, his emotions in disarray as he gave his statement to Detective Chief Inspector Abberline.

'You thought you were doing what, exactly?' Abberline asked.

'Setting a trap,' Babcock sobbed. 'I was so sure that this was just some ham-fisted amateur that if I could tempt him out I could easily detain him until I could summon the police. I even had a police whistle in my purse to do just that, but I never got the chance to use it.'

'Likewise the derringer that you hoped would protect you from harm,' Abberline commented.

'I didn't know it would end like this!' Babcock blubbed, dissolving into tears once more.

Abberline waited patiently for Babcock to compose himself.

'You did a foolish and dangerous thing Mr Babcock. Had it not been for the intervention of Mr Pinkerton things might have ended very badly for you.'

'I know.' Babcock blew his nose loudly on a large handkerchief. 'I can't thank him enough. He literally saved my life. How he came to find us I will never know. It was like a miracle from above.'

'More like good detective work,' Abberline told him. 'Mr Pinkerton was canvassing the drinking establishments in the area, showing their clientele the sketch that I gave you. When he got to the Gown and Taffeta, several people recognised Hutchinson's likeness.'

Babcock raised his eyebrows. 'He went to the Gown and Taffeta? Really?'

Abberline suppressed a smile. William Pinkerton was a tall man, broad shouldered and solidly built. His father, Alan Pinkerton, of whose Scottish heritage he was justly proud, had warned him of the inclemency of the British weather and so he had ventured out in the cold evening with hat, gloves, muffler and greatcoat which gave him the appearance of a large, shambling, bear. 'They say he stood out like a sore thumb,' Abberline said. Babcock had the good grace to make no comment as Abberline continued. 'They were able to give him a fair description of yourself. "A middle-aged trollop in a bad wig" was how they described you I believe.' Babcock pouted in annoyance. 'Cheek!' he said. 'That lot wouldn't know high class couture if it bit them!'

'Be that as it may, it was enough for Mr Pinkerton to recognise his quarry after they had indicated the direction you had both taken upon leaving that establishment. He had, in fact, been following you for some little time, but was unable to properly identify Hutchinson due to the poor lighting. He waited until he was certain he was on the right trail before intervening.'

'He almost left it too late. I really thought my time had come.'

'Fortunately Mr Pinkerton's expertise with a firearm was sufficient to prevent that from happening.'

'Amen to that, Inspector. He saved my life without a doubt.'

'I'm pleased. I will send Constable Colverson in to take a full statement to that effect. You were very fortunate tonight, Mr Babcock. I trust the experience will dissuade you from any future endeavours of this sort?'

'Oh, absolutely, Inspector. From now on, I shall leave policing to the police.'

After dispatching Colverson to take Babcock's statement, Abberline returned to his office where Pinkerton was waiting for him. The big American rose as Abberline entered.

'Well?' he said. 'Did he corroborate my version of events?' he asked.

Abberline waved Pinkerton back into his chair and took his own seat. 'Yes,' he said. 'It was as you said. Hutchinson was about to inflict deadly violence upon Mr Babcock. If not for your timely

189

intervention he would almost certainly not have survived.'

'Then I take it I will not be facing any charges?' Pinkerton asked.

'Normally there would have to be an inquiry into such an event, London not having quite the same relaxed attitude to its citizens discharging firearms with deadly force on its streets, but, under the circumstances, I think an official warning that such action is frowned upon will suffice.'

Pinkerton smiled. 'Is that Scotland Yard speak for it being a clean shooting as we say in the colonies?'

Abberline returned the smile. 'I think you can say that you got your man, Mr Pinkerton.'

Pinkerton nodded. 'Mighty glad to hear it,' he said. 'Do you have any other good news for me?'

'Such as?'

'That job offer I spoke about. Renovations to the Albion Hotel are almost done and with the Huchinson case all wrapped up, I'll be leaving soon. I need to find a bureau chief for the London office before I leave.'

Abberline nodded. 'I am still mulling it over,' he said.

'If you could mull a mite faster, Chief Inspector, I'd be much obliged. As I told you, I only want the best man for the job and I'm looking right at him. If you make me settle for second best my father will never forgive me.'

'Rest assured Mr Pinkerton, I will let you know my decision in ample time.'

'I trust your word Chief Inspector, but is there any chance that you'll ever call me William instead of Mr Pinkerton?'

'Slim to none I suspect,' Abberline said and both men smiled once more.

54

James Maybrick was out of sorts. His stomach had been playing him up for days. His drab of a wife had been no help, pathetic, mewling creature that she was. Was it any wonder that he sought his pleasure elsewhere? His dyspepsia was so extreme that he almost decided to forfeit his routine visit to the bawdy house, but the thought of spending more time at home eventually persuaded him to avail himself of their facilities anyway. Now though, the evening's exertions were weighing heavily on him. The pains in his stomach were increasing, he was sweating and his breathing was laboured. All he wanted now was his own bed. Such a simple pleasure, but one that would forever be denied him.

Several times on his way home, James Maybrick had to stop and rest. Stomach cramps and nausea plagued him incessantly. Cold sweat ran from his brow and his breath came in laboured gasps. Several onlookers paused as he leant against a convenient wall for support. Not one of them offered any assistance, fearing, perhaps that he was simply the worse for drink or maybe a dangerous lunatic. Curse them all he thought to himself. I don't need their help. Never have and never will. James Maybrick is his own man and the devil can take anyone who says otherwise.

It was as his own domicile and the comforts of his own bed came into sight across the park that he noticed the sound of horses' hooves. He paused against some railings. The sounds stopped. He listened. A horse snorted. Nothing more. He struggled on a few more paces. The sound of carriage wheels turning and the clip-clop of hooves began once more. He stopped. The carriage stopped. Chancing a look back he saw a black carriage pulled by a black horse, driven by a bulky figure muffled and be-hatted so as to disguise his features. It was all damned peculiar. A tremor of fear twisted itself in James Maybrick's gut. Fear as only the truly guilty may know. A fanciful notion he told himself. That damn fool Tumblety was spreading rumours and falsehoods and the others may panic like frightened housemaids, but James Maybrick was made of sterner stuff. Best not to take chances though. Leaving the main thoroughfare, he struck out across the park. A horse and carriage would not be able to follow him here surrounded as it was by spiked iron railings. Unfortunately for James Maybrick, the horse and carriage did not need to.

James Maybrick heard the carriage door slam before he had gone a hundred paces. He sensed a presence and, try as he might, could not dismiss it as a fanciful notion. He increased his pace as much as the pain in his innards would allow. And something moved stealthily behind him. Coming closer all the time.

James Maybrick had almost reached the far side of the park before his nerve broke and he cast a fearful glance back over his shoulder. The apparition that presented itself to his horrified gaze made him cry out in abject fear. In truth, it was not totally unexpected. If any demon was going to drag him down to hell for his sins, he would have bet good money it would be in the shape of a monstrous hound.

Shaggy black pelt, crimson eyes, cruel jaws dripping saliva, powerful muscles bunching and relaxing beneath the skin as it loped ever closer. James Maybrick turned and ran even though the effort near tore him in two with the pain that seared his guts. His house was but a few yards away. Once inside he would be safe. He cried out, screaming his wife's name with all the force he could muster.

'Florence! Florence! Open the door. For pity's sake. Open the door!'

James Maybrick saw the drawing room curtains flutter. She had seen him. She would see his distress and follow his instructions. The door would open and he would dash inside shutting and bolting the good solid oak portal behind him. He would be safe. Safe from whatever this monstrosity might be.

But the door did not open. James Maybrick threw himself at it in time to hear the bolts being slammed shut from inside barring him entrance.

'Florence!?' A querulous entreaty and one that he knew deep in his soul would not be answered. James Maybrick turned as his doom sprang upon him with dripping jaws and ripping claws.

'Torn to shreds on his own doorstep,' Colverson said. 'Another witness this time. The man's wife. Claims it was a black dog bigger than any she had ever seen. Once it was done, it turned as meek as you like and ran back across the park. Witnesses say they saw it jump into a black carriage that seemed to be waiting for it. Tame as a poodle it was then. The coachman whipped up the horse and off they went. No sign of them since.'

'In that case, Colverson,' Abberline said, 'I think we need to speak to the grieving widow. See if she can shed some light on the matter.'

55

Abberline doffed his hat and adopted his most solicitous expression.

'Please accept my most sincere condolences on your loss, Mrs Maybrick,' he said.

Florence Maybrick dabbed her eyes with a dainty lace handkerchief. 'Thank you Chief Inspector. Have you come to arrest me?'

'Arrest you? What makes you think I want to arrest you?'

'Because of what I did. To my husband. Oh, do sit down Chief Inspector. Can I get you some tea?'

Abberline acquiesced to the first offer but politely declined the second.

'What is it you think you did to your husband, Mrs Maybrick?'

'Murdered him of course.'

'Murder? Mrs Maybrick, I think the shock may have temporarily unbalanced your thinking. Your husband was attacked on your very doorstep by an unknown assailant.' Abberline had noted that the Maybrick's front door was still tinged with rusty stains and gouged with deep marks that could be nothing else than the claws of a large canine.

'It was a dog,' Florence stated firmly.

'A dog? You saw the attack?'

'I did indeed. A huge black brute it was. It was chasing my husband across the park. He almost reached the house before it caught him but he couldn't get in.'

'He couldn't?'

'No. Because I had locked and bolted the door to keep him out. In the end I thought it was the kindest thing.'

'Kind? Mrs Maybrick, if you witnessed your husband being

chased by a murderous hound it is only understandable that panic set in. Fearing for your own life, your immediate concern may have been for your own safety and locking the door seemed like the best course of action. I'm sure you had no intention of deliberately placing your husband in harm's way.'

'But I did,' she said. 'I decided that a quick, violent death would be preferable to a slow, protracted demise due to the poison I had been feeding him these past weeks.'

'You were poisoning your husband?'

'Yes. He was an awful man. Violent and reprehensible. He frequented houses of ill-repute and brought home vile diseases which he passed on to me. You have no idea how humiliating it was to have to seek medical aid for such things. My doctor was most understanding though. He gave me something that he said would calm James down and to increase the dose if it didn't seem to be working. So that's what I did. And when I realised it was making him ill, I gave him even more, hoping that it would put an end to my misery once and for all. Are you going to arrest me now?'

56

'You want me to do what?' Dr Pettifer protested.

'Test James Maybrick for signs of poison,' Abberline said.

'But the man was torn to pieces. Anyone can see that was the cause of death.'

'Ultimately, yes. But prior to his being mauled to death I have reason to believe he had been poisoned. By his wife, no less.'

Pettifer chuckled. 'Easier to arrest a vengeful wife than an elusive hound, eh, Abberline?'

'Just do as I ask, Dr Pettifer if you would be so kind.'

As Abberline turned to leave, Pettifer called out: 'That's what they're calling you, you know. Inspector Dog Catcher.'

Abberline froze for a second, then, taking a deep breath continued on his way, Pettifer's laughter ringing in his ears.

57

'Are you really going to arrest her, sir?' Colverson asked.

'If the results come back as I expect them to, I may have no option.'

'But on what charge? Not murder, surely. It was obviously an animal attack that killed him.'

'It may well have been a close run thing. Her intentions were clear enough, but I'd like to know what this doctor of hers was up to when he gave her the means to affect such an end.'

'Do we know who he is?'

'She was quite happy to give me his name. Seemed to think he was most understanding.'

'So, who is this paragon of virtue then, sir?'

'Cream. Dr Thomas Cream.'

58

'She did what?' Cream said, affecting as startled and bemused an expression as he could muster with his heart pounding like a steam train in his chest. To have two police officers bearding him in his own office was most disconcerting to say the least and he silently cursed his own weakness in taking pity on Florence Maybrick.

'Progressively poisoned her husband. Apparently following your instructions to steadily increase the dosage in order to achieve the desired effect.'

'That's outrageous! No doctor would ever do such a thing.'

'Then can you tell me what, precisely, you prescribed for Mrs Maybrick?'

'Over the course of time, many things. Some to ease the pain of her many injuries inflicted by that brute of a husband.'

'Then you know her husband mistreated her?'

'She never said as much, but it was obvious. I've seen the signs too many times in my profession to mistake them for anything but what they were.'

'I'm sure that is true, but did your compassion lead you to prescribe something more … permanent by way of a cure for what ailed her?'

'The occasional sleeping draught to help her rest. I may, in passing, have said that giving some to her husband may be beneficial, but by itself it would be harmless. Maybe if she combined it with the other remedies …'

'The coroner found large amounts of strychnine in his system.'

'A common enough substance that could be procured anywhere! Now, unless you intend to arrest me I have patients to attend to,'

59

'Are we going to arrest him, sir?' It seemed to be Colverson's day for asking the same question.

'On the evidence we have so far, I don't think we'd get very far.'

'But you think he's guilty?'

'My nose tells me yes, but I can't take my nose into court and expect to get a conviction.'

'And Mrs Maybrick?'

'Likewise. The poisoning may have been accidental.'

'But the confession?'

'Any good lawyer would plead extenuating circumstances leading to a tragic accident.'

'Then we let things lie?'

'Sometimes, Colverson, that is all we can do.'

60

The Perivale Home for Destitute Women. A bowl of soup and a bed for the night. You have to share a dormitory with twenty other lost souls and sit through a sermon from a beanpole of a clergyman before you can eat your soup, but at least it's dry and no-one's going to try and put his hand up your skirt while you're asleep. Well, no man anyway. A toothless old harridan called Myrtle tried it on a few times but Polly gave her the sharp edge of her tongue and promised a lot more if she didn't give over and that seemed to do the trick.

Polly had kipped in the Home several times and never had any more trouble. Until tonight. She was just drifting off to sleep when she felt someone sit on her bed. Polly groaned softly. 'Sod off, Myrtle,' she murmured, 'before I give you a right slap.'

A voice said: 'That's a nice way to treat a friend I must say.'

Polly felt like ice water had been sluiced into her veins. Her eyes flew open and she sat upright. 'Nell!' she said. 'Oh, Gawd, no, not you!'

Clear as day, Nellie Donworth sat on the end of Polly's bed. If it weren't for the faint luminous glow that outlined her body, Polly could swear she was alive. But she wasn't. Polly's every sense told her so. Nellie smiled ruefully. 'Rum old do, ain't it?' she said.

'But Nell, how? When?'

A voice from further down called out: 'Shut yer yap! Some of us are trying to sleep.'

Polly knew that no-one else could see or hear Nellie, but her own voice would be clear as a bell. She hadn't yet mastered the art of silent communication although she knew that some psychics were able to do so.

Polly slid out of bed and motioned Nellie to follow her. In

stockinged feet she tip-toed to the door and opened it slowly, wincing at the creak it made. She listened intently. If the night matron found her she could be thrown out and that would never do. Hearing no sound of movement she slipped into the corridor, closing the door behind her. She made her way along the landing and down the stairs. The Manager's office would be empty this time of night and Polly figured that would be the safest place to have a chat with her dead friend. The night matron would, most likely, be tucked up in an armchair in the kitchen and Polly saw no sign of her as she reached the big oak door to the office. She eased it open and slipped inside, closing it behind her. Polly sat herself down in a big leather armchair and let out a sigh.

'Nice 'ere innit?' Nellie said, surveying the bookcases and the large desk with ornate brass handles.

'Oh, Nell!' Polly whispered. 'I'm so sorry. What happened?'

'Remember that toff I was hopin' to hook up wiv?'

'Yes.'

'Picked meself a wrong 'un didn't I. I thought he was all right, him bein' a doctor an' all. I knew him from before, see? He did the business when Mary had that little problem. He was nice at first. Bought me a hot chocolate and everything. Bastard must have put summat in it because I came over right queer after that. He said I needed some fresh air, but it didn't do no good. Gawd, it was terrible. Never known any pain like it. Couldn't stand up. I felt ever so sick, then, all of a sudden it all went away. I felt ever so much better. I was standin' up and everything. Except I wasn't. Bloody queer feelin' it was I can tell you. Standidn' there, lookin' down on meself lyin' on the ground in a dirty alley. I seen him bendin'over me and I thought, that's good. He's a doctor. He'll see me right. I mean, I didn't really know what was 'appenin' but I had a fair idea it weren't good, but I thought, he'll sort me out.

But he didn't. Do you know what 'e did? The dirty sod threw up me skirt and whipped off me drawers! The liberty. Not even a by your leave. Nuffink! There's me, lyin' there, knickerless and 'e's 'avin' a right old time. Bloody cheek! Anyway, after 'e'd done 'e just wandered off and leaves me there. By that time I figured out I was done for. I tried callin' for help but no-one could hear me. I wandered about for a bit, but it's ever so lonely when no-one can see or hear you. Then I remembered you sayin' you had this gift like, so I thought I'd come and visit coz it's just not right bein' poisoned and that, and that's not the worst.'

'It isn't?'

'No, coz now they're sayin' I died from the drink and I never touched the stuff! Me Mum was ever so upset when they said that. She finks she knows who done it, but she's wrong. Someone needs to put them straight and you're the only one I can talk to.'

Polly took a deep breath. All thoughts of sleep abandoned. 'Okay, Nell,' she said. 'Start from the beginning. Tell me everything and don't leave nothing out.'

61

'Just because you're the Inspector's errand boy, don't think that gives you the right to sit on your arse all day doing bugger all! You are still a serving police officer, Colverson and your place is out there on the beat, so, unless the Inspector has anything in particular he wants you to do, that is where you will be, do I make myself clear?'

And that, in a nutshell was the gospel according to Sergeant Thicke. It might have been phrased more delicately, but, in essence, Colverson agreed with him and was quite willing to resume his beat duties, especially as Detective Chief Inspector Abberline had a personal matter to attend to and would not require his services until the following morning.

Colverson decided to take the opportunity to stretch his legs and see if he could elicit any useful information from his numerous contacts on the streets of Whitechapel that may help their more serious investigations. Wasn't it Chief Inspector Abberline himself who always said that no detail is too insignificant to ignore and that information is the lifeblood of any investigation?

'Of course, Sergeant,' Colverson said. 'I'll be on my way then, shall I?'

'You do that Colverson, and be quick about it.'

As Sergeant Thicke grumbled his way back to the day room in search of tea and tranquillity, Colverson stepped out into the massed throngs of humanity that populated Whitechapel with a smile on his lips and a spring in his step despite the chill in the air and the promise of rain.

For the first hour or so, nothing untoward presented itself as needing his attention, nor did any of his enquiries reveal anything useful concerning the recent murders. It was then he heard shouting coming from a side street and deemed it worthy of closer scrutiny.

The shouting emanated from a group of four young boys. Colverson was well aware of them from past escapades. Nothing more than youthful high-jinks, but, if left unchecked could escalate to more severe misdemeanours and he had been doing his best to impart some stern words of wisdom whenever the occasion demanded. On this particular day they were congregating in an alley between two shops. The alley was littered with empty boxes and packing crates. The boys were shouting and whooping as they pelted a pile of broken lumber with stones and anything else that came to hand.

'Here now, you boys, what's going on here?' Colverson demanded.

One young miscreant, by name Daniel Banks, turned a flushed, excited face towards the constable.

'We got him!' he announced.

'Got who? What are you talking about?' Colverson said.

The boys crowded around, all talking at once.

'One at a time, one at a time,' Colverson demanded. 'You. Daniel Banks. You tell me what this is all about.'

'We got 'im,' Daniel repeated. 'That black dog murderer. We got 'im!'

'S'true,' another confirmed. 'We saw 'im go into this alley, so we followed.'

'Chased 'im we did,' Daniel interrupted, not to be usurped in his moment of glory. 'Chased 'im wiv sticks and stones until he hid in that pile of crates. We're gonna kill 'im an' skin 'im an' claim the reward.'

'You'll do no such thing!' Colverson told them. 'And what makes you think there's a reward anyway?'

'There's always a reward. My Nan says if you didn't offer a reward no-one would grass anyone up and the coppers wouldn't solve anyfing.'

Colverson had to silently acknowledge that there was a grain of truth in that statement, but he was not inclined to admit as much to a street urchin with a runny nose and holes in his trousers.

'Nonsense,' he said. 'The police do a fine job. Now, stand back all of you and we'll see what we have here.'

'Watch out he don't bite your hand off,' one of them called out as Colverson moved forward and they all sniggered. Ignoring the misanthropic Greek chorus, Colverson approached the pile of crates steadily but cautiously. To be on the safe side he drew his nightstick and circled the shambolic pile of detritus. Lumber of all sorts was piled against the wall creating many nooks and crannies that may provide a hiding place for an animal of some sort. Colverson crouched and used his night stick to move some of the looser planks aside. At the back of the pile he caught a glimpse of movement. Slowly he prodded his nightstick into the cavity, producing a plaintive whimper from inside. As his eyes became accustomed to the shadows, he caught the reflection of two bright eyes.

'Why,' he said softly, 'it's a dog!'

'Told you,' Daniel called. 'It's 'im, that black dog murderer.'

'Nonsense,' Colverson said. 'He's just a pup. Scared out of his wits no doubt by your antics.'

'So there's no reward?' Daniel wanted to know.

'No, there's no reward, but if you want to earn sixpence, I have a job for you.'

'What sort of job?' Daniel asked cautiously.

'I'll give you some money to go to the butchers and get a

205

shilling's worth of sausage meat. Bring it back here and I'll give you sixpence for yourself. And don't even think about running off with the shilling. I know where you live Daniel Banks and I know your father will give you a good walloping for doing such.'

Grumbling at the slander done to his reputation by Colverson's remark, he accepted the commission nonetheless.

As Colverson waited for the boys to return, he settled himself down and spoke gently and softly to the cowering pup. When the boys returned ten minutes later he took charge of the meat and gave them their fee. Telling them to make themselves scarce, he waited until they were out of sight and began feeding small pieces of meat to the dog. At first, the scared pup ignored his hand-held offerings despite obvious hunger. Colverson then broke off a small piece and tossed it close to where the dog sat, hunched and shivering. After a tentative sniff he gobbled the meat down.

'Good boy,' Colverson whispered and tossed another morsel. By degrees, as Colverson tossed the meat closer to where he sat, the small, black dog inched closer. By the time the meat was half gone the dog was comfortable enough to take it from Colverson's fingers. Slowly and gently, Colverson coaxed the pup closer until he was able to stroke his head as he wolfed down the remainder of the sausage meat.

'There's a good boy,' Colverson whispered. 'Now, what on earth am I going to do with you?'

62

The cramped cell at Cobblestones Prison was far less salubrious that the elegant Mayfair address where Abberline had last encountered Madame Olga. The erstwhile medium, although now fully clothed in a simple dress, was still a strikingly attractive woman. Abberline had been intrigued when the message had reached him that a Miss Fanny Kettle had asked to see him at the prison. It took a second before he remembered that Fanny Kettle was Olga's real name. Her trial had been swift and perfunctory, her sentence had been six months and many thought it lenient at that. The message contained no clue as to the reason for her request but, pending further developments, no other more pressing duties laid claim on his time, and Abberline agreed.

Fanny sat demurely enough, but even her drab surroundings and her downcast eyes could not mask the fire that burned within her. Abberline could sense the turmoil within even as he entered the room. As he took his seat Fanny raised her eyes and locked her gaze on his. In other circumstances it would have been enough to send a shiver down his spine, but here, in the confines of Cobblestones, with a burly guard just outside the door, Abberline felt relatively safe. Fanny wasted no time on pleasantries.

'What's happened to Polly?' she asked, her thick Russian accent replaced by her natural East London dialect.

It crossed Abberline's mind to remind her of her situation and that observing the social niceties may well serve her better than surly demands, but there was something in her voice, her manner, that spoke of a deeper concern.

'Polly?' he said.

'My maid. She has nothing to do with this. If you've harmed her

207

…'

Abberline raised his hand and Fanny fell silent. He spoke calmly and slowly. 'The fact that she was complicit, even essential, in enabling you to carry out your deception by providing the voices of the dead would seem to indicate that she was most definitely involved in your criminal enterprise, wouldn't you say?'

'Maybe,' Fanny admitted. 'But she was only doing what I told her. She thought it was a game. If there's any crime here, it's me who should pay for it, not her, you understand?'

Abberline nodded. 'I do indeed understand, Miss Kettle. What I find difficult to comprehend is why a successful criminal such as yourself should have such tender feelings towards her accomplice. Perhaps, and I speculate here, it is because Polly is more than an accomplice. Might she be a relative of some kind? A daughter possibly?'

Anger flared in Fanny Kettle's eyes. 'Cheeky bleeder!' she said. 'How old do you think I am?'

For a second Abberline was flustered. 'I really have no idea,' he said. 'I have always found it indelicate to speculate on a lady's age.'

'Too right it's indelicate! And for your information, Polly ain't my daughter.'

'A sister then?'

'No. Not really. But I brought her up like she was when her Mum died. Her Mum was a good friend to me and I wasn't about to let Polly end up in no workhouse, so I took her and we ran. I always made sure she had a roof over her head and clothes on her back and food in her belly no matter what it took.'

Abberline nodded. There was more to the story than that, he was sure. A lot more he surmised, but Fanny's sincerity shone through like a beacon whenever she spoke of Polly. 'All right,' he said. 'I believe you.'

'You do?'

'Of course. Is there any reason why I shouldn't?'

Fanny shrugged. 'No. It's just I'm not used to coppers believing anything I say, that's all.'

'Well, there's a first time for everything I suppose.' Abberline smiled. 'And you can put your mind at rest. Polly has not been harmed. Not by us anyway.'

'What's that supposed to mean?'

'We don't know where she is. She disappeared into the night whilst Constable Colverson was attempting, and failing, to protect your modesty.'

Fanny laughed, he face lighting up for the first time since their interview had begun. 'Poor bleeder,' she said. 'He didn't know what hit him.'

'I believe you did. Several times as I recall.'

Fanny laughed again. 'Anyone would think he'd never seen a naked woman before. Colverson did you say his name was?'

'Yes. Although I believe he's known as Walt to his friends.'

'Married, is he?'

'Not to my knowledge. Should I ask him? On your behalf, of course. Maybe he could write to you during your incarceration.'

Fanny scowled. 'You can be right nasty when you put your mind to it, you know that? But I'm not going to be here that long. I've got friends in high places I have.'

'If you mean your former clientele, they may be less inclined to bestow their favours on you now they know that you were fraudulently taking their money.'

'It weren't no fraud!' She paused. 'Never mind. But Polly's all right, yea?'

'We haven't been able to locate her, but we are still looking.

When we do find her she will not face charges. We just want a statement from her, that's all.'

'Good.'

'Is that everything? Is that all you wanted to see me about?'

'Yea. But …'

'But what?'

'Do me a kindness if you will.'

'If I can.'

'When you find her, can you bring her to see me? I need to see her with my own eyes to make sure she's all right. Will you do that for me?'

'I will do my best.'

'Promise?'

'I promise. I'll also do you one more favour if you like.'

'What's that?'

'I'll tell Constable Colverson you were asking after him shall I?'

Fanny smiled. Softly, she said: 'You're a good man Mr Abberline. Has anyone ever told you that?'

Now it was Abberline's turn to smile. 'Not nearly often enough,' he said.

63

Emma Abberline was not a woman to give in to emotion lightly. Practical and forthright with a sharp wit and boundless energy. The one chink in her armour was her inability to have children. It was something that both she and her husband dearly wanted but it was not to be. So it was that when Abberline told her of his meeting with Fanny Kettle and her request that he find Polly and make sure she was safe and well that Emma said:

'Of course you must, Fred. You above all people know how dangerous the streets are, especially for young girls. Think how you would feel if it were your own child out there, all alone with no-one to look after her? Fanny Kettle may not be Polly's natural mother but she is her mother in all other regards and her feelings at this moment must be in tatters. She must be sick with worry and you must promise me that you will do all in your power to set her mind at rest.'

Abberline smiled. Knowing how the subject of children struck straight to Emma's heart it never ceased to amaze him how much selfless compassion she could extend to others without once giving in to self-pity. 'Of course,' he said. 'But even if I find her, what on earth shall I do with her? There are houses for destitute women and such like but I can't force her to attend and even if she did, there's no guarantee that she would stay there. With no means of support, not even an illegal one, she is in a delicate position to say the least.'

'Then she must come here.'

'What?'

'You must find her and bring her home to me. We have the room and the means to keep her safe until Fanny is released from prison and the pair of them can establish some sort of life for themselves.'

'You would do that? Open up our home to a known criminal, regardless of the consequences?'

'She is a child, Fred. Children need nurturing and counselling if they are to thrive in this world. Can you deny that we are ideally placed to offer such counselling?'

Abberline sighed. 'Sometimes,' he said, 'it truly astounds me how much love you carry inside you.'

'Fiddlesticks! I'm just being practical. Now, off you go about your business whilst I set up our spare room for our guest.'

64

It was as Abberline was making his way back to Whitechapel that he had a strange feeling come over him. Choosing to walk in order to process the information on the unusual cases that had become his remit he was overtaken by the impression he was being followed. His "coppers nose" had never led him astray in such matters and he saw no reason to doubt its veracity now. Resisting the temptation to look behind him and thereby alert whoever was dogging his footsteps that they had been detected, he increased his pace. Judging the streets sufficiently crowded he stepped suddenly into an alleyway, flattening himself against the grimy brickwork, watching the flow of London's citizenry go about their business.

A baker transporting a tray of bread; two young women laughing and joking; a telegraph boy hurrying on his mission of delivery; an elderly gentleman with a walking stick and a battered top hat. And then …

Abberline took one pace forward and grabbed the young woman by the arm. She gave a squeal of surprise but Abberline's manoeuvre was so swift he doubted anyone else noticed as he pulled her into the alley and clamped a hand over her mouth to prevent any further outcry. She began to struggle but Abberline's grip on her arm was firm.

'Don't struggle,' he instructed her. 'I'm a police officer and I mean you no harm. I just want to know why you appear to be following me.'

Abberline's captive ceased her struggles. 'Good,' he said. 'I'm going to release you now and I want your word of honour you will not scream or attempt to run. I just want to talk. Do I have your word?'

She nodded against his palm and Abberline released his grip. The young woman took one step away from him, turned sharply and lashed out with her boot, catching Abberline a solid blow on the shin.

'Ow!' Abberline shouted, hopping on one foot as he rubbed his injured leg. 'What was that for? You gave me your word.'

'Not to shout or run away, yea. And I didn't. That was for scaring the bleedin' life out of me!'

Abberline gingerly placed his foot back on the ground. 'Hardly a just recompense,' he grumbled. He looked up at his recent assailant. She stood defiant, hands on hips, mouth a thin line, her eyes blazing. 'I know you, don't I?' he said.

'You might,' she said grudgingly.

'Of course! You're Fanny Kettle's maid. The fake psychic.'

'I ain't no fake!'

'We shall agree to disagree on that point. I've been looking for you.'

'You ain't goin' to arrest me.' It wasn't a question. 'I ain't done nuffin' wrong.'

'Fraud, deception, taking money under false pretences …'

'I told you, I ain't no fake!'

'Be that as it may, I have no intention of arresting you.'

'Then why was you lookin' for me?'

'Miss Kettle asked me to locate you and see that you had come to no harm.'

'You've seen Fanny? Is she all right? Can I see her?'

'That might be possible. Now, the more pertinent question is; why were you following me?'

65

A tea shop.

Polly was on her second slice of cake and third cup of hot chocolate before she spoke.

'What are you?' she said.

Abberline smiled and tugged his ear. 'I thought that had already been established. I'm a Scotland Yard detective.'

Polly shook her head and spoke around a mouthful of plum cake. 'That's your job. It's not what you are.'

Abberline frowned at the rather philosophical turn their conversation seemed to be taking. 'You've lost me, I'm afraid,' he said.

Polly sighed. 'Don't be coy,' she told him. 'I know you're not normal.'

Abberline gave a small laugh. 'I assure you I am the most normal person you are likely to meet.'

Polly shook her head vehemently. 'No, you're not. You're like me. You have a gift.'

'A gift?'

'That's what Fanny calls it. It ain't always much of a gift though. Especially when it first started. Fair gave me the willies it did.'

'Oh! You mean your ability to "talk to the dead." '.

Polly scowled. 'And you can take that sarky tone out of your voice for a start,' she told him. 'You're just as bad, 'cept I'm not pretending to be something I'm not.'

'You seem to have convinced yourself that I'm somehow "special". I assure you I'm not.'

Polly studied him quizzically. 'You really don't know?'

'Apparently not.'

'I knew the first moment we met when you handed me your

215

coat and I touched your hand.'

'The spark?'

'That's right. The spark. That ain't normal is it?'

'It's not common but hardly remarkable.'

'No, not like this. I can tell. I just couldn't make out what you were. You're not like me, I'm sure of that. You figured out all the tricks and effects we used to jolly up the séance quick enough, but that could be because you're a good detective.'

'Thank you,' he said.

'I don't think you can read minds either. I thought it could be because you're an empath.'

'An empath!'

'Yea. It means someone who senses the moods and emotions of other people.'

'I know what it means,' Abberline smiled. 'I'm just surprised you do.'

Polly scowled at him. 'Why?' she snapped. 'Just because I'm a guttersnipe you think I don't have a brain in me head, is that it?'

'Not at all. It's just unusual for someone in your position to have such a wide range of knowledge on such topics.'

'You don't know anything about my position, Mr Scotland Yard detective,' Polly said indignantly. 'But if I know anything at all it's all down to Fanny.'

'Ah, the infamous Madame Olga.'

'Yea, and she ain't infamous 'cause I know what that means an' all.'

'Tell me about her.'

'You really want to know?'

'Yes, I do. Miss Kettle impressed me with her sincerity as far as you were concerned. It piqued my interest.'

Polly regarded him in silence for a few seconds.

'Piqued.' Abberline said. 'It means …'

'I know what it bloomin' well means!'

'Of course you do. So, tell me about Fanny Kettle.'

'Fanny's the best. A real good sort. She took me in when I was just a kid. She told me she would look after me and she has done. We had to keep moving about so I couldn't go to school, so she took me to the British Library every day. Taught me to read, taught me my numbers and we just read and read about all sorts of things. And when I got scared when my powers started to come out we went back and found out all about it and I wasn't scared any more. That's when she had the idea for the séances. She said we could both use our talents to their best advantage to make a good living.'

'By hoodwinking vulnerable rich men into thinking they were communicating with their dearly departed loved ones?'

'It ain't a crime if it's true. And you know it's true.'

It was certainly true enough that Abberline had never been able to fully explain to himself how they had been able to produce Martha's name literally out of the air like that. Frequent sojourns to the British Library could easily explain how they had been able to compile facts about the well-known and recently bereaved individuals that formed their clientele, but they could hardly have been able to produce such a dossier on the fictitious Eric Wise. A simple guess then? A mere fluke that it had struck home? Abberline dismissed the thought from his mind.

'Be that as it may, Polly,' he said, 'that is not what we are here to discuss.'

As Abberline reached out for his cup of hot chocolate, Polly impulsively grabbed his hand.

'But it's important,' she said. 'If you don't believe me, you won't believe I can give you the name you want, the name of the

Lambeth Poisoner, and you won't get Fanny out of prison.'

There was no spark this time as their hands met. Instead, there was a slight tremor and a warm pulse that passed from one to the other and back again. Polly stared at their clasped hands, eyes wide, mouth agape. At their first touch, memories had flooded Abberline's mind. Memories of his encounter with Lord Francis Varney, a man who claimed, with some justification, to be a vampire. Moreover, it brought back memories of the Whitechapel fiend known in the popular press as Jack the Ripper whose true nature had never been revealed to the public and whose final demise had, of necessity, been likewise hidden, leaving the murders officially unsolved. A confrontation with the fiend had left Abberline on the brink of death, his life saved by Varney feeding him some of his, Varney's, own blood which had hastened his return to health and saved his life.

'Gawd!' Polly said. 'You're …you're… a vampire!'

'No!' Abberline almost shouted the word. One or two people close by turned to look and Abberline made calming motions to Polly until they had returned to their tea and cake. 'No,' he said, more quietly. 'I most certainly am not.'

'But there's something there, isn't there? I can tell.'

'Whatever you saw, or thought you saw, it has no bearing on the matter currently under discussion and there is certainly no need to be afraid.'

Polly's face became animated and her expression broadened into a beaming smile.

'Afraid? Why would I be afraid? The dead hold no fear for me and this sort of dead … or should that be un-dead? Doesn't matter. I've wanted to meet one for years. You have to tell me all about it.'

'Yes, yes, maybe one day,' said Abberline, flustered. 'But we have more urgent things to discuss.'

'But this means you'll believe me when I tell you that I can give you the name you want because one of his victims came to me and told me don't it?'

Polly continued to beam and Abberline, cornered into agreement, said: 'I will certainly treat it as a serious piece of potentially vital information.'

'And you'll get Fanny out of Cobblestones?'

'If the information proves correct, I will certainly try.'

'Not good enough. Get Fanny out or I ain't sayin' a word.'

'Getting someone out of prison is no easy task.'

'You'll find a way. You're a Scotland Yard detective. And a vampire. You can use your vampire powers to magic her out. Wot a lark that would be, eh?'

'I do not …' Abberline began and then, more quietly, 'have any vampire magic because I am not a vampire and I'll thank you to keep your voice down.'

'You're part one,' Polly told him. 'And that means you can do things other people can't.'

'In some ways, yes, but I can't just snap my fingers and produce Miss Kettle out of thin air!' Abberline said, exasperated.

'But you'll try?'

Abberline sighed. The sign of a good detective is to know when you are beaten. 'Very well,' he said. 'I shall do my best, but it may take a while.'

'I can wait.'

'But not on the streets. Far too dangerous.'

'I can't afford a bleedin' hotel!'

'I have another suggestion. Somewhere you will be safe and I can keep an eye on you.'

'I ain't gonna let you lock me up!'

'Nor do I intend to. Although you may have a most attentive jailer of sorts, but I think you'll get along famously.'

66

'You're absolutely sure you don't mind?' Abberline asked. Polly sat as patiently as she could manage in the Abberline's parlour as Abberline and Emma discussed her immediate future in their kitchen.

'Mind? Of course I don't mind. I said so. It would be an act of kindness. To put her back on the streets would be the exact opposite and an act of gross cruelty. I shall make up the spare bed. And maybe give her some of my old dresses. They may need altering but I'm sure I can manage. Her current outfit is decidedly dingy. What does she like to eat?'

'Uh, cake mainly, I think.'

Emma sighed. 'Never mind, I'm sure she will tell me. I'm sure we will have a lot of interesting conversations whilst you are at work.'

'Yes,' said Abberline a touch dubiously. 'She is an interesting young lady to be sure, but she does sometimes stray into topics that you might call ...unusual.'

Emma raised an eyebrow. 'Really? More unusual than meeting a real life, if that is the correct term, vampire?'

'Yeees,' Abberline drew out the word, having forgotten for a moment that Emma had been privy to all the facts of the Ripper case that had not been permitted to pass into the public domain. 'On second thoughts I'm sure you will get along famously.'

Emma smiled and clasped his hands. 'Oh, Frederick,' she said, 'having her here, it will be as if we have a child of our own at last. Even though it may only be for a short while.'

Abberline felt the familiar pang of regret that the fates had never blessed them with children and he feared that Emma's joy at this temporary facsimile of family life could easily turn to regret

221

and pain upon Polly's departure. That, he reasoned, was a problem for another day and would be met with fortitude and understanding on both their parts should the need arise.

'You are a most remarkable woman, Emma Abberline,' he said.

'And you a most remarkable man, Frederick Abberline,' she responded and kissed him softly on the lips. 'Now, be off with you,' she said. 'You have important work to do and I must see to our guest.'

67

Sergeant Thicke had the nose of a bloodhound and many would affirm a face to match. Now, that olfactory orifice was twitching in a most annoying manner. He prowled Whitechapel Station on the trail of something. Something that should not be there. Something that was making his nose twitch in a most irritating manner.

Only one thing, one creature, usually brought on this level of irritation. But that was impossible. Wasn't it? On his express instructions such a creature was forbidden in the station precincts. This was his kingdom and no-one would dare disobey his edict in this matter. But now, he sniffed, he was sure there was such a creature within his domain and it was concealed behind the door to cell 3. A cell that should be empty. Sergeant Thicke grasped the handle and pulled the door open. And there it was. Plain as day. Worse. The culprit of this incursion lay sleeping like a babe on the hard wooden bunk.

'COLVERSON!' Thicke roared. Colverson bolted upright, startled out of a deep sleep and the black puppy that had been curled up peacefully alongside him leaped to his feet and began barking furiously.

68

'What are you going to call the little chap?' Abberline asked.

'I thought "Constable"' Colverson replied. The pup pricked up his ears and huffed happily.

'Constable?' said Abberline.

'As he's a police dog. Of sorts. Con for short. It's very good of you to offer to take him in, sir. He's ever so intelligent and easy to train.'

'Think nothing of it. It will help to keep Polly amused I'm sure. I expect she will be chafing at the bit until I can work out how to get Miss Kettle released from Cobblestones and caring for a puppy seems just the thing to keep her occupied.'

'Are you any closer to knowing how you'll do that, sir?'

'I have a plan, but it involves seeking the co-operation of Judge Blackstone.'

Colverson frowned. 'Not the most accommodating of Judges,' he said.

'Quite, but under these circumstances, he is the best, if not the only, choice, to agree to my request without asking too many awkward questions. Are you sure he's in good health? Not got any fleas or anything?'

'They reckon he's got gout and he's terribly overweight, and there's that awful wheezing cough …'

'Not Judge Blackstone. Con. Mrs Abberline is most particular about not having any fleas in the house.'

'Oh, he's in tip-top shape, sir. I had him checked out by Mr Carmody.'

'Carmody?'

'A veterinarian. He consulted on that case a while back when a cabby reported his horse had gone missing.'

'Of course. Sounds a very knowledgeable chap.'

'Top of his profession, sir.'

'Hmmm. That gives me an idea, but it'll have to wait until after we've introduced Con here to his new, temporary accommodation.'

69

Love at first sight is a wonderful thing to behold and so it was with Polly and Con. As soon as the pup lolloped across the Abberline threshold on his big puppy paws, Polly descended upon him with a squeal of delight and much hugging, kissing and licking ensued.

'Don't let him lick your face!' Emma advised. 'It's most unsavoury considering where a dog's tongue has been.'

''S'alright,' Polly said. 'I dare say I've had worse than a bit of dog spit in my time,' and returned to rubbing Con's tummy as he lay on his back with his paws in the air.

Abberline smiled encouragingly. 'They seem to be getting along famously,' he said.

Emma humphed. 'And who's going to walk him to make sure he doesn't mess in the house?' she asked.

'Oh, I'll see to that,' Colverson volunteered. 'I'll collect him each morning and take him on the beat with me. He'll get plenty of exercise, and by the time he's back here he'll be so tuckered out he'll sleep right through until morning. You'll hardly notice he's here. And I'll make sure you have a fresh supply of sausages for his supper so it won't cost you a penny, I promise.'

'Well, I suppose it will be all right for a short while. And Polly does seem to be rather taken with him. Do you have a name for him? We can hardly keep calling him "the dog".'

'I was telling the Chief Inspector earlier. His full name is Trainee Police Dog Constable. But he answers to Con for short.'

'Con?' said Emma. 'Well, I suppose it's easy to remember. Con,' she repeated.

As though aware that he was the subject of discussion, Con righted himself onto all four paws and trotted over to Emma where he sat at her feet looking up at her with large, soulful eyes.

'I think he likes you, my dear,' said Abberline.

'I think he simply heard me call his name,' Emma said. 'Dogs respond to verbal signals. It means nothing.' She gazed down at the puppy. 'He does have rather nice eyes though, doesn't he?'

Abberline grinned, detecting a distinct thaw in his wife's demeanour. 'I'm sure he'd let you stroke him if you wished,' he said.

'Oh, I don't think …'

'Go on,' Polly said. 'He's got really soft ears.'

'Has he? Well, maybe …' said Emma tentatively. She bent down and stroked one large ear.

'Oh my word, they are soft aren't they?'

Without taking his eyes from her face, Con leant his head into Emma's palm. Emma let out a small, surprised giggle. 'He does seem a friendly little chap,' she admitted. Con shamelessly butted his head into Emma's hand, his tongue flicked out and licked her wrist. Despite her previous warning about dog's tongues the action elicited another giggle. 'Do you like that?' she said, scratching him under the chin. 'Shall we see if we can find you somewhere nice to sleep?'

'I thought maybe the scullery,' Abberline said.

'Nonsense,' said Emma. 'That's far too cold. He's only young and needs to be kept warm.'

'He can sleep with me,' Polly volunteered.

'Possibly,' said Emma. 'But not on the bed. I'll find some blankets and we can make up a bed for him on the floor. Would you like that, Con? Would that be nice?'

Con gave a doggy smile and a happy wuff, casting a quick glance back at the two police officers and, Abberline would later swear, giving them a crafty wink.

'Well,' said Abberline, 'as things seem to be going so well, we

227

must be off about our business.'

'Hmmm?' said Emma, distractedly. 'Where are you going?'

'We're going to see a man about a dog,' Abberline told her.

70

'You want this man to do what?' Dr Pettifer said, incredulously.

'Mr Carmody here is a veterinarian,' Abberline told him,' and I want you to let him examine the corpses of Druitt, Maybrick and Ostrog.'

'What on earth for?' Pettifer spluttered. 'Do you think this horse doctor can do a better job than myself?'

Carmody, a rotund, red-faced individual, snorted at the derogatory use of the phrase "horse doctor" although, in truth, he had overseen the care of many an equine in his long career. Abberline's opinion about the relative merits of the two medical practitioners he kept to himself.

'I merely wish to ascertain an independent review of the facts from a different viewpoint. Your areas of expertise are linked but different and it may throw a new light on the case.'

Pettifer shook his head. 'I've never heard anything so outrageous. I'll have words with the Commissioner about this, you see if I don't.'

'Do give him my regards,' Abberline said. 'Now, if you would be so kind as to direct us to the individuals in question.'

'They're over there.' Pettifer indicated three forms lying on trolleys covered by sheets. 'But don't expect me to stay here and watch this farce.'

'I'm sure we can manage by ourselves,' Abberline told him.

With an expressive 'Bah!' Pettifer grabbed his hat from the rack and stomped off up the stairs.

'My apologies, Mr Carmody,' Abberline said. 'Dr Pettifer is …'

'A horse's arse?' Carmody volunteered.

'I bow to your expert knowledge in that regard,' Abberline smiled. 'Now, if you would be so kind.'

An hour later, Carmody had finished his examination.

'What do you think?' Abberline asked.

Carmody scratched his head. 'Most intriguing,' he said. 'Both men were obviously killed by some sort of animal. From the bite marks and the claw marks, I'd say it was the same animal, certainly of the same family, but I can't say it's a family I'm familiar with. I'm tempted to say it could be a lion or a leopard, but the injuries are all wrong for that to be the case. In my opinion, and it is only an opinion, mind, I would say they were both killed by some sort of dog, but one larger and fiercer than any I've ever seen. Although it does bring to mind a case I read about a while ago.'

'What case was that, Mr Carmody?'

'A colleague of mine up north was called in to advise on a death that was first attributed to a wolf attack.'

'A wolf? In England? Do we still have a wolf population?'

'Not for many years which was why they wanted my colleague's opinion. He ruled out a wolf attack but concluded it was certainly a dog of some sort. Only happened the once, mind, but if you think it might help I can send you his notes. He was so intrigued by it he sent me all the information to ask my opinion.'

'That would be most helpful, Mr Carmody. And if you could also send me your findings on what you have found today I would be most obliged.'

'Of course, of course. And if you do find out the cause of these deaths, I would be most intrigued to know. There may even be an article here somewhere for the veterinary journal!'

As Carmody cleared away his instruments and the three men said their goodbyes, none of them noticed the skulking figure of Dr Pettifer lurking on the stairs as he turned away and stealthily made his way up to street level.

The next day's headline read:

SCOTLAND YARD DETECTIVE TURNS DOG CATCHER

71

What, Colverson wondered, was the collective noun for a group of Police Constables? An idle of Constables? A workshy of Constables? An ineptitude of Constables?

All these and more would apply to PC's Harrison, Mulcahy and Skinner. Colverson passed them lurking in the corridor on his way to his cubicle. Their animated chatter ceased as he approached, but as he passed, one of them said: 'Woof, woof!' and the others burst into appreciative laughter at his wit and incisiveness.

Colverson paused in his perambulation. Slowly, he turned.

'Which one of you said that?' he asked.

Their faces, still wreathed in schoolboy humour, froze momentarily, the inane expressions slowly collapsing like deflated balloons to looks of chastened chagrin.

'Just a joke, Colverson,' Harrison said.

'A joke? What's so funny about it, Harrison? Come on, tell me.'

'We don't have to tell you nuffink,' said Mulcahy sulkily.

'Yea,' Skinner chipped in. 'You ain't our boss.'

'Am I not,' said Colverson calmly and took one step forward. The three would-be humourists shuffled uneasily, but made no move to disperse although they could easily have done so.

'We may be the same rank,' Colverson continued, 'but I am nothing like you lot of layabouts. Now, what's so funny?'

More shuffling of feet and downcast glances. 'Everybody's saying it,' said Harrison.

'Saying what?'

'You know. Inspector Dog Catcher.'

'Oh, you mean that slanderous piece in the Gazette. I'm impressed, Harrison. I didn't know you could read.'

Mulcahy and Skinner sniggered, but Harrison's face creased into a scowl and colour suffused his cheeks.

'You got no cause to talk to me like that. Just 'cause the Inspector's gone barmy ...'

Colverson moved, but no-one could rightly say afterwards exactly how his nightstick had miraculously appeared in his hand or how he had managed so swiftly to use it to pin Harrison across the throat, up against the wall, replacing any other remarks he may have been planning to make about Chief Inspector Abberline's state of mind with a garbled 'Urkk!'

Harrison's two companions made ineffectual movements that, in those of a more decisive disposition, may have led to their coming to Harrison's aid.

Colverson spared them a momentary glance. 'Stay where you are!' he barked and all movement ceased. He turned his attention back to Harrison.

'Making slanderous remarks about a senior officer could have you up on charges, Harrison, do you know that?' Colverson said.

Harrison contemplated nodding but the pressure of stout English oak across his throat made that course of action unwise. Seeing his predicament, Colverson eased the pressure. Just a bit.

'I didn't tell the Gazette,' Harrison croaked.

'No, but you're more than happy to repeat their lies aren't you? But since you know so much about it, who did tip them off, eh? I'd like a word with them.'

Harrison struggled with his conscience and it was Skinner who came to his rescue.

'It was Pettifer,' he said.

'Dr Pettifer?' Colverson asked.

'That's right,' said Mulcahy. 'He was boasting about it in the pub. He thinks the Inspector is too full of himself and he was going to take him down a peg or two. Makes a nice bit of coin as well,

233

giving tit-bits to the paper about the more gruesome details, he does.'

Colverson paused for a second or two and then released the hapless Harrison.

'Get about your business,' he said. 'If anyone wants me, I'll be in the Morgue.'

When Dr Pettifer returned from a long and largely liquid lunch, he was surprised to find a Police Constable riffling through his paperwork.

'What the devil?' he said.

The constable turned and recognition dawned.

'Oh, it's you,' Pettifer said. 'Abberline's little lapdog,' he sniggered.

Colverson smiled, affability oozing out of every pore. 'That's right. Me,' he said.

'What the deuce are you doing here? You have no right to be going through my papers like this.'

'Chief Inspector's orders, sir. He was rather alarmed that confidential police information had found its way into the pages of the Gazette. He's asked me to do a thorough audit of any medical details that may have been published whilst cases were still actively being investigated. If someone is leaking information, that would be a very serious matter, so the Chief Inspector wants to write a detailed report for the Commissioner.'

Pettifer's eyes widened. 'The Commissioner?'

'Yes, sir. Can't be too careful. He's tasked me with compiling and cross-checking the information. All rather tedious, but necessary, don't you think?'

'I, uh, that is …' mumbled Pettifer.

Colverson picked up a sheaf of papers.

'I'll take these to start with, if you don't mind, sir,' he said. 'And if I find anything ...' He stepped forward so that the two men were almost nose to nose. 'I'll be back,' he said softly.

Pettifer stood motionless as he listened to Colverson's footsteps retreating. Just before the Morgue door closed, he could have sworn he heard a dog bark.

'Colverson!' Abberline beckoned him into his office.

'Yes, sir?'

'I've just had a rather strange conversation with Dr Pettifer.'

'Really, sir?'

'Yes, really. He took great pains to assure me that if I needed any work done relating to any cases, any cases at all, that I was working on, that he would give it his utmost and immediate attention, all in the strictest confidence, of course.'

'That was nice of him, sir.'

'It was, wasn't it. I also saw young Harrison earlier. He seems to have a rather nasty sore throat. I do hope it's not catching.'

'I don't think so, sir. Just something peculiar to Harrison I believe.'

'Good. That's all, Colverson.'

'Thank you, sir.'

As Colverson reached the door, Abberline said: 'Oh, and Colverson.'

'Yes, sir?'

'I value loyalty above all things, Colverson, but don't do it again, there's a good chap.'

'No, sir. Thank you, sir.'

Colverson exited, both men concealing a satisfied smile.

72

The scream jolted Abberline from a deep sleep. As his now conscious mind tried to sift dream from reality he saw Emma leap from their bed and grab her dressing gown from its usual resting place behind the door. He heard the sound of a match being struck and the candle on their bedside table flared into life. Later, Abberline mused that it must have been the mothering instinct that galvanized his wife into action before he could manage even a befuddled 'What...?'

'It's Polly,' Emma told him as she rushed from the room.

'Emma! Wait!' Abberline called, but it was too late to arrest his wife's headlong flight. Abberline scrambled from his bed and grabbed his own dressing gown, following Emma's footsteps to the spare bedroom where Polly had been billeted. Upon his arrival on the scene, Abberline saw Emma holding Polly whose demeanor now seemed more angry than distressed.

'Gave me the fright of my bleedin' life!' she said.

'What did?' Abberline asked.

'Him.'

'Him?'

'That's what I said. Him. Dirty little bleeder. Didn't have a stitch on. Cuddled up right next to me in bed, bold as brass. Not so much as a by your leave. Bloody liberty.'

'You're not making sense, Polly. It was a dream, surely. Alarming but nothing to worry about.'

'Oh, yea? Dream was it? Well, you take a look over there, behind the bed, then tell me I'm dreaming.'

Leaving Emma to console Polly as much as she was able, Abberline moved around the end of the bed and looked into the far corner of the room. He paused, his mouth agape. 'Good Lord!'

he said. There, huddled in the corner was a young boy, not more than five years old, stark naked, his knees drawn up to his chest, his face buried in the circle of his arms, his thin shoulders heaving with muffled sobs.

'Told ya,' Polly crowed. 'Who's dreaming now, eh?'

Emma moved to look over Abberline's shoulder. 'Why, he's just a child,' she said.

'But how did he get here?' Abberline wondered. 'And where are his clothes?'

'And what's he done with Con?' Polly chipped in. 'If he's hurt Con …'

'Hush, both of you,' Emma instructed. 'You're frightening him.'

'Huh!' Polly huffed. 'Serves him right, dirty little devil.'

'Stay back, both of you,' Emma instructed. 'I'll deal with this.'

With a small shrug of deference, Abberline moved back to the doorway, beckoning Polly to do likewise.

Emma knelt down and studied their nocturnal visitor. His skin was pale as milk, his hair, which fell over his forehead, jet black. He seemed to have no obvious injuries and she surmised that his shivering was as much from fear as the cold. 'Hello,' she said, softly. 'My name's Emma. It's all right. You just gave us a bit of a fright, that's all. Can you tell me your name?'

Slowly, the boy raised his head. His eyes were large and dark chestnut in colour. In the flickering glow of the candle light she could see slim slivers of colour in each iris. A bright orange crescent bracketing his pitch black pupils. His gaze was so disconcertingly sad it made Emma gasp. She saw the boy flinch away at her reaction and she smiled in reassurance, but something about his eyes stirred a memory deep inside her mind but it eluded her for the moment like a shadow fleeing the sun.

'That's better,' she whispered. 'You're not hurt are you?' The

237

boy said nothing. No nod or shake of the head to indicate his response.

'No?' Emma continued. 'Are you hungry? Or thirsty?' Still no response from the boy. 'How about a blanket? You must be cold.' Emma reached out her hand to gently touch his arm and the boy shot forward before any contact could be made. Emma sat back with a sharp gasp as the boy threw himself flat on his stomach and squirmed under the bed.

'Emma?' Abberline called. 'Are you all right?'

'Yes, yes, I'm fine. I must have scared him. He's hiding under the bed now.'

'Well, he can't stay there forever,' Abberline said as he and Polly both dropped to their knees to peer into the shadows under the bed.

'Can you see him?' Polly asked.

'No, I … wait, yes, over there. Something's moving …aaah!' Abberline gave a startled cry as a dark shape cannonballed out from under the bed, knocking him aside in its haste.

'Con!' Polly cried, delightedly. 'So that's where you were hiding!'

The puppy jumped eagerly into Polly's arms, licking her face as she ruffled his ears.

'Now where has that blasted boy got to?' Abberline grumbled.

'He must be here somewhere,' Emma said.

'I can't see any sign of him,' Abberline said. 'Give me a hand to shift the bed will you?'

Emma and Abberline took hold of one side of the bedstead each and lifted the bed up and to one side. Beneath, it was empty save for a few dust balls that caused Emma some embarrassment as a meticulously houseproud individual but no-one else seemed to notice. Con continued to gambol around their feet as they searched the bare boards for any nook and cranny that may have concealed a small child. Emma knelt down as if proximity may reveal some hitherto invisible hiding place. 'I just don't understand it,' she said. 'He can't have disappeared into thin air'

Con pounced playfully on her lap as she knelt on the floor, attempting to lick her face. Emma laughed and held the pup at arm's length. 'No, Con,' she told him. 'You're not helping.'

And then she stopped. Holding the pup as still as she was able, she stared into his eyes. Eyes that were dark chestnut in colour with a bright crescent of orange that bracketed his pupils. She let out a small gasp. 'Dear Lord,' she said. 'That's where I saw them before!'

'What are you talking about?' Abberline asked.

'His eyes. They're exactly the same as the boy's.'

'But that's ...'

The pup suddenly became very still, staring into Emma's face with a sorrowful look. 'I think,' said Emma slowly, 'I think that this puppy and the boy are one and the same!'

Events moved rather quickly after that. Having established that the boy was nowhere to be found they decamped downstairs to the kitchen where they sat around the table as Emma dispensed the English panacea for all trauma, hot, sweet tea. Con, still looking slightly abashed stayed close to Polly, still resolutely all dog. They sipped their tea in silence until Abberline spoke up.

'Are we seriously suggesting ...' he began.

'We've all witnessed events that defy logical explanation,' Emma said.

'It's no different from vampires or talking to the spirits when you think about it,' Polly said.

'Yes, but an actual, physical change from a dog to a boy? How is that possible?' Abberline wanted to know.

'Tell us what happened, Polly,' Emma said. 'Right from the start.'

Polly cleared her throat. 'Well,' she said, 'I was spark out. Con was right next to me …'

'On the bed?' Emma said. Her affection for the puppy obviously did not extend to his presence on the furniture, especially not the bed when she had provided a perfectly good blanket for him to sleep on, on the floor.

'Yea,' said Polly defensively. 'He was scared and it was nice to have a bit of company.'

'Perfectly understandable,'Abberline said, avoiding his wife's caustic glance. 'Go on,' he said.

'Well, like I say, I was fast asleep and then I felt something move next to me. I thought it was Con, so I reached out to stroke him in case he was having bad dreams. But I ended up stroking "him". When I realized what I was touching, that's when I screamed. Dirty little bleeder jumped out of bed quick as you like then.' She looked own into the pup's sad eyes. 'Sorry, Con,' she said. 'I didn't know it was you, did I? Otherwise I wouldn't have screamed.'

'Is that all?' Abberline asked.

'All? Ain't that enough?' Polly said.

'But how?' Abberline said. 'I grant you there seems to be no other logical explanation, but even so.'

'There is one more thing,' Polly said.

'Go on.'

'There's something not right about him,' Polly said.

'That much is obvious,' Abberline said.

'All right Mr know-it-all, you explain it then.'

Emma reached out and touched Abberline's hand. 'Let's just stay calm, shall we?' she said. 'It's all rather confusing and I know your policeman's instincts are ruffled by the seemingly inexplicable, but let's hear what Polly has to say, shall we?'

Abberline sighed. Lack of sleep and the turbulent events of the night were making him grumpy. He hated a mystery that defied logic and recent events had catapulted him into the realms of the illogical which upset his equilibrium. 'Yes,' he said. 'You are quite right my dear. I apologise, Polly. Do continue.'

Polly huffed and settled herself, one hand still stroking Con's head. 'Well, when I touched him, the boy I mean, I felt something like when I touched your hand, that sort of something.'

'The spark?'

'Yea, the spark. But not quite the same. I was still half asleep and then scared out of my wits, so I've only just remembered, but I got a sense of something. Something like I get when the spirits are trying to make contact.'

'You think someone from the afterlife was trying to make contact with you through the boy?'

'Yea. And don't look at me like that Mr Part-Vampire, I know my powers are real and so do you or I wouldn't be here would I?'

'All right. I concede that it may be possible, but who, or what was it that was trying to communicate with you and why?'

'Dunno. But I know how to find out.'

'A séance!?' Emma was appalled. 'Here? In our house?'

'It's safe as houses, I promise,' Polly said. 'I've done it hundreds of times.'

'And you agree with this plan, Frederick?'

'It's a trifle unorthodox, I agree, but under the circumstances I don't see any other option. I think we have to at least try Polly's suggestion. If nothing comes of it, we shall be no worse off and will have to think again.'

'Very well,' Emma conceded. 'Polly, what do we need to do?'

'Nothing much,' Polly said. 'We just sit around the table like we are now and hold hands.'

'That's all?'

'That's all. After that, it's all up to me and the spirits.'

73

The room was in darkness save for one flickering candle in the middle of the dining table casting wavering shafts of light on the proceedings and cloaking all concerned in un-natural shades of lambent shadows. The puppy sat next to Polly, leaning against her leg and looking up at her with fearful yet trusting eyes. Polly, Emma and Abberline joined hands.

Abberline had witnessed the mechanics of a séance before, albeit the contrived theatricals of "Madame Olga" so it came as no surprise to him what transpired next. Emma had no such pre-conceptions and he saw the pinched, apprehensive cast to her features and the harsh shallowness of her breath. He squeezed her hand tightly and she turned her gaze towards him. 'It's all right,' he whispered. 'I'm here. I trust Polly. Nothing bad is going to happen I assure you.'

Emma nodded and gave him a tight smile before turning her attention back to Polly and the pup.

Polly closed her eyes and took a series of deep breaths, then she began to speak in a low, clear voice.

'Spirits of the afterlife, I call upon you,' Polly said. 'There is one here who seeks an audience with one of your number. One who is close to this boy … dog … whatever he may be. One who cares about him and wishes to communicate so that we may help him. I implore you to let that one spirit come through so that they may speak to us.'

The silence itself seemed to reverberate, making the very air dense and cloying. Polly opened her mouth and Abberline anticipated another plea to those denizens of the other world, beseeching their co-operation. Instead, a thin trail of mist emerged from Polly's mouth and the air turned chill. Emma gave a small gasp of surprise and Abberline squeezed her hand reassuringly. The mist grew in both volume and substance until it appeared almost solid enough to touch. Abberline resisted that temptation although it taxed his policeman's instinct to the limit not to investigate such a seemingly unique phenomenon to the fullest.

As the spectral fog increased in volume it began to shift and swirl as though stirred by a breeze that could neither be felt or heard by those present. From languid to agitated, the mist combined and coalesced until a definite shape began to appear. After what seemed like an eternity but was, in reality, a matter of seconds, a fully formed figure stood before them. A woman, tall and slim in stature, her hair a raven black, her features fine boned and delicate. But her eyes. Her eyes were her most riveting feature. Large they were and a dark chestnut brown in colour save for tiny slivers of bright orange that bracketed her pupils like crescent moons. Exactly the same eyes as the pup possessed. The vision opened her mouth and began to speak.

'My name is Marta,' she said. 'And I thank you for taking care of my son.' The spectre in their midst reached down and touched the pup on the head. With a soft whine, he began to shake and grow, his very form changing before their eyes. Paws became arms and legs, fur disappeared to be replaced by pale skin and within seconds the boy stood before them once more. Emma let out a small gasp and wrapped her shawl about his shoulders to keep him warm. This time he did not flinch at her touch, his gaze riveted on the ephemeral vision whose name was Marta. 'What is it you wish of me?' the vision said.

'You are this boy's mother?' Polly asked.

'Yes,' she said, an ineffable sadness in her voice. 'How I have longed to see him once more. Having failed him in life I seek to make amends in death.'

'Can you tell us your story?' Polly asked. 'We seek only to understand so that we may help him. Tell us what he is that he can do the things he does.'

Marta seemed to consider this for a while before speaking again.

'I sense a good heart within you,' she said. 'Listen then as I tell you my story. My time here is short and the story a sad one but it must be told for the sake of my child.' She paused and took a deep breath, if such a thing were possible, and began to speak once more.

'We are Fenris. A warrior clan descended from the Great Wolf of legend. The clan chiefs believe it is their destiny to one day bring about the demise of humanity so that pure bred wolf clans can take their place as rightful rulers of this world. To that end, our bloodline must be kept pure. Mating is only allowed between pure Fenris to ensure our progeny carries the Fenris blood from generation to generation. I was a brood bitch, used by the clan for breeding purposes and proud to be so. I produced many litters of pure Fenris who would grow to become proud warriors. It was then I made a fatal error. I met a man. A human. I fell in love. I knew it was wrong, but we lay together and I found myself with child. His child. My condition was in no way unusual and I hoped, I prayed, that my own Fenris blood would dominate and my child would pass as pure Fenris. It was not to be. He was born small and sickly, a puny specimen that the tribe christened Runt because of his size. But I loved him dearly and hoped that the Fenris blood that flowed through his veins would still dominate. Time, however, was against us. The clan chieftans knew he was not pure Fenris and demanded to know who his father was so that they could exact vengeance on the one who had defiled their heritage. I refused to tell them and we were both placed under sentence of death. In desperation I managed to escape with my son hoping to seek out his father and begin a new life. In that hope I was cruelly disappointed. When I found him he was married with children of his own and disowned me. And so we fled again, eking out what living we could, forever fearful that the clan would one day seek us out. I swore that I would ensure my beloved Runt would be safe no matter what, but in that too, I failed. I caught a fever and knew that my time had come. Before I succumbed I taught Runt the skill to turn from human to wolf although, as a mongrel, his wolf form is small and dog-like but may grow as he does. I also told him of the old legends about packs of Fenris/Human half-breeds who live peacefully amongst humanity without bringing danger upon themselves. With my dying breath I bade him to seek out such a pack for only then will he be safe.'

She reached out a spectral hand and laid it upon the boy's head.

'My darling, Runt. I am so sorry I failed you. Know that I love you more than anything in this world.'

The boy gave a small whimper and tears began to trace runnels down his cheeks.

Marta smiled.

'Such a beautiful boy,' she said wistfully. 'Farewell my son, farewell.'

With that, her form began to fade until nothing remained but the faintest wisp of ectoplasm.

The room remained silent until the boy spoke in a small, halting voice.

'Will you be my pack?' he said.

Abberline and Emma spoke in hushed voices as Polly took the boy into the kitchen to give him some bread and dripping.

'That was all most extraordinary,' Emma said.

'I agree, but it does provide answers of a sort to some perplexing matters. We can't ignore the evidence of our own eyes and that in itself lends weight to certain theories.'

'You're not suggesting that innocent puppy is this Black Dog killer everyone is talking about?'

'No, of course not. But if he is but one of an entire tribe, might a full grown adult be capable of such atrocities?'

'I suppose so. But even if that's true, what's to become of the boy?'

'I have no idea. For now, I suggest we keep him with us until this matter is solved. After that, well, normally a child in his position would be handed over to the authorites .'

'And what would they do with him?'

'An orphanage maybe. Or the workhouse.'

A bright spark of anger flashed in Emma's eyes. 'You will not place this child in one of those awful places, Frederick. I forbid it!'

'Then we shall have to consider other options. No workhouse, I promise.'

Emma considered for a moment.' Very well, but I don't want this child involved in anything even remotely dangerous. Is that understood?'

Abberline nodded ascent as Polly entered the room.

'How is he?' Emma asked.

'He's had some nosh and now he seems tuckered out. Nearly fell asleep at the table.'

'I am not surprised. Poor little thing.'

'You can put him in my bed if you want. I ain't going to be getting any sleep for a while, that's for sure.'

'Thank you, Polly, I shall do just that.'

As Emma hurried off towards the kitchen, Polly whispered in Abberline's ear: 'She's a bit of a firebrand, your missus, ain't she?'

'Were you listening at the door?' Abberline asked.

'Just curious,' Polly said. 'But she is though, aint she?'

Abberline smiled. 'She is rather magnificent, isn't she?' he said.

74

The next day when a much sleep deprived Abberline entered Whitechapel station he immediately summoned PC Colverson into his office and shut the door as he told him the news about his dog.

As the young constable was much given to stoicism and had, furthermore, been privy to all the details of the Jack the Ripper case, he accepted the news with a modicum of disappointment and a complete lack of skepticism.

'It's a shame,' he said. 'I was really getting quite attached to the little chap.'

'As were we all, Colverson, but I'm sure he'll be putting in an appearance quite often. In fact, as I understand it, he prefers to remain in canine form most of the time. As he matures that will change and he will master the art of changing to and fro at will whilst remaining human for the majority of his life.'

'And what's going to happen to him in the meantime, sir?'

'Well, as he is strictly your dog after all, you having been the one who found him and rescued him, I took the liberty of speaking on your behalf by saying that I doubted if you would have the desire or the means to raise a human child. Was I correct in that assumption?'

'Most definitely, sir,' said a relieved Colverson.

'My wife, on the other hand,' Abberline continued, 'rather relishes the opportunity and we decided that it would be best if he stayed with us for the foreseeable future.'

'Adopt him you mean?'

'In a manner of speaking.'

'That sounds an excellent idea, sir.'

'I'm glad you think so, Colverson. It does also give us a possible insight into our current investigation.'

'You mean the Black Dog Killer may be afflicted with the same condition as Con?'

'Precisely. It would certainly explain the black cab and the mysterious woman in black who seems to exert some form of control over the beast. Oh, and we changed his name to something more human, as it were. When in his canine form he will still be referred to as Con, but when human he is now Connor.'

'Connor Abberline! A fine name, sir.'

'Connor Abberline? Yes, I suppose he is. I hadn't thought.'

'And a boy couldn't wish for a better father, if I may say so, sir.'

'A father? I suppose I am. Things were so hectic last night I don't think I quite took that aspect in fully. It's a responsibility I shall certainly try my utmost to live up to. As long as his "Uncle Walt" is on hand to share the burden as required?'

'Me? Why, of course.'

'Then that's settled. Now, back to business. This revelation gives us another line of enquiry, one which I hope you will be able to pursue in tandem with finding the link between the known victims and searching for any other related cases that may have been overlooked.'

Colverson blew out his cheeks. 'I'll do my best, sir, but it's a tall order.'

'Quite, but I think I may be able to offer you some assistance on that front.'

'Really, sir? It's not PC Carmichael is it? Only, that office is rather small and stuffy and Carmichael has something of a hygiene issue.'

'Fear not, Colverson. The person I have in mind is of a much more fragrant persuasion. I hope to have secured their services by the end of the day, but first, I have an appointment with a judge.'

75

'Well, well, Abberline, I knew it was only a matter of time.'

Judge Augustus Blackstone, possibly the most corrupt judge to sit the bench in living memory, smacked his lips in pure delight and sipped from a tumbler full of finest brandy. His corpulent frame fairly trembled with delight at the prospect of righteousness brought low. Over the years, Detective Chief Inspector Abberline had been a paragon of virtue regarding crime and criminality that had pierced Blackstone to his flabby soul on numerous occasions, but now, now that upstanding champion of law and order was seeking a favour. Oh, how the taste of that titillated Blackstone's tongue.

'You want to assign a Ticket of Leave to this psychic trollop and put her in your care, is that correct?'

Abberline arranged his features into as blank a mask as his emotions would allow. Dealing with a creature such as Blackstone was anathema to him, but, given the nature of the request, a more upstanding member of the judiciary may have required more evidence before acceding to his request. There being no cause to grant Fanny Kettle a reprieve, a Ticket of Leave was the next best thing. Certain prisoners who posed no threat to society could be released from prison into the custody of a reliable individual who would make sure they did not re-offend for the remainder of their sentence. Once that time had expired they were free to live their life as they saw fit but any misdemeanour before then would see them back "over the cobbles" for their full term of imprisonment with additional charges on top. It was the only way Abberline could affect Fanny's release and, in return, Polly had promised to divulge the name of the Lambeth Poisoner. It was a risk, true, based on Polly's assertion that this information came from the spirit of one of the Poisoner's victims, but Abberline was becoming accustomed to making such judgement calls and felt it worth the risk.

'Yes,' he replied calmly. 'I believe Miss Kettle is truly repentant and, in addition, has the responsibility for a young girl who relies on her as she would her own mother. Miss Kettle is unable to exercise her maternal duties whilst incarcerated in Cobblestones Prison and would benefit from an early release under my guidance.'

Blackstone made an obscene chuckling sound. 'Of course, of course,' he said. 'And the fact that this Kettle doxie is a fine piece of female horseflesh and likes nothing more than to parade around in the all-together doesn't influence your thinking on this matter at all, eh?'

'Absolutely not,' Abberline replied, deadpan.

Blackstone fairly roared with laughter, dabbing tears of merriment from his eyes with a large, grubby, handkerchief.

'By God, Abberline, you're a cool one and no mistake. They say it's the quiet ones you have to watch. And you with a nice little wife at home and all. What's the plan, eh? Set this Kettle whore up in a nice set of rooms somewhere discrete and pay regular visits to see that she's behaving herself, eh, eh?'

Abberline cleared his throat. 'Actually, Miss Kettle will be staying with my wife and myself for the time being. The young girl for whom she has responsibility is already lodging with us, so ...'

Blackstone cut him off with another guffaw of laughter. 'Dear God in Heaven! Three women under one roof and all of them beholden to you in one way or another and you free to take your pick of which one, or maybe more than one? All three if it takes your fancy! I take my hat off to you, Abberline. I never thought you had it in you.'

253

Blackstone continued to chuckle and mutter admiring obscenities as he took up a pen and scribbled the necessary details on the Ticket of Leave docket. He signed with a flourish and slid the paper across the desk.

'Here,' he said. 'Take this to Cobblestones and the woman is yours to do with as you wish.'

'Thank you, your honour,' Abberline said. He picked up the paper and made to leave, closing the door behind him, cutting off Blackstone's raucous laughter. He stood for a moment in the corridor, taking deep, calming breaths. His skin fairly crawled with distaste at Blackstone's insinuations. 'It's not wise to judge others by your own low standards,' he murmured and inside he swore that one day he would see that corpulent, corrupt member of the judiciary brought low. On that day, he was certain, there would be no-one willing to stand up for him or to procure for him his own Ticket of Leave and that would be true justice. For now, he had what he needed to potentially put a most sadistic murderer within his grasp and that was sufficient.

76

By the time Abberline had secured a meeting with Judge Blackstone and another with Cobblestone's Prison Governor, a certain Konrad Dipple, and arranged for Fanny Kettle to be released into his custody, the day was almost gone.

It was mid-afternoon as Abberline led Fanny to a waiting hansom and they began their journey to freedom.

'And Polly really is all right?' Fanny asked.

'Right as rain,' Abberline said. 'Safe, secure and well cared for by my wife.'

'Your wife?'

'Yes. There seemed to be no other means of guaranteeing her safety. Oh, and she also has a puppy to keep her amused. He belongs to PC Colverson really, but he lodges with us when Colverson is unable to house him. There's a rather long story attached to that which I'm sure Polly will tell you all about. Suffice to say it was his arrival that was pivotal in persuading me that her abilities were genuine.'

'So, you are now a believer, Inspector?'

'I am keeping an open mind on the subject. A very open mind.'

Fanny smiled. 'Whatever the reason, I'm very grateful to you. As soon as I'm back together with Polly, we'll get out of your way. I have some friends who can put us up I expect until we can find a place of our own.'

'Out of the question, I'm afraid,' Abberline said. 'There are certain police matters that need resolving first and besides, you are now my responsibility and I need to know where you are at all times to ensure you will not stray from the straight and narrow. That said, it's been decided by myself and my wife, that you and Polly will reside with us for the foreseeable future. It may be a trifle cramped. You will have to share a bed with Polly and probably the puppy, but it will not be too uncomfortable and my wife is an excellent cook.'

'So I'm to swap one prison for another, is that it?'

Abberline smiled. 'A much more lenient regime and much more comfortable surroundings. I even managed to retrieve some of your clothing and other personal items from the Mayfair House so you should be much more comfortable, and this will only be on a temporary basis I assure you.'

'Yes, I'm sorry. You have been very kind to both myself and Polly and I thank you.'

'You are most welcome, Miss Kettle. If what Polly has to tell me proves accurate, that will be recompense enough.'

Their arrival at the Abberline house was greeted with much excited demonstrations of affection from Polly and Fanny and much excited barking from Con who seemed much more comfortable in dog form than in his human guise. Abberline and Emma watched with the beaming smiles of substitute parents until Abberline could attract their attention.

'Miss Kettle,' he said, 'allow me to introduce my wife, Emma. Emma, this is Miss Fanny Kettle.'

Emma stepped forward and took Fanny's hand in hers. 'So pleased to meet you,' she said. 'My husband has told me so much about you. Come, let me show you to your room. I have a feeling that Frederick and Polly have a very important issue to discuss and I think we should leave them to it, don't you?'

With Fanny's acquiescence, Emma led her upstairs, leaving Abberline and Polly alone.

'So,' he said. 'I believe my part of the transaction is now complete. Which means, I think, that you have something to tell me.'

Polly nodded. 'You came through, all right, so it's only fair. The man you want is called Dr Thomas Cream. He's the one who poisoned Nellie. He's the Lambeth Poisoner.'

Once the new arrival had been settled, Abberline put on his overcoat and announced his intention to return to the station for an hour or two.

'Commissioner Warren is intent on keeping me occupied and out of mischief,' he said. 'He has requested that I carry out a full review of the beat constable's rota and present him with a detailed report on how to improve efficiency. Nonsense, of course, but the sooner I get it done, the sooner I can verify Polly's information.'

He kissed Emma upon the cheek and departed. Some ten minutes later, Emma was sitting in the parlour, reading a most interesting article on how to bake the perfect apple pie when there came a knock upon the parlour door.

'Miss Kettle!' Emma said, looking up. 'Do come in. You don't have to knock.'

'I didn't want to disturb you.'

'You're not disturbing me at all. Please, do have a seat. Can I get you something? Tea, perhaps? Or a slice of cake? Do you have sufficient blankets?'

'Nothing, thank you. Your generosity is most plentiful and we are both grateful for it. I just wanted to have a quiet word with you, if I may.'

'By all means.'

Fanny settled herself in an armchair and began to speak. 'I realize that mine and Polly's presence here must be putting you to considerable trouble,' she said. 'I just wanted to thank you.'

'Think nothing of it. With Frederick working such long hours it's nice to have the company.'

'That's very kind, but I'm sure we're not the sort of company a lady like yourself is used to or would want under normal circumstances.'

'Stuff and nonsense! Frederick has told me all about the pair of you and, although your escapades are a mite more colourful than the company I usually keep, he is convinced, as am I, that you are decent and kind people.'

'That's very good of you.'

'Besides, I must admit to being rather intrigued by your past profession. Can I ask you something?'

'Of course.'

'Is it true that you carried out your séances without wearing any clothing whatsoever?'

Fanny laughed. 'Not a stitch!' she said. 'Naked as the day I was born.'

'Heavens! Wasn't that a bit ... chilly?'

'Sometimes. But it was a most effective way of focusing the gentlemen's attention on me rather than on anything else that may have been going on.'

'I'm sure it was, but wasn't it embarrassing?'

'At first, maybe, but you get used to it.'

'I doubt that I could get used to such a thing.'

'You never know until you try. You'd be good at it, I reckon. An attractive lady like yourself.'

'Heavens, I really wouldn't have the nerve.'

'It doesn't have to be in a room full of strangers.'

'Then who?'

'Your husband. I've always found that the undraped female form is a very effective weapon in the armoury of feminine wiles.'

'You think so?'

'I know so. The next time you want a new dress or his agreement on some matter that you think he may be adverse to you'll find it a most useful diversion to prevent him giving it too much thought and securing his agreement in the process.'

Emma smiled. 'That is a most interesting thought, Miss Kettle, most interesting indeed.'

'Please, call me Fanny.'

'And you must call me Emma.'

Having reached that accord, the conversation turned to more mundane matters.

77

Colverson was surrounded by boxes of old Police Gazettes, crime reports and witness statements. The former broom cupboard that had been commandeered for his sole purpose was cramped and stuffy, but he ploughed on regardless, separating the various documents into strategic piles that overflowed the desk and littered the floor.

Abberline opened the door cautiously lest he disturb the constable's train of thought, or, even worse, overbalance a particular pile of information whose significance may never be retrieved.

Muted mutterings came from behind a pile of boxes and Abberline gave a discrete cough by way of introduction. Colverson's head popped up from behind the mountain of paper like a tortoise peering out from his shell.

'Oh, hello, sir,' he said. 'I didn't see you there.'

'Not really surprising,' Abberline said, indicating the detritus of police ephemera that enclosed the constable's activities. 'How goes it?' he asked.

Colverson sighed. 'Slowly,' he admitted. 'There's just so much … paper. It's like looking for a needle in a haystack, but I'll find what we need, sir, you have my word on that.'

'I don't doubt it for a minute, Colverson, but things may progress a tad more swiftly if you had a little more assistance, is that not correct?'

'A bit of help would be appreciated, sir, as long as it's not Constable Bellweather. I'm not even sure he can read.'

Abberline did his best to suppress a smile. 'Have no fear, Colverson. Bellweather is engaged on other duties more suited to his personality and attributes. I believe Sergeant Thicke has him mopping out the cells after a drunken visit from Dingus Magee who spent the night after being found comatose in the gutter outside the Lamb and Trumpet. No, the person I have in mind has much more intellectual acumen.'

Abberline opened the door wider to reveal Fanny Kettle standing in the corridor. 'Miss Kettle has been released into my custody and has agreed to assist you in your search for any connection between the three victims and their similar deaths.'

Colverson could only stand and stare, his eyes wide, his jaw slack with amazement.

Fanny moved forward, smiling beguilingly. 'What's the matter constable?' she said. 'Don't you recognise me with my clothes on?'

78

For Sir Charles Warren to visit a lowly station house was something akin to a Royal visitation. Even Sergeant Thicke drew himself into some semblance of attention as the Commissioner barrelled through the door and marched straight towards Abberline's office.

'Reid!' Sir Charles shouted. 'Follow me at once,'

Inspector Reid scurried in his wake. As Abberline's office door slammed shut, Sergeant Thicke, and everyone else in attendance, visibly deflated like a pricked balloon. Raised voices could be heard. One voice anyway. 'There's trouble and no mistake,' Sergeant Thicke prophesied. For once, his instincts were correct.

Abberline rose from his chair as Sir Charles stormed in. Reid stood, hesitant and bemused. Sir Charles neither asked for nor was offered a seat. Instead he paced, his hands clasped behind his back, his head lowered like a be-whiskered vulture circling its prey.

'Do you know what they're calling you, Abberline?' he bellowed.

Abberline opened his mouth to answer, but Sir Charles gave him no opportunity to confirm or deny his knowledge of station house gossip. 'Dog catcher!' Sir Charles roared. 'Chief Inspector dog catcher, that's what they're calling you,' he said.

'And who might "they" be, Sir?' Abberline asked.

Sir Charles waved a hand to encompass the entire world. 'Everyone!' he said. 'Your colleagues, your subordinates and, inevitably, that damned newspaper that seems intent on dragging the good name of Scotland Yard through the mud.'

'With all due respect Commissioner, Mr Stead's sensationalism is hardly ...'

Sir Charles cut him off with a snarl. 'And you know the worst thing, Inspector? I'll tell you shall I?' Seeing no way of actually preventing the Commissioner from doing precisely that, Abberline remained silent. 'You're not even a good dog catcher!'

'The investigation is on-going, Commissioner. PC Colverson is currently ...'

'Three murders!' Sir Charles roared. 'Three murders of prominent gentlemen. A barrister, a mine owner and a well-respected mill owner, all ripped to shreds by some maniac with a knife and your only suspect seems to be a dog!'

As Sir Charles paused for breath, cognizant perhaps that if he did not his head would likely explode, Abberline saw his chance and began to speak.

'If I may, Commissioner,' he said. 'Although two of the victims were indeed a barrister and a mill owner, the second victim, Mr Ostrog, was not a mine owner. In fact, he was suspected of being nothing more than a confidence trickster who had adopted many aliases and professions to further his chosen career.'

Sir Charles, panting now in an effort to regain control of his breathing and his blood pressure, growled: 'He was well known in society circles and had been visiting Lady Constance Barlow shortly before his death in his capacity as her business advisor,' he said.

'Dispensing false hopes and honeyed words do not a business advisor make, Sir Charles.'

'Are you contradicting me, Abberline!'

'Not at all, sir. I am merely pointing out that there is no obvious connection between the three victims. If we can establish that, we will be one very important step closer to catching the culprit.'

'And yet you still maintain that these three men were mauled to death by a dog?'

Abberline took a deep breath that had aspirations to be an exasperated sigh. 'The wounds inflicted on all three victims are not typical of any bladed instrument. A noted veterinarian has examined all three and concluded that the scratches and bite marks most closely resemble those of a large dog.'

'Druitt was drowned, man. Washed up on the shores of the Thames and yet you still claim he was murdered by this phantom hound?'

'We have an eye witness who saw Druitt chased by a large black dog and his body evidenced claw and bite marks similar to those of the other two victims.'

'And your eye witness is a drunken vagrant who has trouble discerning which day of the week it is let alone anything else!'

'We also have the testimony of Mrs Maybrick who swears that her husband was mauled to death before her very eyes by a large, black, dog.'

'A befuddled housewife who also confessed to poisoning her husband!' Sir Charles threw up his hands in despair. 'This won't do, Abberline, this really won't do.'

'Perhaps with a few more resources, progress would be more rapid, Commissioner.'

'Oh, there will be more resources, Abberline, but you won't be in charge of them.' Sir Charles spun around, searching the room until he alighted on Reid, silent and almost forgotten, standing by the door. 'From now on,' Sir Charles said, 'I want you to hand over all your cases to Inspector Reid.'

'Commissioner, I really must protest ...'

'Protest all you like, Abberline. It's that or immediate dismissal. If you're lucky, Reid may assign you some filing duties until I make up my mind what to do with you. Good day gentlemen.'

With that, Sir Charles Warren swept out of Abberline's office, slamming the door behind him. Abberline and Reid stared at each other for several long seconds. It was Reid who finally broke the silence. 'Bugger,' he said.

Abberline nodded. 'Yes, Edmund,' he said. 'Bugger indeed.'

79

The hubbub in Whitechapel Station following the Commissioner's visit had gradually subsided. Reid sat across the desk from Abberline looking pale. Abberline placed his hand on a pile of folders sitting quietly on his desk.

'This is everything we have on the most urgent cases,' Abberline said. 'Two primary lines of enquiry would seem to be most urgent. The Black Dog murders and The Lambeth Poisoner ...'

Reid held up his hand in a plea for silence. 'Chief Inspector,' he began, 'I would like you to know that I had no idea about the Commissioner's intentions. I had no idea he even intended to visit.'

'Do not trouble yourself, Edmund. The Commissioner and I have a different philosophy when it comes to solving crime.'

'Following the evidence wherever it may lead whatever the consequences?'

Abberline smiled. 'Exactly.'

'And you are convinced that these cases in particular pose a significant threat to the public and should, therefore, be given top priority?'

'I am. In the case of the Lambeth Poisoner, the instances of death by poison in a relatively small area, the sort of victim and the manner of disposal of the bodies is too similar to be accidental. There is a single hand at work here and he shows no sign of stopping unless we can apprehend him before he kills again.'

'And the Black Dog murders?'

'Improbable as it sounds, the wounds inflicted on the victims point to their assailant being a large canine. Whether at the behest of his trainer, using the dog as a weapon or a random series of attacks by a rabid stray, for example, is not yet clear, but there is some evidence to suggest the former.'

'The eye witnesses?'

'Precisely. A carriage was seen on both occasions. A woman seemed to exert some control over the beast but motive is not clear, which is why I think it vital to establish what links the three victims.'

Reid nodded. 'A most noble aim, I'm sure, but all this …' he spread his hands wide in a hopeless gesture, 'on top of a full caseload of more mundane robberies, burglaries, murders. I don't know how I am expected to cope. The Commissioner doesn't seem to understand that our resources are stretched to the limit.'

'I sympathise, Edmund, but I am sure you will devise some method of prioritising your cases. In the meantime, if I can be of any assistance as regards filing, feel free to call on me.'

An expectant silence prevailed for some seconds and then Reid looked up. 'One idea does occur to me,' he said.

'Yes?'

'Well, the Commissioner did give me leeway to employ you as I saw fit and suggested that filing may be the most productive use of your time, did he not?'

'Yes.'

'But he didn't actually say that filing was the only task I was instructed to give you, did he?'

'No, I don't believe he did, if I recall correctly.'

Reid began to warm to his theme. 'Then I would not be overstepping my authority if I were to suggest other, more productive, means of occupying your time?'

'Not exactly, no.'

'Splendid! Then in my judgement, your skills would be best

267

employed in an investigative capacity to shoulder the burden of several specific cases that have hitherto not been deemed serious enough to warrant the time of the detective division or the rank and file. To wit …' and he indicated the pile of files on Abberline's desk. 'Of course, the Commissioner need never know of this arrangement as long as such investigations can be kept relatively discrete?'

'Discretion is my watchword, Edmund.' Abberline smiled. 'And if I may say, Inspector, I predict that you have a long and successful career ahead of you.'

Reid beamed. 'In that case I will leave you to your work, Chief Inspector.'

80

Police Constable William Walter John Colverson. A man who, he liked to think, had the moral fibre to make a fine, upstanding police office. Stern but polite in the execution of his duty and able to deal with any member of the public, be they victim, perpetrator, or simply a concerned citizen, in the manner appropriate to their situation. Women, however, had always been a bit of a mystery. Even more so when, in the course of his duty, he had been required to wrestle a naked, and most attractive, member of that species to the ground and restrain her with handcuffs. He had executed his duty in the most efficient manner possible, taking care to cause as little harm as possible to the lady in question, even though she fought like a hellcat, and to preserve such modesty as possible by the judicious use of his cape even though she seemed quite unperturbed by the amount of bare skin that was on display. Beyond that, he was prepared to consign the whole business to a wry anecdote that he might impart to those generations of constables who came after him by way of warning them of the many unexpected encounters they may experience as they progressed through the ranks.

And yet, now, here he was in a rather cramped space with that self-same unclothed female, although now, thankfully, she was fully dressed, with the instruction that they work together to solve a puzzle that gave every sign of being un-solvable.

Every time Colverson glanced in her direction, visions of their first encounter rose, unbidden, in his mind. She was damnably attractive after all and the mere sight of her caused a red flush to rise from the collar of his uniform to infuse his cheeks. Not only that, but every time he stole a surreptitious glance, she seemed to look up, giving him a, frankly, flirtatious smile with her soft, full, lips and even, white, teeth, which only served to make his discomfort even worse.

All that, he believed, he had the moral fibre to cope with, but her modus operandi differed markedly from his own, making any co-ordinated progress almost impossible. Colverson favoured the steady, methodical approach, studying the facts, noting anything of possible interest and cross-referencing one with another until a coherent pattern of association was established. Only then would he deem his findings to have sufficient foundation to present to his superior officer. His enforced partner in analytical analysis favoured a more scattershot approach. She gave scant attention to each document. Pausing only if some salient word or phrase presented itself and tossing it aside in a most haphazard fashion if she deemed it unworthy of further attention. And the mutterings! Grunts and sighs, even the occasional peal of laughter. All in all it was most distracting and disconcerting.

'PC Colverson!' There was an exasperated edge to her voice. He looked up. 'Yes?' he said.

'I … oh, hang it, I can't keep calling you "PC Colverson". What's your real name?'

As their relationship was one of official police business, Colverson was inclined to remind her of that fact and to insist that the use of his rank and surname was the correct form of address under the circumstances. He knew that Chief Inspector Abberline was a stickler for propriety and had, himself, instructed those inclined to be less formal to adhere to this protocol. Colverson opened his mouth to impart such instruction but instead found himself saying: 'William Walter John Colverson.'

She smiled and Colverson felt the colour rise to his cheeks once more.

'That's a mouthful!' she said. 'What do your friends call you?'

Once again, Colverson steadied himself to re-inforce the fact that this was an official liaison and over familiarity was to be discouraged. What he actually said was: 'Walt.'

'Walt! Then that's what I shall call you. And you must call me Fanny.'

'I'm not sure that would appropriate.'

'As it's my name, I don't see how it can be inappropriate.' She gave him that smile again. 'After all, once a gentleman has seen a lady without her drawers, a certain degree of familiarity is acceptable, don't you think?'

Colverson's thoughts at that moment were best kept to himself and he contented himself with blushing an even deeper shade of red which seemed to please his tormentor no end as she gave a delightful giggle which did not help his condition one iota.

'Was there something you wanted?' he asked.

'I want a lot of things, Walt, but right now I'd settle for divine inspiration, because I don't see how else we're going to make any sense out of all this … mess!' She waved a hand to indicate the piles of papers that littered the desk and floor of their allotted space.

'These are all the reports, the Police Gazette and sundry statements going back five years,' Colverson explained.

'I know what they are,' Fanny shot back. 'I just don't see how we're expected to find anything of interest.'

'It's called research, Miss Kettle.'

'Fanny.'

'All right, Fanny. It's always like this at the start. We cast a wide net and sift out any related information, however slight it may seem. In this case, anything including dogs.'

'Yes, but we've got everything from someone being bitten by a Pekinese …'

271

'Lady Catherine Devonshire. What a to-do that was.'

'… to a sheepdog accused of worrying someone else's sheep!'

'Near caused a riot down at the stock yards that did.'

'And the fact that you can remember things like that is deeply worrying, Walt. You need to get out more.'

'We don't exactly have a lot to go on Miss Kett … I mean, Fanny.'

'Maybe not, but go through it again would you? Remind me.'

Colverson sighed and picked up a file containing a summary of the salient facts thus far.

'The first victim that came to our attention was Michael Ostrog, a con-man who was killed in the parlour of Lady Constance Barlow, apparently by a black hound according to a rather distressed Lady Constance. Inspector Reid carried out the initial investigation, but could really make no sense of Lady Constance's statement and assumed the attacker had to be human. This was supported by the Coroner who has always given little credence to the Black Dog theory. The second victim to come to our attention but the first to die chronologically it seems, was Montague Druitt, a solicitor. A witness saw him being chased by a black dog along the embankment. He jumped into the Thames to escape and drowned, but not before being savaged in several places by his canine assailant which is how we know his murder is connected to the other two. It was some time before his body was washed up which delayed our initial investigation. The third victim to come to our attention was James Maybrick, a mill owner. Chased across the park by a black hound as witnessed by his wife before being savaged to death on his own doorstep. None of these men have any connection that we can find so we're trying to establish a link with any previous dog attacks that might give us a clue.'

'And is that all we've got?'

'We have a witness in the Druitt case who gave us some background information.'

'Let's hear it then.'

'It's all in the report that the Inspector gave you.'

'I know, but I like to hear you speak it out loud. You've got a nice voice.'

Colverson muttered something under his breath and held up the file on the pretence of studying its contents in the hope of hiding another blush that infused his cheeks. His subterfuge did not prevent him from hearing Fanny's amused giggle.

'Druitt was apparently a disturbed sort of person. Some trauma in his past led him to have dark desires which he took out on the girls who worked at the Minnow's Walk brothel. A violent sort, apparently, but in his private life, a quiet, reserved individual even if prone to bouts of melancholy.'

'This trauma he's supposed to have suffered. What was that all about?'

'The witness didn't know. When Druitt was in one of his black moods he didn't make much sense apparently. The only phrase he kept repeating was about Paladins.'

'Paladins?'

'Some sort of order of knights it seems.'

'I know what a paladin is, but why does it seem so familiar?'

'Means nothing to me. Some sort of gentleman's club it seems. Called themselves the New Reformed Paladins apparently.'

'Ah-ha!' Fanny snapped her fingers and shot to her feet, dislodging a pile of papers in the process.

'Careful!' Colverson said. 'It took me ages to put those in order.'

'I knew there was something familiar about that name, I just couldn't recall what.'

'I couldn't find a trace of it anywhere.'

'That's because you've not been looking in the right place. Come on, Walt, we're going out.'

'Out? Where?'

Fanny grinned. 'A dirty book shop, that's where. But don't worry. I'll look after you.'

81

'For gawd's sake gal, look as though you're enjoying it, do. Imagine it's one of them sticks of rock you get at the seaside.'

Rosie Barkham, on her knees and as naked as the day she was born, looked at the item in question, enveloped by her plump fist, and tried to imagine it with Blackpool stamped through the middle. Imagination failed her. 'Looks more like a whelk,' she decided. 'Smells like it an' all.'

Leo Taxil cackled obscenely. Charlie Semple, whose anatomical deficiencies were the object of Rosie's unflattering comparison, gave an affronted sniff. 'I ain't never 'ad any complaints,' he said.

'You do surprise me,' Rosie told him. 'Still, a tuppenny whore ain't fussy. As long as she's got a full purse, she don't care what else don't get filled.'

'And you'd know all about tuppenny whores, you would,' Semple told her.

''Ere, you sayin' I'm cheap?' Rosie wanted to know.

Taxil clapped his hands. 'Children, children, a bit of perfeshonal decorum if you please. We need three more shots yet or the learned gent wot's paying for 'em will be right narked, and if he gets narked, I get narked, savvy?'

A voice from behind Taxil said: 'Need a hand keeping the staff in order, Leo?'

Taxil swung round, a smile supplanting the annoyed grimace on his craggy features.

'Well, as I live and breathe, if it ain't Fanny Kettle! How's tricks, ducks?'

Before Fanny could answer, Charlie Semple protested: 'Never mind that. This is supposed to be a private session, not a peep show for anyone who walks in off the street.' Having delivered his

275

opinion on the matter, he cupped his privates with an air of affronted dignity. Rosie, on the other hand, displayed no such modesty or objection to the new arrival's presence.

'Don't mind him, darlin',' she said, smiling in what she assumed was a coquettish fashion at an embarrassed PC Colverson. 'He's just narked because he's not up to the job.'

'I heard that,' Semple shouted.

'You were meant to!' Rosie shouted back. Rising to her feet, she launched a much more brazen smile towards the flummoxed Colverson, tossing her hair back over her shoulder lest his view of her body be inadvertently obstructed. 'Maybe you'd like to take his place?' she said. 'I'll warrant I'd look like I was enjoying it then,' she said to Taxil.

'Behave,' he told Rosie. 'In the meantime, see if you can raise the dead back there or none of us is going to get paid.' As Rosie retreated, Taxil said: 'How you been keeping, Fanny?'

'Can't complain.'

'Really? Only, last I heard you had a spot of bother with the law and ended up over the cobbles.'

'Old news, Leo. I'm out now and free as a bird.'

'How'd you manage that then?'

'Let's just say I've got a guardian angel.'

Taxil nodded towards the speechless Colverson. 'Is that him? Your guardian angel?'

Fanny grinned. 'Walt, meet Leo Taxil. The strumpet's called Rosie and the shrinking violet over there is Charlie Semple.'

Colverson nodded politely. 'Madam. Mr Taxil. Mr Semple.'

'He's ever so polite ain't he?' Rosie said. 'Tall as well,' she added. 'I like that in a man. Tall and polite.'

Bored with the proceedings, or the lack of them and grateful for any interruption, she came and attached herself to the befuddled constable, linking her arm in his and touching the shiny buttons on his tunic.

'That's a nice policeman's uniform,' Rosie said. 'Does it come off?' she wanted to know.

'Why does every street nymph keep asking me that?' Colverson wondered, crimson faced as he cast around desperately for some appropriate rejoinder. Fanny saved him the trouble.

'Hands off,' she said. 'He's spoken for.'

'I am?' Colverson squeaked.

'Yes, you are. Unless you'd like to ...' Fanny gestured at Rosie and the camera.

'No, no,' Colverson confirmed frantically. 'I'm spoken for. Well and truly spoken for.'

'That's a shame,' said Rosie. 'Sure I can't change your mind?'

'Rosie,' Taxil intervened. 'Leave the poor sod alone and go and wait over there.'

'Spoilsport,' Rosie said. 'I was just having a bit of fun,' she pouted as she moved to sit on a broken down couch, casting the occasional glance in Colverson's direction.

'So,' said Taxil. 'What can I do for you, Fanny? If you're looking for work I can fit you in. Your stuff is still very popular.'

'Your stuff?' blurted Colverson. 'Do you mean to say, you used to do this sort of thing?'

'No, I did not!' said Fanny haughtily. 'Not this stuff anyway. Individual poses of an undraped and artistic nature for the discerning art connoisseur.'

Seeing Colverson's shocked expression, she added. 'A girl's got to live, and you had more than an eyeful when you slapped the handcuffs on me.'

Colverson stared at her, open mouthed. 'That was police business!' he said.

'Ay-ay! Sounds like funny business to me,' said Taxil, grinning from ear to ear.

'Never mind that,' said Fanny. 'That's not why we're here.'

'So why are you here, Fanny? Only I've got to get these shots finished while Charlie's still up to it, if you get my meaning.'

Ignoring his crude allusion, Fanny continued. 'When I used to pose for those art photos I used to get bored whilst you fiddled with your tripod and I'd go down to the bookshop downstairs.'

'I remember. You scared the life out of that vicar who was browsing the nature periodicals. He thought one of the naked nymphs had come to life right in front of his eyes!'

'I was wearing a sheet, but be that as it may, I remember reading one of your pamphlets. Some sort of penny dreadful about Paladins?'

'Oh, yea. The New Reformed Paladins and the Beast Woman of the Forest.'

'A snappy title, don't you think, Walt?'

Colverson's thoughts at that moment were too confused to form a coherent reply so he said nothing.

'Very popular that,' said Taxil. 'I've still got a few downstairs if you want one.'

'Maybe later. If I remember right, you said on the cover that it was based on a true story told to you by someone who had witnessed the whole thing.'

'That's right. I did add a bit of colour to it, but the basic story was supposed to be true.'

'Who told you about it?'

'Why do you want to know?'

'It could help the police solve a murder. Three murders in fact. If it's true that is.'

'Oh, it's true all right, but a good journalist never reveals his sources. Unless there's money involved.'

'You greedy bugger. How much?'

Colverson laid a hand on Fanny's arm. 'Hang on,' he said. 'Scotland Yard does not pay for information.'

'No?' said Taxil.

'No,' Colverson confirmed.

'Then you're out of luck then, ain'tcha?'

'We do, however,' Colverson continued, 'investigate cases of indecency and the use of young women for improper purposes against their will.'

Taxil snorted. 'Young? Her? And she gets paid for her services.'

'You ain't paid me yet,' Rosie called out. 'And you ain't paid me for the last job neither, you old skinflint' she added.

'Seems like this is a prima-face case for investigation to me. Of course, that would mean closing the premises whilst uniformed officers conducted a most thorough search. It might inconvenience some of your clientele whilst the premises is off-limits, possibly for several days, but I'm sure they'd understand, being dedicated art lovers, that is.'

'Several days!' Taxil blurted. 'You can't do that!'

'Oh, but I can,' Colverson's nightstick magically appeared in his hand. 'And whilst we conduct such a thorough search, we can't guarantee there won't be some accidental damage. A lot of this equipment seems quite fragile to me.' To emphasise the point, he smacked his stick into the palm of his hand with a resounding "thwack!"

Taxil sighed like a deflated balloon. 'All right,' he said. 'You keep low company, Fanny, you know that?'

'Maybe, but he's a tiger when he's roused ain't he?' and she winked at Colverson who blushed accordingly.

'Now,' she said. 'Who told you about the Paladins?'

'Me dad, Ambrose. He was a butler to some toff who had a bunch of roaring boys up to his country house. Swears blind they were attacked by some kind of monster.'

'Did he tell you their names?'

'Might have done. I made 'em up when I wrote the story.'

'And your dad? Is he still around?'

'Yea. He lives with me now.'

'Can we speak to him?'

'You can try. He's not all there these days, but he has his moments.'

'Where can we find him?'

'Downstairs. We live behind the shop. Can I get back to work now?'

'Of course. We wouldn't want to get in the way of your art.'

As they made for the stairs, Colverson paused and had a whispered conversation with Taxil. The photographer didn't seem too pleased with what Colverson said, but grudgingly nodded in agreement.

It was as they were making their way downstairs that Fanny made a "humph" sound.

'Something wrong?' Colverson asked.

'You tell me, Walt,' she said.

'I don't know what you mean.'

'I thought it was only the sight of me in the altogether that got you all hot and bothered. Seems I was wrong.'

'Hot and bothered? You mean that young woman? No, it was just a surprise, that's all. She means nothing to me. Nothing at all.'

'Oh! So, it is just me that gets you hot and bothered. That's nice to know.'

In the dark of the stairwell, Colverson could not see Fanny's mischievous smile.

'And what was that you and Taxil were talking about all chummy?' she asked.

'Oh, that was nothing,' Colverson said.

'It must have been something. Come on, Walt, we're partners aren't we? Partners don't keep secrets from each other.'

'If you must know …'

'I must.'

'I told him I wanted him to parcel up any photos and any photographic plates he may have of you and to deliver them to Whitechapel Station for my attention only by tomorrow. Or else.'

Fanny paused. 'My photos? You want them all to yourself do you, so you can look at them whenever you want? I thought better of you, Walt Colverson.'

'No! It's not like that. I don't want to look at them! I just don't want anyone else to look at them either. I just couldn't stand the thought of any debauched lout leering over you like that. It's not right. You deserve to be treated better than that, Fanny.'

For once, Fanny Kettle was speechless. Impulsively, she leaned forward and gave him a peck on the cheek.

'What was that for?' Colverson asked.

'Just because,' she said and wiped her hand across her eyes.

'Are you crying?'

'No. It's just the dust in here. Come on, we've got a suspect to interview.'

'He's not a suspect. He's a potential witness.'

'Whatever he is, he's an old man and if we don't get a move on he may well be dead before he can tell us anything.'

This time it was Colverson's turn to grin in the shadows.

They found Ambrose Taxil sitting in the back parlour of the bookshop. The old man was huddled in an armchair in front of a roaring fire, a blanket over his knees and another around his shoulders. A tankard of ale sat at his feet and his chin rested on his chest. He was snoring loudly.

'Blimey, it's stifling in here,' Colverson said.

'Old bones,' Fanny replied. 'They feel the cold. At least his son thinks enough of him to keep the fire going. More than he does for his models. It's fair parky up there when you're wearing nothing but a bit of lace and a feather in your hair. The draught gets everywhere. You should have seen the size of my goosebumps.'

'All right, all right,' said Colverson. 'Enough now. You've made your point.'

'And what point would that be?'

'You think I'm a prude. An unsophisticated bumpkin. I just think women should be treated with respect, that's all.'

'You know your trouble, Walt Colverson?'

'What?'

'You're a gentleman.'

'I'm a simple copper, that's all.'

'Not so simple. And when I say a gentleman, I mean you're a gentle man. That night we first met ...'

'At Madame Olga's?'

'That's right. You had me at a disadvantage you might say. Most men would have had a good old gander and their hands would have been everywhere, but not you. Even when you put the cuffs on me you asked if they were too tight and then you covered me with your cape. You've a good heart, Walt Colverson. Any girl would be glad to have you.'

'I've not found one yet.'

'Maybe you've not been looking in the right place.'

Their words petered out and they simply stared at each other for a few seconds. Colverson opened his mouth to speak when a voice interrupted them.

'If you two have finished whispering sweet nothings to each other, perhaps you'd tell me what the hell you're doing in my parlour!'

'Police business, Mr Taxil,' Colverson said, then, in a softer voice to Fanny: 'Are you blushing?'

'It's the heat in here.'

They moved forward to stand before the huddled figure of Ambrose Taxil.

'Hello, Mr Taxil. My name's Fanny. You probably don't remember me. I used to pose for Leo.'

Ambrose ran his rheumy eyes up and down her body as though trying to imprint the image on his mind. 'Might do,' he said. 'So many of them parade through here, it's hard to keep track.'

'This is my friend, PC Colverson. We'd like to ask you a few questions. Can we sit down?'

'Please yourself, though I don't know anything the police might be interested in.'

As they pulled up two upright wooden chairs, Colverson realised that, as the official representative of law and order, he should be the one asking the questions, but Fanny had slipped so naturally into the role he reasoned that she would probably have a better chance of eliciting information from the old man than he would and he let the lapse in protocol slide without comment. Play to your strengths, he thought, and Fanny Kettle was, without doubt, a strong woman.

'We'd like to ask you about a penny dreadful that Leo wrote,' she said once they had settled themselves.

Ambrose snorted. 'He writes hundreds of them type of things. Rubbish the lot of them.'

'He said you gave him the idea for this particular one.'

'Did I? No, he's having you on. I don't have nothing to do with that sort of thing. It's a blessing his mother didn't live to see the sort of filth he peddles.'

'This was a special sort of story,' Fanny pressed on. 'He said it was a story you told him from when you were a butler to a rich sort. Something about the Paladins?'

Ambrose took a rattling intake of breath and fixed his eyes firmly on Fanny. 'I should never have told him that,' he whispered. 'I've tried my best to forget it all these years but I still get nightmares.'

'We don't want to upset you Mr Taxil, but it could be really important. Please can you tell us what happened?'

'What happened? I'll tell you what happened.' Flecks of spittle flew from his lips and his emaciated frame shook with emotion as the floodgates of memory opened.

'They went mad, that's what happened. Rich young tearaways, that's what they were. They thought they owned the world. What they did to that poor serving girl don't bear thinking about.' A twisted smile insinuated itself across his countenance. 'But she got her own back, on one of 'em at least. Bit right through his John Thomas, that's what she did! Ripped it right off and spat it out. That's when it really got bad.'

'What happened, Mr Taxil?' Can you tell us?'

Ambrose paused and wiped a hand across his mouth. 'She ran for her life. Through the woods. Stark naked she was. They were all too shocked to start with, but then it sunk in. He was dead, you see, the one she bit. Blood everywhere and that got their dander up. They took up guns, swords, anything they could find and went after her. I followed on, tried to stop them, but it was no good. They chased her through the woods until they got to a gypsy camp. She was one of them, you see. A gypsy. This was her family, but they didn't care. The New Reformed Paladins.' He spat into the fire and watched it sizzle. 'That's what they called themselves. A fancy name for a bunch of degenerates and murderers. They started shooting then and hacking away at anything that moved. I won't say as though they didn't deserve it though. The gypsies. They weren't human, you see. As soon as the fight started, they began to change. Right before my eyes. Turned into savage animals they did, but it didn't do 'em any good. They were slaughtered. Every one of 'em. Maybe they deserved it, maybe they didn't. They were abominations, that's all I know. It didn't last long. Not really, but I'll never forget it. After they were done they all went back to the house and got roaring drunk. Next day they got me to bury their friend in the grounds next to a big old oak tree. They told me to go back to the woods and bury the remains of the gypsies and burn their caravans. Make it look like they were never there. I didn't want to, but what choice did I have? Not that it mattered. When I got there, it was all gone. Bodies, caravans, the lot. Just some blood soaked earth and that was that.'

Fanny reached out and touched his hand. 'It must have been terrible for you, Mr Taxil and I wouldn't dream of pressing you for more details, but there is one more vital service you can do for us if you would.'

'What's that?'

'Can you tell us the names of the men who were present? The names of the men who killed the gypsies?'

Late that night, Abberline and Colverson sat in conference in Abberline's office, studying a file which contained a list of names and a series of notes in Colverson's handwriting pertaining to each name.

'These are the names Ambrose Taxil gave us,' Colverson said. 'We spent the rest of the day checking the police files and the newspaper archives. The first three, William Henry Bury, a builder's merchant, killed in Dundee. Frederick Bailey Deeming, owned a plumbing firm, killed in Liverpool, that was the case that Mr Carmody mentioned had been brought to his attention by a colleague. And finally, Nicoli Wassili, son of a wealthy Ukranian businessman, bit of a playboy apparently, killed in Kent. All in the last few years and all showed signs of being attacked by an animal of some sort. No arrests made in any of these cases. The different times and different locations meant that no-one made the connection between them. The three current victims, Druitt, Maybrick and Ostrog also appear on the list and, having been killed in London and in close succession, made it easier to spot. We can find no trace of Jacob Isenschmid, but that name would tally with the name Druitt mentioned to the girl at Minnow's Walk. Ambrose Taxil claims he was the one killed by the gypsy girl which rather supports his theory that he was buried in the grounds of Granby Lodge where the events are alleged to have taken place. At the time, the Lodge was owned by one Francis Tumblety, the last name on the list. It was sold shortly after these events took place and I doubt if the current owners would like us digging up their garden to verify the fact that they have a murder victim buried there.'

'Nor should we need to, Colverson. But what about this Tumblety? What news of him?'

'Bit of a mystery there, sir. He went abroad not long after. He may be back in this country now, but we haven't been able to trace him.'

'Given the frequency of the latest murders, it may be safe to assume that our avenging angel believes he may be within reach. If that is the case, his quest may be coming to an end, which means we have limited time to warn Mr Tumblety of the danger he is in and to apprehend the perpetrator.' Abberline closed the file. 'This is most excellent police work, Colverson. You are to be commended.'

'Thank you, sir, but the credit should go to Fanny. I mean, Miss Kettle. She was the one who recognised the Paladin connection and I doubt if Mr Taxil would have been so forthcoming to me about the details. She has a real knack for this sort of thing.'

Abberline allowed himself a small smile. 'So, I take it you would have no objection to continuing to work closely with Miss Kettle in the future?'

'No sir,' said Colverson a mite too swiftly. 'That is, if you want me to, sir. I would have no objection at all.'

'Splendid, because we still have to locate the elusive Mr Tumblety and the Lambeth Poisoner is still at large, so it's all hands to the pump, as it were.'

'As you say, sir, but, if I may ask …?'

'Yes?'

'What happens after?'

'After?'

'After this case I mean. What happens to Miss Kettle then? She'll need some way of earning an honest living so as to support herself and Polly.'

'A very good point, Colverson and one I have been pondering myself. Suffice to say, changes are afoot which may have a bearing on the matter. I can say no more for the moment, but I believe both you and Miss Kettle may find yourselves working in close harmony for some time to come. For now, go home and get

287

some sleep. Tomorrow we start afresh, but make no mistake, Colverson, we are much closer now than we have ever been, all thanks to you and Miss Kettle.'

82

Cream jolted awake from a dream in which he had been running through a deep, dark, forest. Branches clutched at his clothes, his skin, holding him back. He turned to brush the entangling foliage away and realized it was not branches at all but his previous victims, wide-eyed, frothing at the mouth, hands hooked into claws. They reached for him, dragging him down to his doom. As he opened his mouth to scream, he awoke, a cold sweat beading his brow, his shirt soaked through. Only the light of a pale moon illuminated the chamber. On shaking legs, Cream lit an oil lamp and inspected his charge. The boy tossed and turned, his skin pale and clammy to the touch. His condition seemed no more advanced but there was no discernible improvement. Cream bathed the boy's forehead with the sinking feeling that he had reached the limits of his medical prowess. Indeed, he doubted that anyone in the medical profession would be able to bring about a more positive solution. No-one in the legitimate medical profession anyway. But maybe those who operated on the fringe of medicine might be able to offer some hope? Nonsense, of course, but since the disease was somehow linked to this damnable curse that turned a young boy into a savage beast, might that change be linked to some malady of the brain and not some physical condition? Cream did, after all, have access to someone who claimed to have mastery over the minds of men. And women of course, especially women, but in desperate times, desperate measures must be employed. The very thought curdled Cream's stomach, but he had no other choice. Before the boy deteriorated beyond all salvation, Cream must persuade Reilly to allow him to ask his brother, James, to help.

Thus decided, Cream left the sick room in search of Reilly. At this time of night, the living quarters were dark and quiet. Cream passed various doors until he came to Reilly's study. No-one impeded his progress and he was just about to knock when he heard soft voices from inside.

'And there's no sign of the man?' Reilly's voice.

'None.' That was a burly fellow called Ryan, one of Reilly's most trusted lieutenants.

'Damn it all, he can't just have vanished into thin air.'

'We've got all our watchers out and about, but there's no hide nor hair to be found. It's like he's a ghost. He was seen getting off a boat in Southampton and boarding a train for London, but since then, nothing.'

'Francis Tumblety may be a devil in human form, but he's no ghost. He's flesh and blood right enough and I want him found!'

At the name Francis Tumblety, Cream froze. Had he heard correctly? He had no idea why Reilly wanted Tumblety, but given Tumblety's many misdemeanours, it could be for any number of reasons. What price would Reilly be prepared to pay to the man who gave him the whereabouts of the object of his search?

As Cream mulled over his options, the door opened and the impressive form of Ryan stood framed in the light that spilled from the room.

'Ah,' Cream said. 'I was just about to knock, but I heard voices and didn't want to disturb you.'

'Doctor,' Reilly called. 'Come on in. You have good news for me, I hope.'

'In a manner of speaking. Perhaps.' Cream entered the room. Timing was crucial, but, for now, he would keep Tumblety's whereabouts to himself. If he could persuade Reilly to allow James to treat Callum and, miracle upon miracle, if James was successful, his bargaining chip would exceed his wildest expectations. Not only would he have his debts eradicated, he may even be able to negotiate enough financial reward to enable him to start a new life far from here. America. That was where Cream had his sights set and maybe, just maybe, he now had the means to achieve his ambition.

83

'What news "Doctor"?'

Cream could not help but notice the inflection that Reilly placed on the word "Doctor". What little patience the man had had worn beyond thin long ago. He was a man used to getting results. His word was law and instant obedience was mandatory.

'It's proving more vexatious than anticipated, Mr Reilly,' Cream managed.

'Vexatious? I don't give a damn how vexed you are, Cream. I want to know if my son is going to live or not. Tell me true, can you cure him or not?'

Cream knew better than to lie, but a little dissembling may just ease the unpleasant truth.

'My methods are producing satisfactory results,' he began.

'Then its good news you have for me then?'

'Ordinarily, yes, but this is by no means an ordinary case.'

'Then it's bad news? Make up your mind, Cream, before I lose my temper.'

'The boy's dual nature complicates matters,' Cream hurried on. 'Every time the consumption recedes, it allows the lupine part of his make-up to come to the fore. It's almost as if the human side of his nature regards the wolf side as a dangerous intruder. He is utilizing his human strength to fend off the wolf and that weakens him once more and allows the infection to re-establish itself. It's a vicious circle that must be broken if he is to survive.'

'And how do you propose that we do that?'

Cream sighed and mopped his brow with a red-spotted handkerchief. 'I am no expert on lycanthropy. I doubt anyone is, not in its medical implications anyway, but I surmise that it is a condition triggered by some reaction in the brain. To allow Fin's human side to fight the consumption, the wolf must be tethered.'

'I do not like to repeat myself, Cream, but in your case I will make an exception. How?'

'That, I am afraid, is beyond my skills, but I know a man who may be able to help.'

'Let another into our secret? I think not. You will go to this man and get him to instruct you in what must be done without discussing the exact nature of the problem.'

Cream shook his head wearily. 'Impossible, I am afraid. Even if I could acquire a basic grasp of the techniques, I would not have the experience to conduct the procedure adequately. This needs to be performed by an expert in their field otherwise the enterprise is doomed to failure.'

For several seconds Reilly remained silent.

'You're sure there is no other way?' he finally asked.

'Not if you want your son to live.'

'Very well. Bring this man here. But I warn you, if one word of my son's true nature gets out …'

'I am aware of the consequences, Mr Reilly, I assure you, and I promise that the gentleman I have in mind is someone of the utmost discretion.'

84

Dr James Cream was just finishing his third whiskey when a knock came upon his door. Cursing, he rose to his feet and opened it to reveal his brother, hopeful of admission.

'Good evening, James,' Cream said. 'Might I come in for a few moments?'

'I'm in no mood for this tonight, Thomas. I don't care how much you owe or who to. I've just lost the woman I love, murdered by the Lambeth Poisoner of all people. My star patient, on whom I pinned my professional hopes, has also been murdered. Shot down in the street by some trigger happy American! My life is in tatters and I want to be left alone in my misery.'

In other circumstances, Thomas Cream would have been delighted to see his brother in such dire straits, especially as he was one of the architects of such misery, but his current mission was one of such urgency that he must strive to undo whatever mischief he had caused. As James moved to close the door, Cream blocked his intention by the timely insertion of his foot. 'What if I told you I had a business proposition for you? One that would seal your reputation for all time and prove to all the doubters that mesmerism is a legitimate science.' The words came out in a rush, underscored with no little note of panic.

'Why on earth would I enter into a business proposition with you of all people?' James said.

'Not with me. Not directly, but I can put you in touch with a case the like of which you will never have encountered before. Hang it all, James, we can't discuss it on the doorstep. Let me in, for pity sake. Hear me out and if you don't like what I have to say you'll never have to see me again.'

'Do I have your word on that?'

'Just let me in, will you?'

'Oh, very well, but this had better be good, Thomas.'

James turned away, leaving Cream to enter of his own volition, closing the door behind him. Once seated with a grudgingly parsimonious scotch, Cream began his tale.

'What if I were to tell you that there is a condition of the mind that creates a distinct and separate entity that is able to assert itself over and above that personality that normally presents itself to the world?' he began.

'I would say you are preaching to the converted, brother dear. I already have … had a client who exhibits such traits. But now he is no more and all I have left is you. Hardly a fair trade in my view.'

Cream swallowed the insult and pressed on. 'Did your other client's disorder manifest itself as a purely mental and emotional separation of character or did it trigger certain physical changes as well?'

'Stop talking nonsense! A superficial alteration in the patient's physiognomy resulting from mental aberrations is nothing more than a distortion of their own features. A bland, passive expression becomes a scowling, anger filled countenance. Stop wasting my time.'

'I'm not talking about changes of expression, James. I'm talking about a fundamental rearrangement of bone and sinew that overlaps basic human appearance with that of a wild beast.'

'Now you're entering the realms of myth and legend! Really, Thomas, I don't know what you're up to but I've had enough of this. I want you to leave.'

'But just suppose, just for a second, that the untapped forces of the mind could bring about such a transformation? Would that not be something that would raise the man who discovered such a condition to the pinnacle of his profession?'

'To even suggest such a thing would be the ruination of my career, what's left of it anyway. I've had enough of this, Thomas. Leave now or I will throw you out.'

At that moment, there came a loud knocking at the front door.

'Who the blazes is that?' said James angrily.

Cream sighed. 'I really wish you had listened to me, James,' he said. 'I really didn't want it to come to this.'

'Come to what? What are you blethering about?'

Cream rose and made his way to the front door, followed by James. Cream opened the door to reveal the massive frame of Jacob Crow.

'James,' Cream said, 'this is Mr Crow. He's come to escort us to a meeting with my employer where you will receive irrefutable proof that what I say is true. I would strongly suggest that you agree to this course of events, James, because, if you do not, Mr Crow would take that as a personal insult.'

'I don't give a tinker's cuss what Mr Crow thinks about anything ...' James's words trailed off as Crow held up one massive hand for silence. James watched the fingers of that hand curl into a fist. Mesmerised by the sight, he watched as the first stayed motionless. Then it moved. Faster than a speeding train, straight towards him. After that, things went decidedly black.

'Ah, there he is. Back with us. I was afraid Mr Crow may have hit you harder than necessary,' Reilly said.

'It was just a tap,' Crow rumbled.

'So it was, but you have the strength of a carthorse, Jacob and Dr Cream here is a delicate morsel to be sure. Leave us now if you would Jacob, so that we can have a wee chat with Dr Cream in private. Wait outside if you will. I shall call if we need your services again.'

Crow nodded and removed himself from the room, closing the door behind him.

James Cream struggled up from the depths of unconsciousness, his head ringing, his jaw aching and he was sure more than a few teeth had lost their moorings.

'Where? …Who? … Why?' No one question seemed sufficient and he seemed incapable of phrasing a single one of them anyway.

'Drink this,' Reilly said, handing him a crystal glass containing a generous measure of rather fine brandy. James did as he was told.

'That's good,' Reilly said. 'Now, introductions. You've already made the acquaintance of Mr Crow and that's your brother, the other Dr Cream over there. My name is Patrick Reilly and this is my wife, Siobhan.' Reilly indicated a strikingly attractive red-haired woman who regarded him with a sceptical expression.

'I take it your brother has told you of the situation we find ourselves in, Dr Cream?'

'My brother has informed me of a malady which manifests itself in physical changes to the human form, yes. He believes it is a disease of the mind and that I may be instrumental in curing this condition.'

'Not quite the full story then, but a start. What do you make of it, doctor?'

'Poppycock. Utter balderdash.'

Reilly smiled and shivers ran up and down James Cream's spine.

'Poppycock is it? Balderdash? You like fancy words, so you do, Dr Cream, but I'm just a poor lad from the bogs of Ireland, so let's call a spade a spade, shall we? My wee boy is a werewolf. A shapeshifter if you like, just like myself and my wife. It's a proud heritage, but this restless spirit within needs to be calmed before it can allow the disease that afflicts him and is stealing his life to feel comfortable enough to leave him. Two enemies, as you might call them, each fighting for control of my son's body. Is that something you think you could help with, Dr Cream?'

James burst into laughter. ' Werewolves? Do you take me for a fool, Mr Reilly? There is no such thing as a werewolf.'

Siobhan snapped impatiently: 'If it's evidence you want, Dr Cream, I'll give it to you.'

She began to unfasten the buttons of her dress. James Cream gasped. 'Madam, I'm not sure what you think you are doing, but this really isn't necessary!'

'Hush now, Dr Cream,' Reilly said. 'If it's proof you need, my wife will oblige. Watch and learn.'

James Cream did as he was bidden and watched Siobhan Reilly remove every stitch of clothing to stand before him naked, the glow from the fire painting her body in shifting shadows. She smiled. 'Watch,' she whispered. At first he thought it was just the shadows from the fire sliding sensuously over her pale flesh, but then he saw the movement, the re-arrangement of bone and muscle beneath the alabaster covering. The distending of limbs, the elongation of the jaw, the growth of the pelt over that smooth, feminine expanse of flesh and, dear God, the hands, the hands that twisted and contorted into razor sharp claws!

James Cream had no idea at what point he began to scream and at what point he wet himself. He only knew that he did both these things as he bolted from his chair, knocking it over in his haste as this "thing" that had, mere moments before, been a most beautiful woman, advanced upon him. All rational thought fled his mind and possible escape through the door did not enter his head. Not that it would have done any good since Crow stood impassive as a mountain on the other side of that portal.

James Cream found himself cowering in a corner as a wolf-like beast advanced slowly upon him, jaws agape. It stopped, regarding him quizzically, sitting upon its haunches. And then it began to change once more. All the reconfiguration he had just witnessed reversing itself until Siobhan Reilly, naked and smiling, sat before him.

'If you now believe in werewolves, Dr Cream,'she said, 'can you save my son or not?'

James Cream was only aware of his soiled clothing, the stench and the feel of it, and the sly grin on the face of his brother at his abject humiliation. Part of him still rejected the notion that he had witnessed an actual physical transformation. Some form of hypnosis, he reasoned. That was a field he was more familiar with. Something orchestrated by his younger sibling for the express purpose of humiliating him perhaps.

Had his acumen not been overcome with grief at Matilda's death he would, no doubt, have seen through the ruse easily enough. Such was the workings of the rational mind. And now he was forced to examine the patient. Well, this would reveal the truth of the matter. He would be in sole control of proceedings and no outside influence could sway his findings.

That the boy was genuinely sick was plain enough, although a skilled actor could simulate such. The boy lay, hollow-eyed and gaunt upon his pillows. His mother whispered sweet words of encouragement to him and then drew back.

James Cream sat on the edge of the bed and pulled out his gold pocket watch. He held it up to the light and gently swung it to and fro.

'Now, Fin,' he said. 'Just follow my watch. It's perfectly safe. Just follow my watch and imagine yourself in your most favourite spot. A field perhaps, or a woodland glade. Wherever you feel safe and warm. Then let your eyes close. Your lids are getting heavy. Feel yourself floating, floating, safe and warm and comfortable.'

With a soft sigh, the boy's eyes drifted shut. James Cream pocketed the watch.

'Listen to my voice, Fin. Focus on it. Concentrate. Open your mind. Let me in so that I may see what is troubling you.'

It was then that the beast attacked.

The deepest pits of hell are naught compared to the darkest depths of the human soul.

Such it was when James Cream communed with the mind of Fin Reilly. Not even George Hutchinson's sadistic alter-ego had presented itself in such an obscenely aggressive manner. At least he had been able to communicate with the entity he had christened Spring Heeled Jack. This was a monster of a very different sort.

Bestial images, dark and blood-red, threatened to overwhelm him with slavering jaws and howls of inhuman fury. No quarter asked or given, it's only desire was to rend and kill, it's only motivation a savage, primeval fury that knew no bounds. A lesser practitioner may well have been overcome by such an onslaught and even James Cream, for all his vaunted confidence, was almost washed away by such an onslaught. There was no reason here, no pathway to meaningful dialogue. And yet … Beneath the power and the fury, there was something else. Some slim thread of more human emotion. Fear. That was it. Not the creature's fear of James Cream. Oh, no, that was obvious. But a fear emanating from the child whose mind and body housed such a creature. Not fear of the creature itself, but fear of dying, fear of leaving his parents, fear of the unknown. And in that fear he had summoned up this protector to repel the invading organism that was attacking his mortal shell, unaware that in so doing he was freeing that other being's desire to conquer and destroy. Extraordinary! What a paper this would make! Before the swirling mass of dark emotions could prove overwhelming, James Cream beat a hasty retreat to find himself sweating profusely and shaking in every limb. His voice wavered as he spoke.

'When I snap my fingers, Fin,' he said, 'you will awake from your trance.'

James Cream snapped his fingers in front of Fin Reilly's face and the boy's eyes drifted open with a sigh.

'Well, doctor?' Reilly's voice. 'Do you think you can help my son?'

'I ...' James Cream coughed to clear his head. 'It will not be an easy task, but I believe it is within my power to do so. I will need daily sessions with your son. How many is impossible to say and I can offer no guarantee.'

'But it is possible?' Siobhan now.

'Yes, I believe so.'

'Then name your price, doctor,' Reilly said.

'Price? I ... well, your permission to document my findings and present them to the medical fraternity would be more recompense than any monetary reward.'

'No.' It was a flat refusal from Reilly. 'No-one will know about this and that's final.'

'But I can assure you of my complete discretion Mr Reilly. I will mention no names, although ratification would be a great advantage, I believe I can still present a most compelling case study.'

'Your discretion be damned, doctor! Cure my son and I'll pay you a king's ransom, but if one word of this comes out in public I'll come looking for you and you won't like the face I am wearing when I find you. Our heritage must remain a closely guarded secret. Not even my most trusted lieutenants, not even the redoubtable Mr Crow, know our true nature and that is how it shall remain. Do we understand each other, doctor?'

James Cream swallowed hard. It was a bitter blow to be denied such a privilege, but there was nothing to stop him from writing a paper anyway. All he had to do then was find another such shape-shifter who would be more willing to step into the public domain. That, surely would be permissible? It was a risk, but then all life is a risk is it not?

'Yes,' he said. 'I believe I understand you perfectly.'

'Good. But I'm a fair man, so I ask again. Name your price.'

'I don't really know, I … wait, there is one thing.'

'Name it. If it's mine to give, you shall have it.'

'My fiancé, Miss Matilda Clover recently met an untimely demise.'

'My commiserations.'

'Thank you. She fell victim to the Lambeth Poisoner. The police seem unable to apprehend the villain. I thought with your connections …'

'Set a thief to catch a thief, eh, doctor?'

'I wouldn't put it quite like that.'

'That's because you are too polite, doctor, but I am not offended. I have no illusions about what I am. I believe I may be able to locate such an individual for you. And if I do, what then?'

'Then? Why, I would seek an equivalent measure of revenge for his black deed.'

'And would you wish to carry out this revenge yourself?'

James Cream felt the blood drain from his face. 'No,' he

muttered. 'I would be content to know that a just punishment had been exacted.'

'Let us be plain, doctor. In return for your services, you wish me to identify this Lambeth Poisoner and to kill him on your behalf in as slow and painful a way as possible. Is that the size of it?'

'I … yes, it is.'

Reilly smiled and held out his hand. 'Then you have yourself a deal Dr Cream.'

James Cream and Patrick Reilly shook hands. In such a manner are deals made with many a devil.

He let him name his own fee! And what a fee it was. Nothing less than the life of his own brother if he did but know it! Outrageous. Thus did Cream's thoughts run. Curse him. James always has the luck. But there was one thing James did not have. The name of the one individual Patrick Reilly wanted above all else save the life of his son. Let James do his work. Should he fail, the deal he had struck with Reilly would be null and void, and Cream's life would be safe, but Cream would still have the knowledge to re-negotiate his own bargain. A clean slate and enough money to finance a new life for himself. In America. That was his dream and it was almost within his grasp. But if James succeeded … His own fate then did not bear thinking about. Time would be of the essence. Would Reilly delay paying his debt to James in order to carry out his own mission? Quite likely, but it was still an enormous risk. It was one that Cream had no choice but to take. He must hold his nerve and pray that, for once, the fates would smile upon him.

85

Dr James Cream. Expert in ailments of the body and the mind. Especially the mind. But this was something beyond even his experience. Society women and their daughters, oh, he could handle them. He could cast a veil over their insipid minds and make them dance a jig. Sometimes quite literally. It was a lucrative profession with considerable additional benefits, but professionally unfulfilling. Until, that is, he encountered George Hutchinson. Seemingly an unpromising dullard upon their first encounter, he soon proved to be quite unique. A distinct and most malevolent personality inhabiting the same mind, most unique indeed, and such a fascinating case study with a live specimen to exhibit like a performing monkey at a side-show! Oh, yes, that would be his ticket to fame and fortune. With George in his pocket he may not even have had to marry Matilda Clover for her father's fortune, but still, one can never have too much money and he did feel a certain affection for the girl. Having lost both Matilda and George in the same week in the most cruel of circumstances plunged him into a deep depression, but now he had a chance to redeem himself. When Reilly forbade him from using Fin as a case study it was a severe blow, but he knew better than to disobey the cold-eyed criminal. Still, knowledge once gained cannot be forgotten. If one such condition exists, there are bound to be more. James Cream vowed to find them. Whether or not he could save the child was almost immaterial, but the technique he had used on George was most effective and he had no doubt that a similar devise would work here. First, he must invade the boy's mind and seek out the malevolent entity and reach some sort of accord. Dr James Cream rolled up his sleeves and set to work.

Children are easy to put under. They had no natural defences, no cynicism to counter James' commands. Communicating with the malignant entity may be much more difficult. How does one talk to a wolf?

Quite easily in point of fact. As soon as Fin succumbed, the wolf appeared, defending his territory, attacking in the only way it knew how. An alarming change that made James sweat profusely came over the boy's features. A twisting and re-arranging of the facial muscles, pushing the flesh into shapes and directions no human being could possibly attain.

'Get … out!' The voice was a snarl.

James was used to George's alter-ego manifesting a different vocal pattern, but this was a beast given voice and it chilled him to the bone.

'I only wish to talk,' James said.

'No … talk …get … out!'

A singular mind with a singular objective. How much could the animal mind really understand? How much control would the human side of Fin's nature have over his wolf counterpart?

If James could not establish a meaningful dialogue his cause was lost. Taking a deep breath, he prepared for battle.

Several hours later, a drained and shaking James Cream held a council of war with his brother and the Reillys.

'The beast is well-nigh impossible to communicate with,' he said.

'That beast,' said Reilly, 'is a wolf. The sacred spirit of our clan and one we hold in high esteem.'

'Of course, of course,' James muttered, ignoring his brother's smirk. 'What I mean to say is that this wolf persona has one purpose and one purpose only and that is to protect Fin from any

305

and every form of harm.'

'A noble intent,' Siobhan murmured.

'Quite so, but having identified the tuberculosis as an enemy, it has engaged it in a battle to the death. Each time the disease withdraws, the wolf follows it, intent on eradicating it. When attacked, the virus responds by renewing its own efforts, thus trapping them in a perpetual cycle that will only end when Fin is physically incapable of sustaining such a battle any longer. It is most bizarre.'

'Then there is nothing you can do for the lad, doctor?' Reilly said.

'There may be a chance. I did persuade the bea … the wolf, to allow me to speak with Fin directly. The wolf was suspicious but perceived me as little or no threat and I was able to exchange a few words with your son. He is terribly weak of course, but I think he understood the need to make the wolf stand down so that the disease could be purged from his system without interference. The only question is how?'

'And do you have an answer to that question, doctor?' Reilly asked impatiently.

'I think so. Potentially anyway. A former client of mine had a similar problem. Nothing of the strength of the wolf, but I believe the same method of control may be effective. In that case I gave him a rhyme to recite whenever he felt his control slipping. In his case a simple nursery rhyme, but for Fin we would need something much more straightforward because of his weakened condition.'

'And you can contrive such a phrase?'

'That part should be quite straightforward, but there is a complication.'

'Which is?' Reilly was becoming more and more agitated with

James' circumlocution and the good doctor pressed on quickly.

'This spell, if you wish to call it that, is only effective if the person suffering from the affliction keeps chanting it. Obviously, Fin could not be expected to keep chanting long enough for the tuberculosis to be purged from his system.'

'And the solution to this would be, doctor? And be quick about it before I lose my patience.'

'I need to change the intention of the incantation. Rather than temporary release, Fin must be persuaded to banish the wolf identity from his mind forever.'

'You would have him separate himself from his birth-right!' Reilly exploded. 'Never!'

Siobhan touched him on the arm. 'If this can be done,' she asked James, 'will my son live?'

'Nothing is one hundred percent certain, but I believe, yes.'

'And if it is not done, or it fails?'

'Then he will certainly die.'

Reilly took several deep breaths. 'And after the disease has left his body, can this spell be undone? Can you give him another incantation that will re-unite him with his wolf self once more?'

'Those are uncharted waters, but, theoretically, yes, although I would strongly advise against it.'

'And why would that be?'

'You told me that the change is premature in your son, that he had not matured enough to exert the necessary control over the wolf. That being the case, the wolf has had free rein these last weeks. He has tasted freedom and he likes it. If your son survives and the wolf is subsequently released, he, not Fin, will become the dominant personality. Savage and uncontrollable. If your son is to survive with any shred of humanity or free will, the wolf must be caged permanently.'

'It's a hard choice you ask of us, doctor,' Reilly said.

'Or no choice at all,' Siobhan said. 'If it's a choice between having our son back, hale and hearty, or having a wild, uncontrollable beast, what would you choose?'

'We don't know that for certain, my love,' Reilly said. 'The doctor here said it was uncharted waters which means, at best, he's guessing, is that not so, doctor?'

'To a large extent, yes. But what I do know for certain is that if things are left as they are, your son will die of tuberculosis within the week. Is that not so, Thomas?'

Cream was jolted into attentiveness suddenly, not anticipating to be involved in this conversation. 'I … yes, I concur with my brother. It's the wolf that is preventing my treatment from bringing Fin back to full health. If that obstacle is not removed, his health will continue to fail and he will surely die.'

'There you have it,' said Siobhan. 'We really have no choice at all, do we, Patrick?'

Reilly scowled and then reached out for his wife's hand, his features softening. 'No, I suppose not. Very well doctor. You have our permission to try this treatment. When can it be administered?'

'As soon as the next seizure manifests itself. But I suggest that the boy's mother be the one to explain to him the urgency and the necessity of such a plan. If you are willing that is?'

'There is nothing I would not do for my son, doctor.'

'In that case, there is just the matter of the trigger word or phrase. It should be something that Fin is familiar with. Do you have any suggestions?'

After a moment's silence, Reilly said: 'There is one word that should suffice. Our clan, doctor, is called the Fenris. We are named after the giant wolf of Norse legends, a creature so huge and fierce that the gods themselves feared him. Feared him so much that they chained him with a mystical chain for all time, only to be set free at Ragnarok, the battle at the end of the world, when he would break his chains and kill the gods. Fin knows those tales well. He knows the name given to the chain that bound Fenris and its purpose. I believe that will serve your purpose, doctor.'

'It will indeed. And what is this name?'

'Gleipnir.'

That night, as most nights, the disease and the wolf did battle for the life and soul of Fin Reilly. James Cream and Siobhan Reilly sat at the boy's bedside, hoping and praying that this would not be the final battle for the boy's life. At length, the seizure passed and the wolf retreated.

'Now,' whispered James. 'Now I shall put Fin under the influence and ask him to listen to your voice.' So saying, he took his watch and began the, by now, familiar ritual.

'Listen to my voice, Fin,' he said. 'I have your mother here and she needs to speak to you most urgently. Listen to what she has to say for it is most vital that you do.'

James motioned Siobhan forward and she began to speak to her son in soft whispers. He gave feeble nods and groans that James took to be understanding and, at length, Siobhan sat back.

'Fin,' James said, 'you have heard your mother's words of wisdom. Do you understand what you must do?'

The boy nodded feebly.

'Good. Rest now and when the time is right, do what you must.'

Fin closed his eyes and his head lolled back against the pillows. James withdrew to an armchair and Siobhan continued to sit by her son, speaking in a soft voice as she recited over and over the old Norse legends of gods and monsters and a giant wolf known as Fenris as the boy slept.

It was as dawn was breaking that James was rudely awakened from a fitful doze by a voice screaming: 'GLEIPNIR! GLEIPNIR! GLEIPNIR!'

No sooner had James stumbled to his feet than the door burst open to admit Patrick Reilly with Thomas Cream hot on his heels. Siobhan Reilly still sat on her son's bed, holding the boy in her arms as he screamed the name over and over. 'GLEIPNIR! GLEIPNIR! GLEIPNIR!'

Gradually his voice diminished into silence and Siobhan laid him back against the pillows.

'Has it worked?' she said. 'Has it worked?'

Thomas Cream moved to the bedside. He checked the boy's pulse, and touched his forehead. 'His fever is less,' he said. 'His pulse is still weak, but steady. The next few hours will tell, but I believe you have done it brother. The boy is alive and the disease seems to be in remission.'

86

'How is the patient today?' Cream asked.

Siobhan beamed. 'Sitting up and taking notice, doctor,' she said. 'He's eaten some broth and there's colour back in his cheeks.'

'Excellent. And his ... convulsions?'

'Not a sign of them. Your brother calls in most days to ...what does he call it? To reinforce the conditioning, that's it, but he says it's only a precaution.'

'Good. And you continue with the regimen I have suggested?'

'Clean sheets, plenty of fresh air, regular as clockwork.'

'Then the danger seems to have passed. I'm pleased.'

'And it's all thanks to you and your brother, Dr Cream.' Reilly's voice came from an open doorway and the man himself exited from his study, extending his hand for Cream to shake.

'Much as we would like to take the credit for this miracle,' he said, 'I feel it was due more to the lad's remarkable constitution than my medical skills that have pulled him through.'

'Modest as always, doctor, but I'll hear none of it.' Reilly put his arm around Cream's shoulder and ushered him towards his son's room. 'After you've checked the lad over, perhaps you'll do me the honour of joining me for a celebratory drink?'

'I would be delighted. There is one small matter I would like to discuss with you, if I may?'

'Of course. See to the lad and then join me in the study,'

Reilly was in an unsurprisingly good mood and Cream took this as an omen that his bargain would find favour. He sipped his drink and settled back in a comfortable armchair, Reilly sitting opposite him.

'Now then Dr Cream,' Reilly said. 'What is it you would speak to me about?'

'I would like to review the terms of our bargain,' he said.

Reilly still smiled but a coldness crept into his demeanour. 'A deal is a deal, Dr Cream. You cure Fin and I wash away all your debts owed to me. It is done and cannot be undone. You have my gratitude, Dr Cream, you and your brother, and I acknowledge that we would not have had his services if not for yourself but re-negotiating the terms of our agreement was never on the table. I thought you understood that?'

Cream swallowed nervously, his previous confidence dwindling slightly. 'Of course, of course,' he said. 'What I have in mind is not so much a re-negotiation, more of an additional agreement that you may consider worth your while. If I were to give you certain information, which I believe you desire, what might the price be for such a service?'

'That would depend upon the situation. I have already agreed to carry out an additional task for your brother and I fully intend to do so as soon as Fin is up and about and it can receive my full attention. Is that not already extra payment enough?'

Cream felt a cold sweat break out on his brow. There is some time yet, he thought, before Reilly begins to set his men on the trail of the Lambeth Poisoner. If I can seal this deal quickly enough I may yet be well out of harm's way before all is lost. 'You have been most generous, Mr Reilly, but I believe the information I have for you may be worth even more than you have already promised.'

'Then spit it out, man. I'm keen to hear what it is you think I would be willing to pay for.'

Taking a deep breath, Cream set out his case. 'During my treatment of your son, I happened to hear, quite by chance, that you were seeking a certain individual who had done you great

312

wrong.' Cream saw Reilly stiffen as the implication of his statement sunk home. 'I know not of any details,' he hurried on, 'but it seemed that this search was of utmost importance to you and, if I were able to give you the location of said individual, might it be worth a small extra consideration?'

'Don't play me for a fool, Cream,' Reilly snarled. 'This matter is one of family honour that must be avenged. It would go hard with anyone who sought to take advantage of my good nature in such a matter.'

'I wouldn't dream of doing so, Mr Reilly. It is by the merest happenstance that I possess this most vital information. As such it is worthless to me, but if it is something that you desire …' he let the thought trail off.

Reilly sat back and folded his hands beneath his chin. 'What makes you think I won't get Jacob Crow to simply beat the information out of you?' he said quietly.

Now there was an option that Cream had not counted on. Thinking fast, he said: 'I rely on your reputation as a fair man in business dealings, Mr Reilly. That and your integrity that led you to acquire my services to treat your son. The trust you placed in me to be discrete in such a matter led me to believe that we held a rapport between us as gentlemen should. Was I wrong?'

Reilly let out a peal of laughter. 'By all the gods, you're a chancer Cream! I like that in a man. Tell me what you know, and, if it proves true, you shall have your reward and then some.'

Breathing somewhat more easily, Cream said: 'The person you seek is, I believe, one Francis Tumblety. The reason that you have not been able to locate him thus far is that he has only just returned to this country after many years abroad with a new name and a new profession. The man you seek now goes by the name of Wu Feng, a supposed Chinese magician currently performing at the Alhambra Theatre. Whatever your business might be with him, I suggest you conduct it swiftly, since he is about to enter the final week of his run and after that, who knows where he might be.'

87

'We've been given his name by two separate sources, both of which link him to death by poisoning. Why don't we just arrest him?' Colverson wanted to know.

'It's still just circumstantial,' Abberline said. Along with Polly and Fanny, the two police officers were holding a council of war of sorts. The case of the Black Dog murders had stalled momentarily until the final potential victim on Taxil's list could be found and focus had shifted to the case of the Lambeth Poisoner.

'A clever, or even a competent, barrister would tear our case to shreds,' Abberline continued. 'One source is a highly emotional battered wife who openly admits to having poisoned her husband. Cream would simply deny any wrongdoing since strychnine is a commonly available substance and we may well end up having to prosecute Mrs Maybrick for attempted murder when the poor woman has suffered enough. And as for our other source …' he paused. 'I'm sorry, Polly, but the word of one of Cream's deceased victims simply wouldn't be admissible in court.'

'But I could prove it,' Polly said. 'Let me hold a séance for the judge and I'll convince him it's the truth.'

'They wouldn't allow it, Polly. And even if you did convince one judge, he couldn't direct the jury to convict on that alone.'

'Then I'll do it for the whole bleedin' jury!' Polly said, exasperated.

'It still wouldn't work. A verdict has to be supported by English law and there is nothing in the statutes that take account of psychic phenomenon. Aside from that, it would open the floodgates for any less legitimate psychic to come along and hoodwink the jury into believing anything they wanted. Our evidence needs to be more concrete.'

'Then what can we do?'' said Fanny. 'We can't just let him carry on killing people.'

'We can watch and wait. Try and find someone who can link him with the other victims, particularly on the nights of their deaths. We know he targets women, so let's see if any men have succumbed to poison since he started his activities. We may find that he has been advising other wives on the most discrete way of removing their spouses. Observe his movements as best we can to see if he approaches other women who rebuff his advances, take their statements, try and build a case against him for corroborating behaviour.'

Fanny let out a long sigh. 'Sounds like a lot of bloomin' hard work for precious little reward if you ask me,' she said.

'That's what police work is mainly,' Colverson said, dourly.

'Maybe there's a way to speed things up a bit,' said Polly.

'How so?' Abberline asked.

'How about someone poses as a street girl. Gets talking to him, then, when he tries to slip her pills or whatever, she gives a signal and you move in and arrest him.'

'Set a trap, you mean?' Colverson said.

'That's right.'

'It might work,' said Abberline. 'As long as our Trojan Horse didn't solicit the poison in any way. But who could we get to act as bait?'

'What about Babcock?' Colverson suggested. 'It worked well enough for him when he flushed out George Hutchinson.'

'And he nearly paid with his life, so I don't think he'd be too keen to repeat the experience. Besides, however skilful his make-up, Mr Babcock could not be as alluring as the Poisoner's other victims. Death is not his only aim in these cases, he also has a more … personal agenda.'

'You mean he has it off with them after they've snuffed it,' Polly said.

'Quite.'

'So, it needs to be someone young and attractive, like Nellie.'

'Exactly. Any subterfuge would be too easily spotted, but who could we find to take on such a role?'

'Gawd give me strength!' Polly said. 'It's a wonder you lot solve any crimes at all! You're looking right at her. Me! I'll do it.'

'No!' A chorus of voices as Fanny, Colverson and Abberline all voiced their objection.

'Why not?' said Polly. 'It was my idea.'

'Actually, it was Babcock's idea,' Colverson pointed out.

'And as I said, he nearly got killed,' added Abberline.

'Far too dangerous,' said Fanny. 'And you aren't that good an actress. But I am.'

'What?' said Colverson.

'I'd be perfect,' said Fanny. 'I'm used to running scams and if I could fool Lords and high class gents into thinking I was a Russian psychic, I reckon this would be a doddle.'

'You'd have to keep your clothes on this time,' Colverson said.

Fanny grinned and punched him on the arm. 'Cheeky sod!' she said.

'But it was my idea!' Polly said. 'I want to do it, for Nellie's sake.'

'Your motives are admirable,' said Abberline, 'but Fanny is correct. It's far too dangerous. It requires finesse that only an experienced performer could manage.'

'Then you agree?' said Fanny.

'Hold on a second,' said Colverson. 'I'm not sure about this at all.'

Fanny reached out and closed her hand over his. 'I know how to

317

look after myself and I wouldn't dream of doing it if I didn't know you were nearby, ready to come to my rescue and keep me safe.'

Polly and Abberline exchanged looks.

'Are you two keen on each other?' Polly asked.

Fanny and Colverson exchanged embarrassed glances. 'Well, we have been working together quite closely,' Colverson admitted.

'And we have formed, what you might call, an understanding of sorts,' Fanny said.

'You are!' Polly grinned.

Before Fanny and Colverson could utter any more explanations, Abberline gave a discrete cough. 'I take it there are no further objections to this plan of action?'

Having received no further response save three heads shaking, he said: 'Splendid. Then I suggest we work out the details.'

88

Thomas Neill Cream was in rare good humour. His reputation as a skilled medical practitioner had never been higher, he was debt free and had the promise of a goodly amount of cash that would soon be his which would enable him to book passage to America and set himself up in whatever business he saw fit. Life had never been better. Only one thing remained to be done to make it perfect. For that, he needed a woman. One last kill before his departure for the New World. This one needed to be special. None of the gin-soaked drabs that comprised many of his previous prey. The young woman he had bumped into on the street, what was her name? Hattie? Sally? Nellie! That was it, Nellie. She had been exceptional. Young, ripe, flawless. He had enjoyed her. He needed someone equally as inviting. None of the clientele of the Dog and Duck met his requirements and he was about to move on to pastures new when the door opened and in she walked. No, not walked, sashayed with an air of confidence that put her head and shoulders above her sisters. Older than Nellie but younger than many he had dallied with. The flush of youth tempered with a degree of maturity. How he loved to see that flush of vitality wither and die as they swallowed his little pills. How the pleading look clouded their dimming eyes as the pain took hold, how their bodies shook and twisted until the blessed stillness of eternity claimed them. Then he was free to do as he wanted and he wanted this woman so much it was like a red hot poker twisting his innards.

She made her way through the throng, exchanging a smile, a word, a touch on the arm. He heard her laugh, throwing back her head, baring her smooth, white throat. In the normal run of things, her very self-confidence would have been off-putting, but

Cream was a new man now, a physician of unparalleled skill with a pocket full of money coming his way and a virgin land ahead of him to ravage to his heart's content. Yes, life was good and he had no doubt that this woman would be his before the night was out.

Earlier that afternoon, Abberline, Colverson and Fanny went over the rudiments of their plan.

'We know that the Poisoner approaches his victims on the street,' Abberline said. 'We've been able to ascertain that most of his victims had been seen in various drinking establishments shortly before their demise, but had always left alone.'

'We think he uses these places as his hunting ground,' continued Colverson. 'He selects his victim and, if they leave alone, he follows.'

'Once they have reached a secluded enough area,' Abberline said, 'he approaches them on the pretext of doing business. Moving to an even more secluded alley or back street, presumably for reasons of privacy, he persuades them to drink or eat something which contains the poison. Once the poison has done its work, he commits an act of gross indecency. If our plan succeeds, you must, on no account, ingest anything he may give you.'

Colverson produced a police whistle and handed it to Fanny. 'Take this,' he said. 'Once he offers you anything to eat or drink, blow on it three times and we'll come running. Once we have whatever it is he's offered you, we can test it for poison. If it's positive, we'll have him.'

'We have the advantage of knowing what he looks like,' Abberline said. 'So we can follow his movements until he's decided which establishment he's going to use. We will secrete ourselves, in disguise of course, in that establishment before you begin your, uh, performance, so we shall be able to follow him directly he leaves to follow you, so we won't be far away. Is all that clear?'

'As crystal,' Fanny said. 'Honestly, you men, you'd think I'd never done this sort of thing before.'

'You haven't,' said Abberline. 'Not with a murderer as your target. Just because he's never used physical violence before doesn't mean he won't if he thinks he's been hoodwinked.'

'I … that is, we, just want you to be safe, Fanny. That's all,' Colverson said.

Fanny patted his hand. 'I know,' she said softly. 'And I appreciate it, I really do. But now I need you both to bugger off so I can get ready for my performance.'

And what a performance it was!

In their respective guises as two honest labourers and a saucy nymph of the night, Abberline, Colverson and Fanny had trailed Cream from his lodgings to his final destination of the Dog and Duck. He had considered two other hostelry's before deciding on this particular establishment. The trio had waited as he went inside each only to re-appear in a matter of minutes finding them not to his satisfaction. Having ensconced himself within the portals of the Dog and Duck, Abberline decided that this was their best chance to make their move.

Abberline and Colverson went in first. The place was crowded, but not too crowded. They ordered two tankards of ale and found a corner table from which they could survey the room. Cream was situated at the other end of the bar at a small table almost hidden in the shadows, but from where he could also observe all that transpired within. In due course, Fanny made her entrance. She was "dressed down" as she called it. Nothing too flash, but nothing too drab. She allowed her personality to shine through her pedestrian appearance as she "worked the room". A smile here, a laugh and a joke there, charming her way through the populace. A burly fellow made a grab for her and Colverson half rose from his seat. Abberline laid a restraining hand upon his arm.

'Steady,' he warned. 'Remember why we are here. Miss Kettle is more than capable of dealing with the likes of him, I'm sure.'

Reluctantly, Colverson sat back down.

'There,' said Abberline. 'She has everything under control.'

The altercation had ended with a smile and a laugh and Fanny continued her perambulation, but Colverson was still unhappy.

'Shouldn't she be focusing on Cream?' he asked. 'All this parading about, all this flirting, it's dangerous.'

'Miss Kettle is playing a finely judged game,' Abberline told him. 'Cream may be a cold blooded killer, but he's no fool. He wouldn't risk giving his victim poison in a crowded bar, it would create too much of a commotion and he would be sure to be remembered. This is his hunting ground. He selects his prey then waits for them to leave. He follows shortly afterwards with no-one the wiser and no-one to make the connection. See how he hides himself away? Avoiding all contact? When he leaves it's as if he never existed.'

'I suppose so,' Colverson grumbled. 'I just wish there were some other way.'

Abberline smiled. 'I had a feeling that you and Miss Kettle would make a fine team, but do I take it that Polly was right in her assumption that there is a more personal connection here than meets the eye?'

'I don't rightly know,' Colverson lamented. 'She's friendly enough. Takes pleasure in teasing me, even makes flirtatious overtures when the mood takes her, but ...'

'But what?'

'I mean, look at her now. Working her wiles on every man in the room. She's intelligent, witty, beautiful even. A free spirit. What could she possibly see in me? I'm just a boring copper.'

'You sell yourself short, Colverson. True, policemen are a breed apart, but few have your integrity, your determination, your eye for detail. You have exceptional potential.'

'Thank you, but when it comes to women, I'm baffled. She completely confounds me.'

'Such is the prerogative of all women, Colverson. I take it that you trust Miss Kettle's judgement on all aspects of the case so far?'

'Of course.'

'Then why do you doubt her judgement when she makes romantic overtures? Unless you think it nothing but a cruel deception, do you not think that she may have good reasons for her actions?'

Before Colverson could reply, Fanny made her exit with a wave and a cheery goodbye.

'She's leaving,' Colverson said. 'And our man is still sitting there nursing his ale.'

'Patience, Colverson. He won't be too keen to be seen to be hot on her heels, but he won't wait too long for fear of losing her. There, see? He rises.'

Cream left his table and, pulling his hat down over his eyes, made his way quietly and unobtrusively to the door. As it closed behind him, his departure created nary a ripple in the atmosphere of the bar.

'Now, we too must bide our time,' Abberline said. 'If we follow too closely, he may spot us and it will all have been for naught.'

'But Fanny's out there all alone.' Colverson was champing at the bit.

'Then we must use our judgement to make sure the risk she is taking is worth it. We agreed with Fanny the direction she would take upon exiting so a brisk pace will bring us within earshot of any misadventure she may encounter.'

'Then can we go now?'

'Yes, Colverson, we can. The chase is on.'

If he had been a whistling man, Thomas Neill Cream would have whistled as he walked the darkened streets of Whitechapel. For once, everything seemed to be going his way. Once Reilly had finished his last bit of gruesome business, he would have enough funds to commence his new life in a land with less restrictions than gloomy old London and freedom was what he craved to give his predilections full rein. There was the slight annoyance that, once he had received his well-deserved recompense, Reilly would devote his energies to unmasking the Lambeth Poisoner and his success in that endeavour would never do. Still, Cream was certain that even Reilly's resources could not lead to his disclosure before he had boarded a ship to America and that would be that. A new country, a new name and a new career. Yes, all in all, a cause for a cheerful whistle if ever there was one. And the cherry on the cake was the enchanting nymph of the night that had caught his eye. A treat he felt he rightfully deserved. His timing had to be perfect. As he exited from the pub he had caught sight of her skirts disappearing around the corner. He moved quickly but quietly as was his practice, closing the gap but giving his quarry no cause for alarm. She had been looking for trade, of that he was sure, but none of the cloddish denizens of the Dog and Duck had caught her eye. Cream felt sure that his more sophisticated appearance would find more favour. She was a tricky one though. Her route seemed random and convoluted. Twice he thought he had lost her, only to catch a glimpse as she made her way through the side streets and alleys he was so familiar with. You won't lose me that easily my girl, he thought. Sure enough, as he rounded a corner, there she was, stationary, leaning nonchalantly against the wall of an alleyway between two shops. The light was poor, but good enough to see her welcoming smile.

'Hello, my ducky,' she said. 'How would a nice gentleman like you like to spend some time with a girl like me, eh?'

'I'd like that very much.' Emboldened, Cream advanced to arm's length.

'Of course, time is money,' she said.

'Naturally.' He took some coins from his pocket and handed them over. What did it matter? He would retrieve them from her corpse soon enough.

'That'll buy you a really nice time, that will,' she said, pocketing the coins.

'Good. But it's a chilly night. What say we have a tipple before we begin?' Cream produced a silver hip flask from his pocket and unscrewed the cap.

'You go ahead, ducks,' she said. 'I've got to keep a clear head if I'm going to do more business tonight.'

Cream shrugged and took a deep swallow. He held out the flask. 'Just one mouthful won't hurt,' he said

'I need to keep awake. Can't make rent money if I'm snoozing it off in a doorway.'

Cream laughed. 'In that case, I have just the thing.'

From his inside pocket he produced a small paper bag. From it, he emptied two white tablets into his palm.

'These will keep you going all night long, I promise. You can trust me, I'm a doctor.'

Now it was her turn to laugh. 'You're a cool one and no mistake,' she said. She eyed the tablets. 'Ah, well. I suppose it won't do no harm.'

She picked up the tablets and Cream proffered the flask once more. 'Swallow them straight down,' he said. He watched a she raised her hand to her mouth to take the tablets, then took the flask from him and drank.

For a second, Cream had thought she would be difficult, but he had practiced his art and knew she could be persuaded. The contents of the flask were innocuous enough. Something to loosen their inhibitions, that's all, gain their confidence. The pills were whatever would cure what ails them or so he would say. Something to keep them awake, to keep out the cold, to relax them if this were their first time – how many times had he heard that one from some gin-soaked harridan – an all-purpose panacea with only one true purpose.

He took back the flask.

'Shall we get started then?' she asked.

'Momentarily,' he said. Methodically he screwed the top back onto the flask and placed it in his pocket. 'Just give the tablets time to do their work, shall we?'

'Do their work? What do you mean?'

At this point, Cream could wish for better illumination. He loved to see the fear appear in their eyes, the first intimation that all was not well.

He watched as she slumped back against the wall, one hand clutching at her throat.

'Relax,' he told her. 'It will all be over soon.'

She began to cough and double over, clutching her stomach. She groaned and shook, falling to her knees. He watched her convulsions with detached interest, tapping his foot impatiently. The longer she took to die, the longer he would have to wait for his pleasure, the thought of which was already fanning the flames of desire within.

Finally, she lay still. He waited to be absolutely sure and then he moved in to position her in the most accommodating manner to suit his purpose.

It was then that he heard the sound of laughter. At first, he thought he had been discovered, but no, the sound was coming from the erstwhile corpse at his feet. A corpse that moved, sat up and propped herself up against the wall.

'I wish you could see your face,' she said and held out her hand where two white pills nestled peacefully. She raised her other hand to her mouth. It contained a police whistle. She gave three loud blasts and the sound of running footsteps heralded the arrival of two figures.

Uttering a curse, Cream turned and fled.

'After him, Colverson!' Abberline yelled as he, himself, took off after the running figure.

Colverson paused momentarily. 'Are you all right?' he asked Fanny.

'Fine and dandy,' she replied. 'Now get going. I'll be right behind you.'

Colverson took off down the alley as Fanny scrambled to her feet and followed on as swiftly as she could.

A trap! How could he have been so foolish? But all was not lost. The alleys and byways were his playground. He knew every inch of them. Knew every dead end, every double-back and shortcut. He would lose his pursuers, of that he was sure and once free he would lie low. A day or two at most and Reilly would give him the funds to make his escape, he just had to keep running.

Those in dogged pursuit soon became aware of his plan to evade capture.

'Split up,' said Abberline. 'He can't evade all of us, but be careful. Sound your whistle when you have him, both of you.'

Grimly, the chase continued, winding and circuitous until it became obvious that his intention was to wend his way back to the more populated areas where he might more easily lose himself in the night-time throng.

As this realisation dawned on all three, they re-doubled their efforts to forestall his plans, but his greater knowledge of the terrain kept him tantalisingly ahead of them. Lungs bursting with effort, Cream emerged back onto the main road which was crowded with revellers, cabs and delivery men going about their trade. A few more seconds and he would be swallowed up by their masses, if only he could catch his breath. It was as he gulped in a lungful of much needed oxygen that he heard the shrill blast of a whistle. He glanced towards the sound and saw one of his pursuers emerging from a side street.

'He's on the High Road!' Colverson shouted in the hopes that his companions were within earshot.

Uttering a vile curse, Cream took off in the opposite direction with Colverson in hot pursuit.

Shoving his way past disgruntled passers-by, Cream heard the sound of pounding footsteps getting inexorably closer.

Suddenly, a figure appeared to bar his path. The treacherous doxy who had led to his downfall positioned herself in front of him, grabbing him by his coat and heaving him to the side to slam into the wall.

From the corner of his eye, he saw her male companion racing ever closer. Panic, deep as a poisoned well, rose up inside him and gave him strength he did not know he possessed. He slammed his fist into the woman's stomach and had the satisfaction of seeing her double over with a grunt of pain. He pried her hand from his coat collar and shoved her with all his might, sending her flying from the pavement to stumble into the road. Cream heard the sound of pounding hooves, the shout of a panicked cab driver. Someone shouted 'Fanny!' and then the male pursuer was there, right next to him but veering into the street where he grabbed the woman and swung her back to safety on the pavement. An heroic act, indeed, but too late to save himself. Cream saw the man struck by the side of the cab and fall beneath its wheels. He heard a scream of pain and the woman yelled 'Walt!' but Cream didn't wait to see the outcome of the disaster his actions had precipitated.

His legs felt unequal to the task, but he willed them into movement.

A brief flicker of hope illuminated his dark soul. 'I'm free!' he thought. 'I'm free!'

And then a fist took him full force in the gut and he staggered, bent double and retching as another figure, or maybe the same one, he was never sure, struck him on the chin, straightening him up momentarily before he fell backwards onto the pavement.

As he lay there, he saw the face of the third pursuer looming over him, his face like fury and the barrel of a revolver an inch from his nose.

'If my constable is hurt, or worse,' the figure said, 'I promise you, you'll pray that I pulled this trigger.'

With an almost inaudible sigh, Cream passed into unconsciousness.

89

'This is all a terrible misunderstanding! I am innocent, I assure you.' Cream sat in an interview room at Whitechapel Station, a dark, dispiriting square bereft of windows but with an abundance of peeling paint and undefined smells left by its previous malodourous occupants. Cream's stomach hurt and there was a long, purple bruise along his jaw, both gifts from the man who sat opposite him, Detective Chief Inspector Abberline.

'We have a witness,' Abberline said. 'One who will testify in court that you pressed her to take two tablets which, having been analysed, were found to contain a lethal dose of strychnine.'

Cream made a dismissive noise. 'Some tawdry street doxie? She's lying. No-one will believe her word against a respected member of the medical fraternity.'

'This particular "street doxie" is an undercover operative in the employ of Scotland Yard. I think her testimony will stand scrutiny.'

Cream paled, throwing his bruised jaw into even starker relief. 'It ...it was all a mistake,' he said. 'I am a medical man, I carry many tablets about my person. The young lady was complaining of a headache. I simply aimed to give her a palliative to ease her pain, that is all.'

'Which is it, Dr Cream? A lying street doxie, or a simple mistake?'

'I ...I ...uh ...'

Abberline continued, sparing Cream the trouble of further fabrications.

'We also have corroborating evidence from Mrs Florence Maybrick who has made a statement claiming you gave her tablets to feed to her husband in ever increasing doses to cure what ailed him. They too contained lethal doses of poison.'

'A distraught housewife! I explained all that.'

'Another mistake then, Dr Cream?' It seems you are beset by them. What about Miss Matilda Clover? Was she a mistake also?'

'I don't know what you mean.'

'Miss Matilda Clover. Daughter of Sir Edward Clover. I believe you met the young lady at one of your brother's assemblies.'

'I may have done.'

'The late Miss Clover has been positively identified as one of the Poisoner's victims. Lured to her doom by a note, ostensibly signed by her putative fiancé, your brother James, whilst she was attending a meeting of the Gentlewomen's League. When questioned about the note, your brother denied all knowledge of such events.'

'What has that to do with me?'

'Miss Clover was so entranced by the missive, thinking it heralded a long awaited proposal, that she showed it to several of her companions leaving it behind in her haste to meet her paramour. When we compared the note with samples of your own handwriting taken from your rooms, they bore a striking similarity.'

'But that just supposition,' Cream spluttered. 'It proves nothing.'

'By itself, maybe not, but your handwriting bears a marked likeness to your brother's. Something that could easily deceive a young woman in love and, since Dr James Cream was giving a lecture at the time Miss Clover received the note, he could not possibly have been the sender.'

Cream opened and closed his mouth like a stranded guppy.

'Furthermore,' Abberline continued, 'you may like to know that Sir Edward Clover was most pleased to discover that we have someone in custody for his daughter's murder. So pleased, in fact, that he went straight out and engaged the services of Sir Reginald Percy QC to prosecute the aforementioned detainee.'

'Sir Reginald Percy!' Cream gasped.

'You've heard of him, I take it. A most celebrated Queen's Counsel with a remarkable success rate in every case he has prosecuted. Of course, if you had sufficient funds to engage a defence barrister of equal calibre, you may just be able to argue a case of unfortunate mistakes on all counts. Do you have sufficient resources to do that?'

Cream remained silent.

'No, I thought not,' Abberline said. 'And then, of course, there are the charges of attempted murder of Miss Fanny Kettle who you callously pushed in front of an oncoming carriage and the severe injuries sustained by Police Constable Colverson when he saved Miss Kettle's life. We have numerous witnesses to those events I assure you.'

'Stop!' Cream held up his hands. 'All right, all right. Maybe there is a case to answer.' Suddenly the drab, cold little room seemed unbearably hot and he licked a bead of sweat from his upper lip. 'What if I could give you some information. Information that you are in desperate need of. Would that go some way to mitigating the charges against me?'

'You're co-operation on any matter would be passed on to the presiding judge at your trial. It would be up to him what he makes of it.'

'But would it save me from the noose?'

'Conceivably. What information are you talking about?'

Cream took a deep breath. 'The Black Dog murders,' he said.

'What do you know of the Black Dog murders?' Abberline asked

'I know who is committing them and who his next and final

victim will be. After that, he will be gone and you will never catch him. You may not even have time to catch him now since he plans to strike this very night.'

'Tell me all you know,' Abberline said.

90

St. Thomas' Hospital. Men's Surgical Ward. A way-station for those unfortunates not completely whole in body or in spirit.

Police Constable William Walter John Colverson was dozing when he heard his name called as if by an angel. His first thought was that his time had come and he was being summoned by some celestial roll call to meet his maker.

As his eyelids fluttered open his misinterpretation of events was apparent although the vision that greeted his eyes was no less angelic nor any less welcome for that matter.

'Fanny!' he said, startled. 'What are you doing here?'

Her unblemished brow creased in irritation. 'Where else would I be, you great lummox?' she said.

Colverson struggled into a sitting position. 'I just meant, how did you get past that dragon of a ward sister. She's very strict about visitors.'

Fanny's lips curled in a smile, most fetchingly in Colverson's estimation. 'She wasn't always a ward sister,' she said. 'Years back she was a street nymph like many an upstanding member of the community. It wouldn't do her reputation any good if that news got out, so we came to an arrangement. She lets me visit whenever I like and I keep my mouth shut.'

'Is there no end to your wiles? Colverson grinned.

'Not that I've found,' Fanny said. 'She even let me bring a friend.'

'A friend?'

Fanny made a clicking noise with her tongue and a black, furry shape jumped up onto the bed.

'Con!' Colverson said, ruffling the dog's ears who returned the favour by licking Colverson's face before settling down by his side with his head resting on Colverson's thigh.

'I thought you'd like to see him,' Fanny said. 'More than you'd care to see me most like.'

'Why do you say that?'

Fanny's composure broke and her face configured itself into a sorrowful expression, her eyes glinting with unshed tears.

'Oh, Walt!' she said, her voice breaking with emotion. She nodded towards Colverson's bandaged foot. 'Is it bad?'

'Bad enough,' he told her. 'Could be worse though. Only lost two toes. It'll make walking a beat difficult but I'll recover right enough.'

'Two toes!? And it's all my fault.'

'How do you make that out? I don't recall you driving the cab that ran me over.'

'It wouldn't have happened if you hadn't pulled me out of the way.'

'If I hadn't, you'd have been squashed flat!'

'And so could you have been!'

'But I wasn't. We both lived to tell the tale.'

They were silent for a while before Fanny said: 'No-one's ever done anything like that for me before.'

'I don't suppose you make a habit of nearly getting run over do you?'

'You know what I mean. You risked your life to save mine. That's not something I'll ever forget.'

'Just doing my duty, Miss.'

'If I thought it was just that …' she paused and then leant forward and kissed him hard on the lips. His arm went around her and the embrace lengthened, the kiss becoming less fervent and more gentle as time went on. Someone in one of the other beds raised a cheer and cackled happily. Finally, breathless and blushing, they disengaged and stared into each other's eyes. No words were spoken but some profound sort of understanding had been reached and they both knew it.

'When you get out of here,' Fanny whispered, 'I'm going to nurse you back to health, you see if I don't. And then …'

Colverson took her hand. 'And then?' he asked.

Fanny smiled, her old confidence returned. 'And then we'll have one hell of a time, you and me, you can bet your life on that.'

Colverson smiled. He may be two toes light, but he was a very happy man.

91

Colverson was still basking in his new-found euphoria when he received his second visitor of the day.

'How are you feeling?' Abberline posed the question as he stood, awkwardly, by Colverson's bedside. Hospitals had always unnerved him. Something about the smell. Illness in general unmanned him in a way that nothing else did, even when his first wife, Martha, was dying he tried to distance himself as much as possible from the day-to-day mechanics of decay and dissolution. It was something of which he was mortally ashamed.

Colverson was pale but otherwise in fine form, his damaged foot hidden beneath blankets and bandages.

'Not too bad, sir,' he said. 'Considering. They say I can go home soon.'

'Well, that is good news.'

'They need the bed for more deserving cases I expect.'

There was an awkward pause before Colverson said: 'Don't suppose I'll be pounding the beat anytime soon, eh, sir?'

'Possibly not.'

'Or ever, like as not, I expect.'

'There is a certain level of fitness expected from serving officers, it's true,' Abberline confirmed.

'Thought as much. Still, I knew the risks when I joined. No point crying over spilt milk as they say.'

'Do they? Yes, I suppose they do, but I wouldn't worry too much about not being able to pound a beat anymore.'

'No?'

'No. There is one final piece of business that I have to attend to which should be completed this evening one way or another.'

'The Black Dog murders?'

'As you say, the Black Dog murders.'

'You mean you know who is responsible?'

'If this evening's events play out as expected, yes, I believe we do.'

'I'm sorry I'm going to miss that, sir.'

'Can't be helped. I have someone in mind that will, I am sure, offer valuable assistance in your stead, even if not up to your standard.'

'Very kind of you to say so, sir.'

'And once that business is complete, I believe I may have some news that may shed a new light on the future for both of us.'

92

No-one would argue that Siobhan Reilly was the queen bee when it came to keeping the bawdy houses belonging to the Reilly clan under control. With her flaming red hair and flashing green eyes she could transform from a picture of exotic beauty to a fearsome harridan in the blink of an eye and not one brothel madam, no matter how hard-bitten could stand before her wrath without quailing. For that reason, Siobhan took it upon herself to make the weekly collection run to all the establishments under their control. Her regular driver was a lanky, cross-eyed individual called Tommy Mann. This morning, like many another, he stood waiting with the usual black carriage outside the warehouse that served as headquarters and domicile for Patrick and Siobhan Reilly.

Jacob Crow sat nearby on an upturned packing crate ostensibly taking the morning air. In reality he was waiting for a glimpse of Siobhan Reilly as she left to make her rounds. Simply put, Jacob Crow was in love with Siobhan Reilly but dared not speak of such emotions lest he brought calamity down on both their heads. After his wife had so cruelly deceived him, Crow's heart had turned to stone within his breast. Or so he thought. That deadening of emotion had enabled him to resign himself to his fate at the end of a gallows rope with nary a qualm. That he had been spared such a fate mattered little. In all vital respects, Jacob Crow regarded himself a dead man. It was only when Siobhan Reilly took pity on the morose and solitary creature that he had become that his emotions began to thaw. She asked him to recount his many escapades in the boxing ring and reciprocated by telling him tales of her youth in the green fields of Ireland. She laughed and smiled and made him feel whole again. Was it any wonder that he fell beneath her spell as so many had before? The fact that she seemed blissfully happy with her husband and devoted to their son was the only pang of anguish that could not be resolved. That being the case, he contented himself with such brief glimpses as he was able to contrive until she once again had time to sit and talk.

He watched her now as she emerged from the side door that led to their private quarters. She wore a blue dress and bonnet and carried a large leather satchel that would soon be filled with coin. She greeted Tommy Mann with a dazzling smile.

'How goes it, Tommy?' she asked.

'Fine, ma'am. Just fine,' he told her.

Siobhan paused and frowned. 'Isn't your Katie about to drop?' she asked.

'That she is ma'am. Her waters broke this morning. Her mother's with her now. By the time we get back it should be all over bar the shouting, and there's sure to be plenty of that.'

'Land sakes, man, what are you doing here?' Siobhan said. 'Your woman's about to give you a child and you should be by her side giving her comfort and support.'

A dubious look crossed Tommy's face at the idea of being in such close proximity to such an event. 'I have my duties here, ma'am. Mr Reilly's been very good to us and I don't want to let him down. Besides, childbirth is rightly a woman's thing isn't it?'

'Nonsense,' Siobhan shot back. 'When Fin was born, Patrick was by my side the whole time and I was grateful for it.'

Tommy's eyebrows shot up. 'Really?' he said.

'Really. So, off with you now and let us know if it's a boy or a girl so we can toast their health.'

'But the collection rounds …'

'They'll be taken care of, have no fear. Now, be off with you, and no skulking in the ale house until it's over or I'll hear about it and I won't be pleased, hear?'

'Yes, ma'am. Thank you, ma'am.'

Jacob Crow grinned to himself as Tommy Mann scuttled off into the morning throng.

'Now,' Siobhan said, 'I need to find another driver. These takings won't collect themselves.'

'I'll drive you,' Crow volunteered. A chance to spend more time in Siobhan's company was not to be passed up.

'Have you nothing else you'd rather be doing?' she asked.

'I've had my morning run and a sparring session's fixed up for later, but right now I'm at a loose end.'

'Well, we can't have that, can we? I will accept your gracious offer Mr Crow. Let us away.'

She linked her arm in his and they made their way to the cab.

93

Limehouse Lil ran a respectable establishment. Everyone knows that because she tells them often enough. Her girls are clean and willing and she pays her dues to her patron in full and on time. Everyone knows who her patron is and no-one gives her any trouble.

Until now.

Siobhan Reilly came a-knocking as she usually does with that big, brown, leather satchel to receive her share of the takings. The girls were all still abed after a heavy night and Lil received her in the parlour as usual.

'How's tricks, Lil?' Siobhan asked as she entered. Lil was seated at the table, her hands clasped in her lap to stop them from shaking, her face white beneath her layers of rouge and powder.

'Fine and dandy, Mrs Reilly,' she said.

Siobhan paused, frowning. 'Mrs Reilly?' she said. 'Why so formal, Lil? And where's the tea and cakes? We usually have a good old natter, you and me. Isn't that so?'

'Not today,' Lil said. 'Today is different.'

'How different?' Siobhan tensed and sniffed. There was fear in the air and more. Close by she could smell trouble in the form of a masculine scent. Different from the usual musky odour that permeated an establishment of this sort. Without another word, she turned and headed for the door only to be blocked by a roughly dressed individual, his face masked, holding a gun.

'Not so fast, lady,' he said. 'You have something I want and I mean to get it.'

Siobhan swung back to Lil. 'You set me up, you cow!' she spat.

Lil started to wail. 'It's not my fault, mistress. They threatened me. They have guns!'

'They?'

Another figure, much like the first, stepped through the door that led to the kitchen.

'Not thinking of leaving us are you?' he said.

'Hand over that satchel,' said the first, 'and we'll be on our way, no harm done.'

'You want it? Come and get it,' Siobhan said.

'Oh, we've got a feisty one here,' said the second.

'Then do as the lady asks, brother,' said the first.

As the second lout moved to do just that, a shadow passed across Siobhan's face. So swift and so subtle was it that it could almost pass for a trick of the light. Her features began to shift and change and a bright yellow light seemed to shine from her eyes.

The second thug paused, disconcerted, momentarily blocking his partner's line of sight. It was all the delay Siobhan needed.

With a snarl, she swung the heavy bag at the second thug, knocking his gun arm up and away. Reflexively, he pulled the trigger, loosing a shot into the ceiling with an explosion of sound. On the downswing, Siobhan used the bag to smash into the side of his head, toppling him back to sprawl across the table.

Lil leapt up out of her chair and commenced to scream, but Siobhan had other things on her mind. Having temporarily disabled one assailant, she now had no-one between her and the gun held by the first miscreant. But he had other things on his mind as well. The shock of her actions had momentarily disconcerted him but now he realised that this easy meat was anything but. In fact, he would have sworn on a stack of bibles that she wasn't even human. Her face was distorted, her mouth and nose elongated into a snout and her hands had claws! Claws that now slashed at his gun arm, drawing blood even through his thick coat and cutting deep to the bone. He screamed as Siobhan

343

launched herself upon him, bearing him to the floor, his gun falling from useless fingers.

'Shoot her!' he screamed as he saw her jaws open, revealing sharp canine teeth. 'For God's sake, shoot her!'

His companion, scrambling upright, did just that. Two shots rang out, each finding their mark. More by luck than judgement. Siobhan howled as the bullets thudded into her flesh, one in her upper arm, the other into her leg. It was a howl that would have split the moon in twain had that celestial object been its recipient. Instead, it heralded the pounding of heavy footsteps, already alerted by the sound of gunshots. The parlour door was burst asunder and Jacob Crow erupted into the room.

Siobhan had rolled to one side, her feature still half animal. Crow took that in, but forced the sight to the back of his mind lest it confound his actions. That this misshapen, bloodied creature was Siobhan Reilly he had no doubt and his duty was clear.

First, he grabbed the wrist of the man who still held a gun. Crow squeezed and twisted and there was a sharp crack. The man screamed but Crow paid him no mind. Crow hefted him up and slammed him down upon Lil's dining table, splitting the wood and sundry bones in the process. A heavy boot to the head knocked the man insensible which gave Crow leave to turn his attention to his companion who was scrabbling on his knees for his fallen weapon. As his fingers closed upon the gun, Crow stamped hard upon his fingers. More sharp cracks and more howls of pain followed. Pinning the man to the floor with his boot, Crow rained blows upon the felon's unprotected head until that object resembled nothing so much as a squashed fruit.

Crow glanced around. Lil was a huddled mass in the corner, weeping and wailing fit to burst but she was a lesser concern at this moment. Crow ripped the curtain ties from the velvet drapes and tied the two assailants up like Christmas turkeys. He gave each one another hefty punch to ensure oblivion for as long as possible.

'Someone will be back to pick these two up,' he told Lil. 'Do not untie them, even if they beg you, and keep everyone out of this room. Understand?'

Lil nodded and wiped a hand across her eyes. Satisfied he had done all he could on that front, Crow knelt beside Siobhan who lay groaning softly.

'Be still,' he told her. 'I'll see you safe.' He picked her up as easily as if she were a child and carried her out to the waiting carriage, placing her inside as gently as possible. She groaned and her eyes flickered open. 'The money,' she said.

'Forget the money,' Crow growled.

Siobhan clutched at his sleeve. 'We never forget the money,' she said.

Crow nodded and ran back inside, re-emerging moments later with the battered leather satchel. He threw it inside the carriage and mounted the driver's seat. Whipping up the horse, they took off at speed. Siobhan needed a doctor. A hospital was out of the question. Too many questions would be asked and, after what Crow had witnessed, the strange cast that had come over Siobhan's features, he knew that questions would be the very last thing required right now. James Cream was still at the warehouse he knew, tending to Fin's rehabilitation, although why a second Dr Cream was necessary Crow could not fathom. Nonetheless, he would have to suffice.

Crow's arrival at the Reilly warehouse was greeted with much consternation and activity. Crow carried Siobhan inside, shouting for Reilly and James Cream alternately. When both gentlemen were in attendance and Siobhan had been passed into the medical man's care, a grim faced Reilly demanded an explanation. Crow gave him a succinct reiteration of events and Reilly despatched men to collect the instigators of this catastrophe and to impress upon Limehouse Lil the importance of discretion.

'You've done well, Jacob,' Reilly said, 'and you have my gratitude. We'll talk later, but now I must be at Siobhan's side.'

'One more thing,' Crow said.

'Then make it quick, man.'

Crow looked about to make sure they were not overheard. 'When she was shot, Siobhan attacked the two robbers.'

'She's a feisty one all right, that much I know.'

'But when she did, she … changed.'

Reilly stiffened. 'Changed?'

'Her face, her hands, her teeth. They became like an animal.'

Reilly sighed. 'I had meant to confide in you, Jacob, that's the truth, but it's an awful hard thing for a man to understand. I was waiting for the right time, but it seems fate has decided that for me. Let me see how Siobhan fares and then I'll have a tale for you that will explain all.'

Some hour later, Reilly summoned Crow to his office and sat him down with a glass of whiskey.

'The doctor thinks Siobhan will make a full recovery,' he said.

'Good news,' said Crow.

'Indeed. He has removed the bullets and staunched the flow of blood. For a man who focuses on the mind, he's actually quite accomplished in practical matters, even more than his brother I dare say, but the bullet to her leg damaged the bone. She'll have trouble walking for a while and shall need to have splints to aid recovery. But she's strong and I have no fear that she'll weather

346

this storm and come through right as rain.'

'I'm glad.'

'And it's all thanks to you, my friend. Had you not been there, I don't know what would have happened.'

'I was just doing my job.'

'Your job you call it? No, I think not. This was above and beyond the call of your duty to me and I want to reward you.'

'I have little use for money. You see to my needs very well.'

'You've a kind heart, Jacob, and one day that may be your downfall, but if you will not take coin, perhaps you will accept a kind of promotion.'

'Promotion?'

'Aye. An elevation into the higher reaches of my organisation. The role, if you will accept it, of Siobhan's protector, at least until she's fighting fit again. And also as a trusted confidant on certain matters that no doubt have perplexed you since the events of this morning.'

Crow considered silently and then nodded slowly. 'I would be honoured,' he said.

'Good man. Now, let me get you another drink and I will tell you that tale so you may fully understand the transformation you witnessed earlier.

The shadows were lengthening into evening before Reilly finished his tale.

'It's a lot to take in, I know,' he said. 'What do you make of it, Jacob?'

Crow thought for a second, then said: 'If I hadn't seen it with my own eyes, I would have thought such things impossible. I don't fully understand all you have said, but I have no reason to doubt your word.'

'And does that, in any way, alter your feelings about your loyalty to me and my organisation?'

'You have been good to me,' Crow said. 'I have found a home here and a purpose. I am content.'

Reilly smiled. 'I hoped you would feel that way. Now, as I have explained, I have a mission to avenge my family's murder. That mission is almost at an end and after that, who knows what the future may hold, but I promise you that you will always have a place in my household for as long as you wish.'

'I shall do my best to deserve such an honour, but what of the two robbers? They also saw Siobhan's transformation. As did Lil'

Reilly sat back. 'Lil will keep her mouth shut, of that I am sure. She's so befuddled at what happened, she's not sure what she saw. As for the other two. Downstairs in the warehouse at this very moment. Two brothers they are. David and William Hawksworth. Two chancers who sought to elevate themselves at my expense. I have a score to settle with them especially as they witnessed something they should not have seen. I cannot let them flap their gums, so their silence needs to be assured. Permanently. You get my meaning, Jacob?'

Crow nodded. 'The Thames is well known for keeping secrets,' he said.

'And that does not perturb you in any way?'

'They tried to kill Siobhan,' Crow said. 'I would have done the deed myself there and then, but I did not wish to deprive you of the satisfaction.'

Reilly smiled. 'You are a strange man to be sure, Jacob Crow, and I am proud to call you friend.'

Reilly held out his hand. Crow enveloped it in his huge paw and they shook. 'Let us seal our new relationship with a small errand,' Reilly said. 'There is something I wish to accomplish this very evening and, normally, Siobhan would accompany me, but, as it stands that is not possible. Once I have seen to her comfort and posted sufficient guards to ensure her safety until my return, you and I will take a little trip across town.'

94

'But I want to come with you.'

'Siobhan, my love, you're injured. You need to rest. Stay here and see to Fin. I'll take Jacob with me. Now that he knows our true nature, there's no reason not to.'

'But I want to be there, Patrick. When you get final retribution, I want to be by your side.'

'I know you do, my darling, but it wouldn't be wise.'

'Then wait. Wait until I'm well. When my bones have healed, I'll be able to turn and we can both savour the kill. Hunting together as we used to.'

'And that is a wonderful thought, but it has to be tonight. It's his final performance and after that he could be gone to who knows where. If I don't take the opportunity when it's right in front of me, I may never get another chance.'

'Your mind is made up, then?'

'It is, my love, it is.'

'Then tell Jacob to look out for you. I expect you back in one piece or there will be hell to pay.'

Reilly chuckled. 'A promise that would inspire any man to herculean efforts. Rest, my love. After tonight, the world will be ours once more and free of care and obligation.'

95

In their cab on the way to the Alhambra Theatre, Abberline recounted all the facts as he knew them to his travelling companion, William Pinkerton.

'And you really think the killer is this man Reilly who can turn himself into a wolf?' Pinkerton asked.

'It would answer all the questions we have been asking ourselves. I would be sceptical if I hadn't witnessed such a transformation myself, although in that instance, it was just a puppy. As for whether it's Reilly or not, I only have Cream's word for that. Even if it is Reilly, it's still possible that he's using a vicious animal as his murder weapon and there is no supernatural element to be found here at all.'

Pinkerton considered for a moment. 'Of course, back home we have many such legends, especially among the Indian peoples. We have the loup-garou and the rougarous stories which are the closest to what you describe, and many other shapeshifting myths of all kinds. I wasn't aware that Europe also shared these stories.'

'Oh, we're chock-a-block with legends of all sorts. Demons, elves, sprites, devil dogs and the like. You Americans seem to forget that we are a much older culture than yourselves. Any legends you may have were probably transported to your shores by the Vikings or some other early adventurers, not to mention the European settlers that colonised the New World in more recent times.'

Pinkerton chuckled. 'You may be right at that, but I still look forward to seeing such a beast in the flesh.'

'Be careful what you wish for,' Abberline advised. 'But I thank you for providing some reinforcements for what may prove to be a wild goose chase.'

'Think nothing of it.'

'A show of force may well scare him off and I would never forgive myself if I let him slip through my fingers at this stage of the game. Normally I would have Constable Colverson as my companion, but he is recovering from injuries sustained in the Lambeth Poisoner case.'

'He's a good man. I am sure he'll pull through just fine.'

'The doctors assure me that is so, although he has lost two toes on his right foot which may well curtail his police career somewhat.'

'Not if he were to be offered a private commission with a premiere detective agency by someone in a position to choose his own staff,' Pinkerton smiled.

Abberline let the remark pass. 'Ah, here we are,' he said. 'The Alhambra Theatre.'

The lobby of the Alhambra Theatre was crowded. Abberline scanned the faces but saw no sign of Patrick Reilly. He was well acquainted with the smiling Irishman's features since it was well known that he indulged in numerous criminal activities but had yet to be found guilty of anything. Abberline could have persuaded Edmund Reid to mobilise a squad of men but such a heavy police presence may have simply caused Reilly to change his plans. The same result would apply if Tumblety was warned and hidden away. Putting a member of the public at risk, however serious his alleged crimes may have been, did not sit well with Abberline, but, if Cream was telling the truth, tonight would be Reilly's last chance to kill Tumblety before the erstwhile Wu Fang departed for parts unknown, potentially putting himself and Reilly out of Abberline's reach. As to the method of the kill, Cream could not be drawn. Smuggling a dog that size into a crowded theatre unseen would be a feat of magic in itself, but, desperate as it was, this could be Abberline's last chance to bring the murderer to justice.

With Colverson in the hospital and no other resources available, Abberline had called upon the only other companion available to him.

'Any sign of him yet?' Pinkerton asked.

Abberline shook his head. 'No. This may all be a wild goose chase. Cream is not the most reliable source. It's doubtful Reilly would seek to enter the theatre from the front, potentially with a massive hound in tow, but it was worth a look. Come, backstage is our best bet if he plans to attack inside the theatre, but if his past kills are any indication, he will wait until Tumblety leaves the premises. In that case, we need to be ready.'

As Abberline and Pinkerton made their way to the Stage Door where Abberline's credentials would gain them access, they passed a cab parked a little way down the street in the shadows, a great bear of a driver sat hunched in the driver's seat patiently waiting.

Once the two men were out of sight, the driver knocked on the roof of the cab. The door opened and Patrick Reilly stepped down. He glanced up at Jacob Crow. 'This won't take long, Jacob. Mr Tumblety's final performance will be short but memorable.'

'I'll be here,' Crow said.

'If anything should go wrong …'

'I'll be by your side in a matter of seconds,' Crow said.

'No, Jacob, you will not. Remember what I told you? I have entrusted you with my most precious treasures. My wife and my son. Your first and only duty is to make sure they are safe. Are we in agreement on that, Jacob?'

Crow nodded.

'Good man.' Reilly sauntered towards the Alhambra's open doors and disappeared inside.

Backstage was a bustle of activity. Performers coming and going, stagehands shifting scenery, arranging props in readiness for the star performer's farewell performance.

Pinkerton scratched his head. 'I just don't see how anyone could smuggle a giant hound dog in here without being seen,' he said.

'Nor I,' Abberline admitted. 'Which seems to support the theory that the attempt will be made after Mr Tumblety leaves the theatre.'

'Or it seems to favour the other theory that the beast is not a hound at all but a man in the guise of a beast.'

'There is that alternative, but, man or beast, no-one in their right mind would attempt an assassination in a theatre full of people, surely.'

'Tell that to Abraham Lincoln,' Pinkerton muttered.

Both men stopped and considered the implication of that statement.

'You really think there's a possibility of the attempt being made whilst Tumblety is on stage?' Abberline asked.

'Stranger things have happened.'

'But the chosen method of despatch. A gigantic hound is far more difficult to conceal than a pistol.'

'More likely to cause panic though. Easier to get away in the crowd. John Wilkes Booth had no intention of doing so, but this guy may be different.'

'Then we must divide our forces, William. You proceed to the auditorium and be on the lookout for anything suspicious whilst I remain here and keep an eye on Mr Tumblety from the wings.'

Pinkerton smiled broadly. 'You called me William!' he said.

'I suppose I did,' Abberline admitted.

'Does that mean you consider me to be a close enough confidant to consider my offer of future employment?'

'Tonight's events may have a significant impact on both out futures. Let us see how they play out and review the situation in the morning.'

'Fair enough. In the meantime, may I call you Frederick?'

Abberline gave a small smile. 'Whilst I am on duty, I think Inspector will suffice.'

96

As the moment for Wu Feng's entrance approached, the activity backstage increased as the final props were set up behind the backdrop in readiness for it to be elevated into the rafters for the grand reveal. Abberline scanned the gantry for suspicious activity, prowled the nooks and crannies of the wings and backstage area much to the annoyance of the stagehands and the scenery shifters who urged him to 'get out of the way' on more than one occasion. Even though his "copper's nose" was on high alert, he detected nothing more than the amount of tension and excitement you would expect from people employed in such an endeavour. It was all most frustrating.

More than once, Abberline debated whether it was his duty to warn Francis Tumblety of the danger he was in and to persuade him to cancel his performance, but with no concrete evidence to back up his claims, the man would be within his rights to refuse him. Certainly, the Commissioner would have dismissed such a request outright and, whether Tumblety had committed some transgression in the past to warrant his being the target of such a vengeful entity was a moot point. The word of a senile old man and a soon to be convicted murderer was the only thing that linked all the victims thus far. No evidence of the actual crime had ever been found and no crime had ever been reported. Abberline was acting on instinct alone, but had not Polly's identification of Dr Cream proven to be correct? And had that information not come from the shade of one of Cream's victim? If ever there was a case when instinct deserved to be given its due, this was it.

As Abberline mused upon the various aspects of the case, a hush fell over the backstage area. Turning, he saw a figure that purported to be a tall Chinaman with a drooping moustache, dressed in brightly patterned silk robes making his way along the corridor to stand in the wings. If this was indeed Francis Tumblety, his makeup was quite remarkable.

On stage the last act was leaving to scattered applause awaiting the arrival of the legendary Wu Feng.

In the auditorium, William Pinkerton prowled the aisles as Wu Feng went through his act to astounded gasps and appreciative applause. Pinkerton had to admit that the man was a polished performer and it was difficult to tear his eyes away from the stage and remain focused on his task.

Look for something suspicious Abberline had said. A massive wolf-like creature would be suspicious enough, but other than that, it was difficult to know what else would qualify.

A tall man left his seat and began walking down the aisle, but would that qualify as suspicious? People moved around the auditorium all the time for many reasons.

When the man removed his coat and dropped it on the floor, his actions became more noteworthy. Pinkerton squinted in the gloom. Was he barefoot? He cast a glance at the aisle seat the man had vacated and there, sure enough, a pair of boots stood to attention. In the second it had taken Pinkerton to register this fact, several startled gasps and exclamations reached his ears. Looking up, he saw that the man had now removed the rest of his clothing and was striding towards the stage stark naked. Several ladies in the audience were alternately gasping in outrage, swooning, or jockeying for position for a better look as their male companions were rising from their seats, uttering condemnations and oaths, moving to intercept this outrage to public decency.

The cause of this consternation seemed unperturbed, picking

up his pace until he was almost running. It was what happened next that started the real panic amongst the mass of theatregoers. Some thought it was simply a trick of some sort, albeit in very bad taste, to mark the end of Wu Feng's engagement. Others thought the gates of hell had opened up in a London palace of entertainment.

Whatever opinion they held, they all agreed that they had never seen the like before. The naked man was changing his shape right before their eyes. His bones and muscles stretching and bunching, his skin sprouting thick, coarse hair, his features elongating into a muzzle until, in the place of a man, there now loped an enormous black wolf heading straight for the stage.

Trick or no, the nerves of many patrons were stretched beyond breaking point and they rose, en masse, seeking an exit and no doubt composing stern letters of complaint about this outrage.

The only thing passing through William Pinkerton's mind was: 'So that's how you smuggle a wolf into a theatre!'

Pinkerton drew his revolver but the buffeting around him prevented him from firing off a shot. Forging against the tide, he fought his way past the press of panicked citizens.

'ABBERLINE!' he screamed. 'HE'S HERE!'

From the wings, Abberline could hear the commotion of the audience but could not see the terrible transformation that had caused it. He heard Pinkerton's shout above the hubbub and stepped forward onto the stage itself where all activity had come to a standstill.

Wu Feng stood centre stage still staring into the audience. His two female assistants were screaming and running for cover. Abberline raised a hand to shield his eyes from the glare of the spotlights just in time to see a huge, dark shadow take a prodigious leap that took it clear of the orchestra pit, across the footlights on a direct course for the frozen Wu Feng.

Abberline took one step forward and hurled himself full length at the master magician.

The snarling shadow of death collided with them in mid-flight and all three went sprawling.

Abberline rolled over, drawing his revolver. The wolf creature scrabbled to its feet, inch long claws skittering across the boards of the stage, lips curled back from razor sharp teeth and lunged.

Abberline brought his revolver around but was unable to bring it to bear as the massive jaws closed upon the weapon and tore it from his grasp, flinging it away with a contemptuous toss of its head into the orchestra pit.

The screams and shouts of the panicked masses receeded in Abberline's head as he stared up at the huge canine face that loomed above him. In the large, dark eyes he saw the same orange crescents that he had observed in Con's eyes but now they held murderous intent. Strings of saliva dripped from the beasts muzzle onto Abberline's chest and the creature's snarl sent vibrations into the marrow of his bones.

Visions of the mutilated corpses of Maybrick, Druitt and Ostrog flashed through Abberline's mind and he wondered if Dr Pettifer would celebrate when his own remains joined them.

But then the beast turned away. Abberline was obviously considered to be no threat and he had more important business to attend to.

Turning, the beast advanced upon the cowering form of Wu Feng who held up his hands in pointless supplication.

'Please!' he whimpered. 'No!'

Whatever spark of mercy he hoped to ignite within the breast of the Black Dog died a'borning and the animal leapt upon the prone figure, massive paws pinning him down, his jaws looming over his victim, savouring the moment.

The transfusion of vampire blood that had saved Abberline's life during his hunt for the Whitechapel fiend known as Jack the Ripper had forced him to admit that vampires were real. His continued existence provided further proof of that, and the improved state of his health continues to afford undeniable testimony to the efficacy of their blood. Ever since that day, Abberline's senses had become sharper, his "copper's nose" more acute as a result. His physical health too has improved greatly. The common cold seems to no longer hold sway over his constitution, his reflexes are much improved and his physical strength seems magnified. Not, of course, to the level of a proper vampire, but certainly beyond what would normally be expected of even a moderately fit and active man in his late forties. In introspective moments, Abberline would even acknowledge that these improvements have also led to an increase in self-confidence that even someone of his exemplary record could not be expected to possess. Nonetheless, even such an artificially elevated state of confidence would not allow him to leap upon the back of a full-grown werewolf bare handed and try to wrestle him from his prey.

And yet, that is precisely what Abberline did. As the beast turned his attention to the unfortunate Tumblety, Abberline scrabbled to his feet. His revolver lost, he took two steps forward to facilitate whatever momentum there was to be had and jumped, landing at full stretch upon the back of the Black Dog.

Whether his action was the result of his vampire heritage or an act of sheer stupidity, Abberline could not tell, but, having reached his intended target, he had nothing left to do but make the best of it.

The beast gave a surprised grunt upon the impact, but its strength was such that he barely budged. In desperation, Abberline clamped his legs around the beast's mid-section and wrapped both arms around its neck, squeezing with all his might.

The beast heaved and staggered, releasing Tumblety momentarily, seemingly surprised at the strength and audacity of its attacker.

Abberline was breathing hard now with the exertion as he increased the pressure of his hold on the beast's throat, choking off his air supply.

The Black Dog began to shake and buck in an effort to rid itself of this nuisance. Abberline clung on grimly, his face buried in the thick, coarse fur of the creature's back.

When its gyrations proved futile, the Black Dog reared itself up on his hind legs and crashed down onto its back, slamming Abberline into the stage with enough force to drive all breath from his body. His hold weakened . The beast tore itself free and turned upon his tormentor. Any largesse he may have bestowed upon Abberline in their initial encounter now fled as he opened his jaws wide, his fetid breath like a blast furnace in Abberline's face. The detective threw up a defensive arm but knew it was pointless. He closed his eyes and prepared for the worst.

And then two shots rang out. Abberline felt the beast shudder and howl in pain. He opened his eyes to see the creature swaying, blood staining its pelt, his eyes fixed upon the opposite side of the stage where William Pinkerton stood, Colt .45 in hand.

In its fury, the beast attempted to charge the American, but its gait was uncertain. Even though, had it reached its target, it still had the power and the fury to do considerable damage. It never got the chance. William Pinkerton continued firing with deadly accuracy until the hammer clicked upon an empty chamber. The beast swayed drunkenly and then toppled with a crash that shook the entire stage. It lay there, panting and bleeding until the rise and fall of its sides slowed and finally ceased.

Skirting cautiously around the carcass, Pinkerton crossed to Abberline and helped him stagger to his feet.

'Are you all right?' Pinkerton said.

'Battered and bruised, but I'd have been a lot worse if not for your timely intervention.'

'I'd have been here sooner, but the crowd …' he gestured helplessly.

'Think nothing of it,' Abberline said. 'Your timing was impeccable.'

'My timing? What about yours? God damn, you rode that thing like a bucking bronco. I've never seen the like.'

'Not something I'd care to repeat, I assure you, but look.' Abberline pointed towards the spot where the Black Dog had lain but moments before. Now the form of a man lay, unmoving, in its place, blood seeping from numerous wounds.

'He turned back at the end,' said Pinkerton.

'Which rather poses the question, is he a man who becomes a beast or a beast that becomes a man?'

A low moan prevented further speculation on the matter as both men turned to the recumbent Tumblety.

'He's alive!' said Pinkerton. 'You got there in time to save his life.'

'All in the line of duty,' Abberline said. 'Now I really must sit down as I feel rather faint.'

97

Jacob Crow saw the panicked crowds running from the Alhambra's doors and knew the deed was almost done. It was only when he heard the shots ring out that he abandoned his instructions and leaped down from the cab. People were still crowding the doorway but he pushed and shoved his way through the human tide.

'Out of my way!' he yelled. 'Out of my way!'

By the time Crow had reached the main auditorium he knew he was too late. He could see Reilly's body lying on the stage, saw the two men standing over him with pistols in their hands. He couldn't tell if Reilly had completed his mission or not, but whatever way the fates had fallen, he had paid a terrible price. Nodding grimly, Crow charged back out to the street and mounted the cab. His duty now was clear. He would carry out Reilly's last command and make sure that his wife and son were safe.

The Reilly town house was its usual deceptively quiet self as Crow pulled the cab into the stable block. The warehouse at the rear of the premises, he knew, would be its usual hive of activity. Jumping down, he handed the reins to the stable-boy with the instruction to harness up a fresh pair of horses to the large carriage, then he hurried inside and upstairs where yellow lights still burned.

He burst into the sitting room where he found Siobhan Reilly sitting, waiting, her damaged leg propped up on a footstool.

Before she had time to question him, he barked: 'Pack. Quickly. For yourself and Fin. Take whatever money is to hand. We leave within the hour.'

Stark fear etched Siobhan's face as she struggled to her feet.

'What happened?' she said. 'Where's Patrick?'

'Patrick won't be coming. They were waiting for him.'

'No!' It was a rebuttal wreathed in anguish. 'The police? They took him? We must make plans to get him released. 'We have lawyers …'

Crow shook his head. 'Not arrested,' he said.

'Not …?' The wail she gave now was like a soul in torment. She hobbled forward and beat her fists against Crow's chest.

'No. You should have protected him. Why didn't you?'

Crow enclosed her fists in his own. He couldn't bear to look into her tear-stained face.

'He didn't want me to,' he said. 'He made me swear that if he didn't come back I was to get you and Fin out of harm's way. The police will be here soon enough and you can't be here when they arrive. You know that, don't you?'

Although shudders still shook her body, Siobhan nodded. 'I'll go and pack,' she said.

Less than forty minutes later, Crow carried the sleeping Fin to the carriage and placed him inside before helping Siobhan in behind him. He mounted the driver's seat and whipped the horses into motion. The men working in the warehouse and on the dock watched them go. The more intelligent amongst them read the signs and quietly disappeared into the night. The rest would have to take their chances. It was the end of an era.

Where Crow was headed he did not know. His first duty was to get Siobhan and Fin as far away as possible. Siobhan had packed two large suitcases which were now lashed to the roof of the carriage and carried the faithful leather bag full of a week's takings. It wasn't a fortune, but it would suffice.

'We will avenge him,' she told Crow. 'Promise me we will avenge him.'

Crow had nodded and now, as he drove them into the night, he knew that he would do whatever Siobhan desired of him. Reilly had been good to him and he bore the man no ill-will, but a small, selfish part of him hoped that when time and vengeance had healed her wounds there may be a slim chance that Siobhan Reilly would turn to him for comfort and solace. The thought warmed his heart and soul as the moon looked down.

98

Commissioner Warren was on the verge of his habitual apoplexy where Detective Chief Inspector Abberline was concerned. 'You call this a report, Abberline?' he roared.

Abberline took a long suffering sigh. 'I believe it conforms to the standard format required by Scotland Yard, yes. Have I made spelling errors?'

'Don't be flippant with me Abberline,' Warren snarled. 'This travesty is nothing but fairy tales and fantasy! Men who change into wolves? No-one in their right mind would believe that and God only knows what the press will make of it if word gets out.'

'There are dozens of eye witnesses who will testify to seeing the transformation,' Abberline said.

Warren made a dismissive noise. 'Theatre goers who were paying good money to see a "magic show"! Delusional, the lot of them and every one victims of a gas leak that addled their senses no doubt. I'll have that theatre torn apart to find the cause of that leak, you mark my words. Where is this man, Tumblety now? Can he be interrogated?'

'I doubt you'll get much out of him. He had a full mental breakdown. He's currently in the mental ward of Cobblestones Prison until it can be decided what to do with him.'

Warren made a grunting noise. 'As for Reilly. A known criminal. Bawdy houses, robbery, burglary, smuggling, he had his sticky fingers in every larcenous pie imaginable. Including murder. Why he chose these particular victims is difficult to say, but I expect we can find some shady dealings in their past that we can connect to Reilly. A falling out among thieves, that's what it is. The man obviously trained a dog to be a vicious killer and let him loose on those he felt had wronged him as a sort of lesson to any others who may contemplate doing the same. Yes, that's the story we will give to the public.'

'And you think I trade in fairy tales,' Abberline muttered.

Warren rose up in righteous anger and tossed the report across his desk. 'You will throw this travesty away and write it again as I have suggested. Do you understand me?'

'Perfectly,' said Abberline.

'Good. Then get out of my sight and get on with it.'

'No.' The word came out softly in direct inverse proportion to its impact upon the Commissioner of Police.

'What did you say?' he demanded.

'I said "No". My report stands as a true record of these events. If you choose to ignore it, I can't stop you, but I will not lie if asked about the truth of the matter.'

'By God, Abberline, that is outright insubordination! I'll have your job for this.'

'Too late Commissioner.' Abberline drew an envelope from his pocket and passed it across the desk.

Warren looked at it suspiciously. 'What's this?' he asked.

'My letter of resignation. Effective immediately.' Abberline rose, tipped his hat and left the office, leaving Commissioner Warren open mouthed and fuming.

367

99

William Pinkerton was roaring with laughter, tears streaming down his face, dabbing at his eyes with a red and white spotted handkerchief. 'By all the saints, I wish I had been there to see the look on his face!' he managed between chortles.

Abberline allowed himself a smile. 'It was rather satisfying, I must admit,' he said. 'But I'm afraid it was nothing but an empty gesture unless your offer of gainful employment is still open.'

'Damn right it is! Does that mean you accept?'

'I rather think it does.'

Pinkerton leapt to his feet and grasped Abberline's hand in a vice-like grip, shaking it enthusiastically. 'That is something truly worth celebrating,' he said, gesturing at the tray of tea and cakes that lay before them. 'With something stronger than tea.' He crossed to a drinks cabinet and began pouring two overly generous measure of whiskey.

'I will, of course, want free rein to employ my own staff,' Abberline said.

'Wouldn't have it any other way,' Pinkerton said, delivering the abundant libation and taking his seat once more. 'You will have a generous budget to spend how you wish on anything that enhances the business, and that includes personnel. Who did you have in mind?'

'PC Colverson for a start.'

'Wouldn't expect anything else. A fine man and a great asset.'

'I would also like to offer a post to Miss Fanny Kettle. She was invaluable in discovering the true nature of the Black Dog murders as well as showing her bravery when we apprehended the Lambeth Poisoner. Her organisational skills are exceptional and she has a winning way with people of all sorts. I rather thought she would serve as the face of the agency as it were.'

'Couldn't agree more.'

'I would also like to find a place for young Polly. Her more unusual skills also proved of immense use and, as you seem to think cases of this sort may be on the increase, she would also be an invaluable asset.'

'Sound thinking. Anyone else?'

'Not at present, but, as both Fanny and Polly are technically homeless, I was wondering if they could occupy some of the rooms on this floor which were not being used for official business. Purely temporarily, you understand.'

'Forget temporary. If the whole lot of you want to take up residence here, free of charge of course, and live over the shop as it were, I would be delighted.'

'Thank you. I'm sure Fanny and Polly, and probably Colverson, would be only too grateful to take you up on the offer. For myself, I think I will remain in my family home. For the time being anyway.'

'Whatever suits you best Inspector.' He paused. 'I guess I can't call you that anymore, can I?'

'No, I suppose not. That will take some getting used to.'

'So what do you want to call yourself? Pinkerton's have no official ranks, just agents or detectives. How about Captain?'

'Flattering but I have never seen myself as a Captain.'

'What then?'

Abberline thought for a moment. 'Despite my acrimonious departure, I still have a fondness for Scotland Yard and since my full title there was Detective Chief Inspector, I rather think Chief may be suitable? What do you think?'

'That sounds just fine and dandy. Chief Abberline it is.'

'But my friends can call me Frederick.'

The two men smiled. 'Well, Frederick,' Pinkerton said and raised his glass. 'Here's to the start of a new career and an on-going friendship.'

'May they both stand the test of time,' Abberline said as they chinked glasses.

'Of that, I have no doubt,' Pinkerton said and they drank to seal the bargain.

100

Thomas Neill Cream aka The Lambeth Poisoner was tried for his crimes and sentenced to hang, his plea for leniency due to his informing on Patrick Reilly going unheeded. He was executed at Newgate Prison on 15th November 1892.

Author's Note

I hope you enjoyed The Black Dog Murders.

The keen eyed amongst you may have noticed that many of the characters in **The Black Dog Murders** are based on real people. As usual, I have taken the liberty of moving them in space and time and altering their personalities and motivations in order to fit the story that I wanted to tell. If you feel inclined to look any of them up, feel free. They are all fascinating in their own right and you won't be disappointed.

Gary Orchard
April 2025

www.ingramcontent.com/pod-product-compliance
Ingram Content Group UK Ltd.
Pitfield, Milton Keynes, MK11 3LW, UK
UKHW020633131125
8941UKWH00042B/406